HENRY KNOX

VISIONARY GENERAL OF
THE AMERICAN REVOLUTION

Mark Puls

palgrave
macmillan

HENRY KNOX
Copyright © Mark Puls, 2008.
All rights reserved. No part of this book may be used or reproduced in any
manner whatsoever without written permission except in the case of brief
quotations embodied in critical articles or reviews.

First published in 2008 by
PALGRAVE MACMILLAN™
175 Fifth Avenue, New York, N.Y. 10010 and
Houndmills, Basingstoke, Hampshire, England RG21 6XS.
Companies and representatives throughout the world.

PALGRAVE MACMILLAN is the global academic imprint of the Palgrave
Macmillan division of St. Martin's Press, LLC and of Palgrave Macmillan Ltd.
Macmillan® is a registered trademark in the United States, United Kingdom
and other countries. Palgrave is a registered trademark in the European Union
and other countries.

ISBN-13: 978–1–4039–8427–2
ISBN-10: 1–4039–8427–1

Library of Congress Cataloging-in-Publication Data
Puls, Mark, 1963–
    Henry Knox, visionary general of the American Revolution / by Mark Puls.
       p.   cm.
    Includes bibliographical references.
    ISBN 1–4039–8427–1 (alk. paper)
       1. Knox, Henry, 1750–1806.   2. Knox, Henry, 1750–1806—Influence.   3.
Generals—United States—Biography.   4. United States. Continental Army—
Biography.   5. United States—History—Revolution, 1775–1783—Campaigns.
6. United States—History—Revolution, 1775–1783—Artillery operations.   7.
Military engineers—United States—Biography.   8. Cabinet officers—United
States—Biography.   I. Title.
E207.K74P85   2008
973.3'092—dc22
[B]
                                                                    2007037222

A catalogue record of the book is available from the British Library.

Design by Letra Libre, Inc.

First edition: February 2008
10 9 8 7 6 5 4 3 2 1
Printed in the United States of America.

CONTENTS

For Matthew Puls with great affection

ACKNOWLEDGMENTS

This book has benefited from the generous support and help provided from many sources to a grateful author. I wish to express my thanks, especially to Gerald W. Puls, Sheron Puls, Leslie Rivas-Lynch, Donald S. Lynch, Gabriella Rivas-Lynch, Michael Puls, Noosi Puls, Denise Edwards, Jeremy Pearce, Lisa Zagaroli, Dr. Svetlana Mishulin, Motoko Huthwaite, and Michael Mercatante. I am also indebted to Alessandra Bastagli, editor at Palgrave Macmillan, for her guidance and creativity. I would like to thank Billie Rae Bates for helping prepare the manuscript. I am also thankful for the work of the staffs at several libraries and institutions, especially at the Library of Congress, the Massachusetts Historical Society, the Gilder Lehrman Collection at the New York Historical Society, the Montpelier General Henry Knox Museum, the Museum of Fine Arts, Boston, and George Mason University.

With respect to General Knox, I can say with truth, there is no man in the United States with whom I have been in habits of greater intimacy; no one whom I have loved more sincerely, nor any for whom I have had a greater friendship.

—George Washington to John Adams

ONE

LOVE AND WAR

Nine-year-old Henry Knox entered the Boston bookstore, leaving his childhood behind. The boy, blond and tall for his age, could see shelves of books and boxes of fine stationery adorned with floral designs imported from London, along with writing materials, inkwells, quills, pamphlets, and writing paper neatly laid out for customers. His days of playing with friends or attending school would be replaced with the bookshop's chores and adult concerns over money and the support of his family.

His life had been turned upside down that year, 1759. His father, William Knox, a once-prosperous shipbuilder, left the family after his business collapsed in the midst of economic hard times sweeping the American colonies. Plagued by debt, the disillusioned Knox boarded a ship bound for St. Eustatius in the West Indies, leaving his family with no means of financial support. Henry was left to care for his mother and his three-year-old brother. His older siblings, John and Benjamin, had left home years earlier to earn a living as merchant seamen, never to return to Boston.

His mother, Mary Knox, pulled Henry out of Master John Lovell's prestigious Boston Latin Grammar School, an elite primer for students aspiring to attend Harvard College, and set aside whatever hopes she had for him to offer his labor to Messrs. Wharton and Bowes, who had taken over a fashionable bookshop from Daniel Henchman on the south side of Boston. Taking pity on the family, Nicholas Bowes agreed to hire Henry and provide him with whatever paternal attention and moral guidance the now-fatherless boy needed. Mary took solace that her son could continue his education in a bookstore, in an atmosphere of literacy and learning, frequented by the most educated and influential people in Boston.

His employers showed Henry around the store and pointed out the books that might be helpful in furthering his education—volumes on mathematics and history, Greek and Latin classics, and literature—telling him that he could take any home to study. His employers said they would tutor him in the craft of binding and repairing books and teach him everything about the trade. Henry was then put to work, running errands and doing chores around the shop, helping customers, and making deliveries.

He had been saddled with substantial responsibilities, but Henry accepted his role as provider with a secret pride, believing he needed not only to save his family from financial ruin but to reverse its downward spiral. The once-proud Knox name was still revered in Scotland, where his ancestors had descended from nobility. His lineage could be traced to William Knox, lord of Gifford, a manor near Edinburgh in the Scottish Lowlands. William had been the older brother of John Knox (1514–1572), the renowned Reformation preacher who furthered the Protestant movement in Scotland, turning the country predominantly Calvinist and gaining the enmity of the Catholic monarch, Mary Queen of Scots. Religious conflicts between Catholics and reformers drove many Scotch Presbyterians, including Henry's family, to resettle in Northern Ireland.

In 1729, Henry's father, seventeen-year-old William Knox of Derry, Ireland, a town near Belfast, sailed to America with a congregation led by the Reverend John Morehead. Reaching Boston in 1730, they established the Church of Presbyterian Strangers on Bury Street. The first names on the church's baptismal records were Knox and Campbell, the families of Henry's father and mother. William was a shipbuilder and merchant, and construction yards for vessels thrived along Boston Harbor. Because lumber and labor was plentiful in America, ships could be built 20 to 50 percent cheaper than in England. The colonies would soon produce a third of all British ships.

William bought a wharf along Boston Harbor to dock imported goods, a construction yard, and a picturesque two-story, wood-sided home with a gambrel roof and two fireplaces on Sea Street (later renamed Federal Street), near Summer, that overlooked the harbor. A picket fence bounded the property, and a garden provided vegetables.

When William began his courtship of Mary Campbell, his future looked promising. The couple exchanged wedding vows before the Reverend Morehead on February 11, 1735. Henry was born in the family's prosperous home on July 25, 1750, the seventh of ten sons, of whom only four survived to adulthood: John, Benjamin, Henry, and his younger brother, William. An energetic child, Henry was fond of playing with toy soldiers. He and his boyhood friend, David McClure, who later became a prominent Connecticut clergyman, were intrigued that a man had tried to "fly" by jumping from the steeple of Boston's North Church, in what may have been an early demonstration of parachuting. The boys climbed to the roof of a small building owned by Henry's father and slid down a long ship oar to feel the sensation of an airborne flight.[1]

His parents recognized that Henry was intelligent and inquisitive. They applied for his admission to the Boston Latin Grammar School—founded in 1635, a year before Harvard College, by Boston Puritans—then under the direction of John Lovell, an educator considered "the pride of Boston's parents and the terror of its youth."[2] The school was open to students from all social classes, and its alumni included Benjamin Franklin and Samuel Adams. For his admission exam, Henry read verses from the Bible before the stern-faced Lovell.

The school was a one-room brick building with a bell steeple on the south side of School Street, constructed in 1748 to replace a wooden structure from the opposite side of the street. The school bell rang at 7 A.M. to open classes in the summer and 8 A.M. in the winter. Instruction extended until 5 P.M. with an hour break at noon. After classes broke, Henry and the other students attended a nearby writing school. He studied Greek and Latin and was introduced to European history along with math and practical sciences. When snow covered the ground, Henry and his classmates, who included future patriot Josiah Quincy, brought sleds to school. After studies, the boys would coast down the incline of Beacon Street before heading home in the evening darkness.

Shortly after Henry's brother William was born in 1756, the family's finances began to collapse. The colonial economy slumped into depression, in part because Parliament passed a currency act in 1751 that prohibited the provinces from issuing paper money. The shortage of money led to a sharp drop in prices, and many businesses went bankrupt. William Knox's business failed, and he began to sell off his property. Items within their home began to disappear to satisfy creditors. When Henry was eight, his father sold the home in which he and his brothers had been born to move to cheaper housing. Within a year, his father had disappeared from his life as well.

★ ★ ★ ★

If Henry had ever wished to be rid of the drudgery of school, it was unlikely that he wanted to trade it for a job in a bookstore. Yet he harbored an ambition to distinguish himself and did not neglect his studies. During idle moments in the shop, he read, submerging himself in *Plutarch's Lives* of ancient Greek and Roman leaders. He enjoyed the romantic adventure of ancient battles and characters from antiquity. His knowledge of Latin from the grammar school enabled him to teach himself to read French and gain passable fluency in speaking. He read classic histories and philosophy.

Henry possessed a genial, gregarious personality, and he enjoyed dealing with customers: clergymen, merchants, seamen, mothers, and daughters. He especially enjoyed talking to veterans of the militia, who stirred his imagination with stories of battling French soldiers and Indians in the ongoing war for control of the Ohio River Valley, which had exploded into a world war between Britain and France. With rapt attention, he listened to tales of the unsuccessful expedition led by Massachusetts governor William Shirley to capture Fort Niagara in 1755 and the victorious siege of Louisburg three years later to protect the gateway of the St. Lawrence River. Henry must have imagined himself as a soldier, transformed from his obloquy to the heroic status of the men who showed their scars from these illustrious battles to the awe and hushed reverence of onlookers. Confined to a bookstore, he longed for adventure.

Whatever hope he harbored for his father to return and restore the family was dashed when he was twelve years old. Word reached Boston that William Knox had died in the West Indies at the age of fifty. The cause of death is unknown. Feelings of abandonment must have haunted Henry. Any child would have wondered if his father had thought about him and longed to see his son. Why had he not returned? Did his father realize that his son was supporting the family? Henry's memory of his early childhood, the comfortable home on Sea Street or playing at his father's construction yard, must have seemed as illusory as a dream.

Henry sought friends among the tough juvenile street gangs that fought for dominance of Boston's winding streets. He was taller than most boys his age, and he developed a muscular, athletic build. He enjoyed fighting, which provided him the chance to vent his conflicting emotions and the anger he felt over being abandoned by his father and put to work by his mother. Henry became part of a gang from the south side of Boston near the docks, boys whose fathers were shipyard workers and seamen and tavern owners. Their rivals came from the north end, on the other side of the Common, boys from families of merchants and mechanics and dockworkers. In tests of toughness, the gangs fought each other in bloody fistfights. Henry became the champion of his neighborhood and frequently took on the leaders from the rival gang. For at least three years, he was known as the best fighter in the area.

The opposing gangs engaged in a ritual parade on November 5, or "Pope's Night," which invariably led to a battle for dominance. Each gang marched from its neighborhood carrying effigies of the pope and the devil. When the columns met near Union Street, a fight erupted to capture each effigy and chase their defeated foes through the streets. During one of these processions, the south side's effigy was erected on a cart, which lost a wheel during the procession. Knox bent over, nudged his shoulder under the axle, and bore the weight of the cart as the march proceeded. Everyone began to talk about his unusual strength.

Yet inside the bookstore, the rough and aggressive Henry was transformed. He impressed customers with his pleasing personality, intelligence, and his politeness. Radical Whig leader Samuel Adams thought Knox was "a young gentleman of a very good reputation."[3] John Adams, a young lawyer from Braintree who had recently opened a practice in Boston, thought Knox a "youth who had attracted my notice by his pleasing manners and inquisitive turn of mind." Some of young Knox's questions concerned the political controversies swirling around Boston over British tax measures, which began to cost the bookshop revenues and customers and greatly concerned his employers. In 1767, Parliament passed the Townshend Revenue Act, which placed a duty on tea, glass, red and white lead, paper, and paint in an attempt to raise £20,000 to pay the salaries of royal governors and crown officials as well as for British troops in America. In opposition to the measure, Samuel Adams spearheaded a Continental boycott of British goods. The bookshop canceled orders from London and saw a sharp drop in business.

Shortly before his eighteenth birthday, Knox took time off from his clerking duties to watch the local militia parade through town to celebrate the birthday of King George III. Governor Francis Bernard's troop of guards, whose ranks came from the sons of the leading families in Boston, led the vanguard of the procession, which included the town's regiment followed by a train of artillery under the command of Lieutenant Adino Paddock, a Boston chair-maker with a shop along Boston Common. Paddock had a reputation as an efficient, disciplined drillmaster. The soldiers mustered in King Street, where the riflemen fired three rounds. The artillery regiment responded with a booming shot from each of their new field pieces. The three-pound brass cannons, the pride of the town, had arrived in February aboard the ship *Abigail*. The Massachusetts general assembly had sent two aging cannons to London to make a cast for these new guns, which bore the insignia of the province.

Henry, impressed with the artillery company, which Paddock put through the choreographed movements of a mock battlefield engagement, decided to join its ranks. The company, proudly known as The Train, had formed in 1763 under the direction of Captain David Mason. Paddock, an ardent Tory with loyalty to the British, took over command in 1768. Unlike the governor's guards, the members of the artillery unit were not among Boston's leading families, but were mostly sons of south-end shopkeepers, shipyard workers, and blacksmiths, silversmiths, and cobblers. Although they were amateur soldiers, they had gained great proficiency thanks to instruction from a group of British gunners two years earlier. In the late autumn of 1766, a regiment of British artillery arrived in Boston on its way to Quebec. As it was too late in the season to proceed up the St. Lawrence River, the soldiers quartered in the militia barracks on Castle William Island, a fort in Boston Harbor, where they remained until the following May. Over the winter, the professional soldiers took the time to instruct and drill members of The Train in the intricacies of firing cannon with precision.

Henry took his place among the ranks drilling under Paddock, learning how to load and fire a cannon and how to maintain it. He quickly realized that learning to be a competent soldier encompassed more than just valor, honor, and duty; there was an underlying, dispassionate science to military art. To build entrenchments and fortifications, he needed to learn engineering and geometry, as well as the calculus involved in gauging distant targets and firing guns with accuracy. He pored over the bookshop's volumes on military science, such as *Sharpe's Military Guide*, and borrowed books from the Harvard library. He had already spent years preparing himself for life as a soldier by studying French under the then-widespread belief that war with France would erupt again someday, and he had also familiarized himself with biographies of famous generals and by reading Julius Caesar's *Commentaries*. Knox longed to distinguish himself by earning military laurels. But unlike most militia at the time, he saw the need to apply in-depth study to the craft and take an analytical approach to battlefield tactics. He learned how to design fortifications that would protect musket men while allowing them a clear view of the field and providing vantage points to unleash enfilading fire in all directions. He learned the best ways to transport cannons weighing several tons, how to survey a position to find its topographical strengths and weaknesses, and where to place the most effective entrenchments. Within months, Knox became a skilled engineer and military tactician.

The political controversies between England and the colonists also provided Henry with opportunities to learn the craft of being a soldier. In August 1768, two ships sailed out of Boston Harbor bound for Nova Scotia. The governor of the province, Francis Bernard, let it be known that their mission was to transport troops of Irish regiments to Boston to occupy the town and quell agitation and resistance over Parliament's tax measures. On September 28, the ships sailed back into the harbor. On the first day of October, two regiments landed. Knox could watch the soldiers disembark and march in an impressive military parade along the length of Long Wharf, which led into town, with beating drums and glistening bayonets. Each man carried a cartridge box of sixteen balls, the allotment usually packed when entering enemy territory. The British battleship *Hussar* provided protective cover from the landing with seamen ready to open fire on any resistance from the townspeople, who could do nothing but watch in apprehensive silence.

The regiments took up quarters in unoccupied houses and public buildings in town. Knox watched the soldiers drill on Boston Common and Brattle Square to the sounds of an ear-piercing fife and the pounding of drums. The townspeople were incensed by the sight of the armed men. In the evenings, the Sons of Liberty, a secret Whig society that undermined British tax measures, played soothing and patriotic melodies on violins and flutes to calm residents.

Boston became an armed camp, and spectacles such as the public flogging of military deserters became frequent at the Common. The British commanders ordered that a cannon be placed directly in front of the Massachusetts Provincial House, which had been converted into a barracks. Knox watched the professional artillerists practice their maneuvers and carefully studied their movements. Like many in town, he seethed at this threat to his freedom.

As he entered adulthood, Knox was uncertain what his future held. He made tentative plans to open his own bookstore, but he placed this dream on hold until the boycott of English goods ended. Foremost on his mind was the support of his aging mother and younger brother, who by then was entering his teen years. Knox remained in the employment of Nicholas Bowes and supported the boycott, which caused deep tension and financial hardship in Boston. Henry was friends with several of the Sons of Liberty, including

Benjamin Edes and Jonathan Gill, publishers of the *Boston Gazette*, and Paul Revere, the silversmith and sometime dentist.

On a cold winter Monday, March 5, 1770, Knox crossed the Charles River to visit friends in Charlestown. Returning home that evening, he walked through Cornhill along Boston's crooked and icy streets and was only a short distance from home at around 9 P.M. A fresh coat of snow had fallen, and the night was clear. Boston was without street lanterns; the only light came from a half-crescent moon and the glow from windows. Rumors had circulated for the past two days that residents should avoid walking the streets because soldiers had vowed to avenge a beating of several of their comrades by the workers at Gray's Rope manufacturing factory the previous Friday. Knox ignored such warnings. More than six feet in height and an able fighter, he had little to fear.

Only minutes before Knox was to pass by the customhouse and town hall, a British officer crossed King Street. A boy who served as a barber's assistant yelled at the redcoat, "There goes that mean fellow who had not paid my master for dressing his hair!"[4]

A sentry by the name of Hugh White, who had been involved in the fight at the rope plant, was stationed in front of the customhouse. He walked up to the boy who had insulted the officer and said, "Show me your face."[5]

"I am not ashamed to show my face to any man," the boy said defiantly.

The sentry struck him in the head with the butt of his musket, and the boy fell to the ground stunned before staggering off, yelling that he thought he would die from the blow.

A witness rang a fire alarm for the townspeople to run to the rescue. Knox, hearing the clanging bells, began to pick up his pace. A group of soldiers also rushed up Exchange Street. Seeing that there was no fire, the soldiers began to clear the streets, before gathering at their station near the town house. Officers ordered the men to their barracks at the main guard not far from the customhouse.

The injured boy returned with friends to taunt White and throw snowballs and ice. "There is the soldier who knocked me down!" he yelled, pointing to the sentry. The soldier felt threatened and outnumbered. As objects were hurled at him, he quickly loaded and primed his musket.

"The lobster is going to fire!" yelled one boy.

By then Knox had arrived at the scene and recognized a potential disaster. He ordered the boys to stop harassing White. A Tory who stood nearby thought that Knox did "everything in his power to prevent mischief on this occasion."[6] Knox then turned to the sentry, warning, "If you fire, you must die for it." Under British law, any soldier who fired on residents without orders from the civil authorities was subject to capital punishment.

"I don't care!" White yelled to Knox. "If they touch me, I'll fire."

The boys continued to threaten and taunt the soldier. "Fire!" shouted one.

"Stand off!" the sentry ordered, and he retreated to the door of customhouse. Pounding on the door, he shouted: "Turn out, main guard!"[7]

A servant rushed from the customhouse up to the main guard and screamed to the soldiers, "They are killing the sentinel!"

The captain of the day, Thomas Preston, ordered a dozen men out. As Preston made his way toward the customhouse, townspeople lining the streets yelled insults and profanities. The soldiers fell out with bayonets fixed, knocking townspeople out of the way to get to the scene.

The sentinel was surrounded by at least ten townspeople as the soldiers arrived in front of the customhouse, and in minutes another fifty followed them up King Street. The servicemen pushed their way through the crowd, using bayonets and the butts of their muskets to clear a wedge, before lining shoulder to shoulder in a semicircle to protect the sentry. Knox raced to Preston and pulled on his coat to get his attention, pleading with him not to ignite the situation.

"Take your men back again," Knox demanded. "If they fire, your life must answer for the consequences."

"I know what I am about!" the captain shouted.

The soldiers began to load their muskets, and Knox saw some of the soldiers attack the townspeople with bayonets. He estimated that the crowd had grown to about eighty people. A group of about a dozen agitators began to taunt the men. "You are cowardly rascals," one resident sneered, "for bringing arms against naked men."

"Lay aside your guns, and we are ready for you," shouted another. "Come on, you rascals, you bloody backs, you lobster scoundrels, fire, if you dare. We know you dare not."[8]

As Knox was warning Preston to calm down, a British private named Hugh Montgomery was hit by a stick, which clanged against his musket and caused him to lose his footing. Rising, Montgomery yelled for his comrades to fire. Shots erupted in a flash against the darkness. Preston, standing near Knox, asked Montgomery why he had fired without orders. Before Preston received an answer, he was struck by a club and knocked down, submerged in the chaos of the panicked crowd.

Knox, at the foot of the town house, turned to see townspeople fall. A second round of shots discharged, then the frantic mob fled screaming in terror. Knox heard the people cry "fire, damn your blood," and could see the body of Crispus Attucks, a fifty-year-old black man, who had been struck in the chest by two balls and killed instantly. He saw John Gray, an owner of the rope factory, who had been hit with a fatal shot to the head. James Caldwell was hit twice in the back and died on the spot. Eight others were wounded, two mortally.

Of the eleven victims, only one had played a part in the clash with the soldiers. Knox was stunned. He had desperately tried to prevent the bloodshed. He had thrown himself in the midst of the conflict, risking his own life. As he stood looking at the crimson stains in the fleece-white snow, he heard church bells begin to ring. People poured out into the streets. Regiment drums sounded men to arms.

After the initial flight from the scene, townspeople dragged the wounded away as the infuriated British reloaded their muskets and lowered their sights. Preston stopped them from firing by striking their flintlocks with his hand.

"This is our time," one of his men exclaimed angrily.

Many of the residents were unaware that shots had been fired. Soon news of the shooting spread, and residents raced to the corner of King and Exchange streets, where they were horrified at the sight of blood and bodies.

"To arms! To arms!" Knox heard them cry. Many townspeople were ready to form battle ranks and drive the troops into the harbor.

A townsman told Preston that as many as 5,000 people were gathering at an adjacent street, inflamed by cries to kill the soldiers. Battle drums beat to produce a madding, thunderous chorus, and Knox could see residents crowd between the customhouse and the town house. The lieutenant governor of Massachusetts, Thomas Hutchinson, rushed to the scene and appeared on a balcony overlooking the crowd at about 10 P.M. He urged townspeople not to give in to angry passions and to trust that justice would prevail through legal means. He asked the British officers to send their troops back to the barracks. "The law," he pleaded, "should have its course." He said that he "would live and die by the law."

Magistrates then arrived, looking for witnesses to the shooting. Knox told them that he had seen the tragedy unfold. He gave an affidavit in which he stated that he had warned both White and Preston against firing and that by the time he arrived, no one was throwing snowballs or anything else at the sentry. Statements were taken until 3 A.M., and Preston and the other soldiers who fired their muskets were later arrested.

Knox was most likely among the 1,200 people who attended a town meeting at Faneuil Hall on Tuesday morning. There townspeople approved a statement demanding the removal of troops from Boston's borders. A committee of fifteen was chosen, led by Samuel Adams, who met with the lieutenant governor and Colonel William Dalrymple. They agreed to remove the Twenty-ninth Regiment, in which the accused soldiers served, but said the other regiment in town, the Fourteenth, would remain.

Knox watched as thousands of residents from the surrounding towns of Roxbury, Charlestown, Braintree, Dorchester, and Cambridge showed up in Boston, muskets in hand, ready to defend the town. The two regiments consisted of a mere 600 soldiers. By nightfall, it was likely that they would be surrounded by 10,000 colonists.

As tensions mounted, an afternoon town meeting was held. To accommodate the overflow crowd, the meeting was moved from Faneuil Hall to the Old South meetinghouse. The townspeople found the solution offered by royal officials of removing one regiment and maintaining another in Boston unacceptable. The cry went up, "Both regiments or none, both regiments or none." Another committee was chosen to issue the demand for the troops to vacate the town before the royally appointed lieutenant governor and Colonel Dalrymple. They agreed to withdraw the troops and station the soldiers in the barracks of Castle William Island in Boston Harbor. The evacuation would take two weeks. Knox took his part in a guard detail to stand watch over the town until the evacuation was complete.

On Thursday, March 8, Knox attended the funeral of four of the slain townsmen. Shops were closed and bells tolled in slow, solemn cadence not only in Boston but in neighboring towns. At 4 P.M., several hearses formed a procession on King Street at the scene of the tragedy. They proceeded up Main Street followed by 15,000 to 20,000 mourners, who marched four and six abreast through the narrow lanes. The *Boston Gazette* reported, "The distress and sorrow visible on every countenance, together with the peculiar solemnity with which the whole funeral was conducted, surpass description."[9] The bodies were placed in a vault at the Granary Burial Ground, to be held until the spring thaw allowed for burial. Paul Revere was commissioned to produce an engraving showing a line of British soldiers firing on the inhabitants, which was widely distributed.

With the troops confined to Castle William Island, a sense of normalcy returned to Boston. When passions subsided, many residents realized that war had been narrowly averted, and Whigs and Tories tried to ease strained relations.

On April 12 in London, Parliament acknowledged the success of the boycott and repealed all the duties on imports to America except for tea. When news of the repeal reached the colonies, merchants began to relax the prohibition on British goods. By May, the tactic was abandoned in Albany, Providence, and Newport, followed by New York businessmen in July and by Philadelphia importers in September. By October 12, Boston merchants decided that it was futile to persist in barring British goods and agreed to return imports to their shelves. This was the moment that Knox had been waiting for. Finally, he could order books from London. He began his plans to open his own bookstore and leave the employment of Nicholas Bowes.

Two weeks later, on October 25, Knox testified in the trial of Captain Thomas Preston. On the witness stand, he was questioned by prosecutor Robert Treat Paine. Knox reported that he had warned the accused officer not to allow his men to fire, an act that was deemed a capital offense, and that although the sentry was visibly shaken and afraid, he was not in danger. John Adams and Knox's former classmate Josiah Quincy provided legal defense for Preston. Upon cross-examination, Knox said that he heard people in the crowd yell, "Fire, damn your blood."[10] In his closing argument, John Adams said that Preston could not have ordered the men to load because Knox had stopped him as he approached the scene, and by that time the men had already loaded their muskets. Conflicting testimony in the case led the jury to acquit Preston.

In the second trial over the massacre, which involved the eight soldiers who fired their muskets, Knox provided the same testimony. In December, six of these men were acquitted, while two were found guilty and given a light sentence. Suffolk County sheriff Stephen Greenleaf branded their right thumbs with a hot iron to denote their conviction. Preston sailed for England and was awarded £200 by the government for his troubles relating to the shooting.

Following the trial, Knox focused more of his attention on his plans for a bookstore. He found a suitable shop opposite William's Court in Boston, and he sent an order of £340 for books to Thomas Longman and Sons of London on April 22, 1771. Within eighteen months, his orders totaled £2,066 in value.

Four days after his twenty-first birthday, his friends, the publishers Edes and Gills, ran an announcement of the opening of Knox's store in the *Boston Gazette*: "This day is opened a new London Bookstore by Henry Knox, opposite William's Court in Cornhill, Boston, who has just imported in the last ships from London a large and very elegant assortment of the most modern books in all branches of Literature, Arts and Sciences (catalogues of which will be published soon) and to be sold as cheap as can be bought at any place in town. Also a complete assortment of stationery."[11]

Knox's shop became a favorite for Boston's fashionable set to lounge in and discuss the latest topics or literary offerings. Knox was young, well liked, and handsome. His genial personality and charm attracted young women, who in turn brought to the shop young men who might not otherwise be disposed to reading. His friend Henry Burbeck said that "Knox's store was a great resort for the British officers and Tory ladies, who were the ton [vogue] at that period."[12]

The leading lady in Henry's life, his mother, died that year, eleven days before Christmas, at the age of fifty-three. The cause of her death is unknown. As he laid her to rest, Henry could reflect on the tribulations of her life. She had endured ten pregnancies and watched six infant sons die; she had been abandoned by her husband and left to care for two children. But she had lived to see Henry grow into manhood and open his own business, and for him to gain a measure of respectability in Boston and restore the family's reputation. He could take solace that he had faithfully stood by his mother and saw to her needs in her last years. His only remaining family connection was his fifteen-year-old brother William, whom he put to work helping run the bookstore.

Henry's store quickly outgrew the property at William's Court. He moved to another location near the town house in the center of Boston. He posted notices around town, advertising that he also bound and repaired books, journals, ledgers, and other volumes at short notice and sold books in all languages, arts, and sciences along with a complete line of stationery. He competed with seven other bookstores in Boston and was inventive in advertising books using the novel idea of including blurbs from the literary magazine *Critical Review*.

When he was not tending his shop, Henry continued his military training. During periods of peace, colonists maintained militia companies ready to protect the frontiers against American Indian attacks and in anticipation of another war with France. In the case that such a war occurred, Henry believed colonists should be prepared. In 1772, he cofounded the Boston Grenadier Corps, an offshoot of Paddock's Train. Knox was second in command. The company designed and ordered tailors to make splendid uniforms, and Knox and orderly sergeant Lemuel Trescott drilled the men in the evenings, choreographing their movements and training them to load and fire cannons and perform battle maneuvers as well as to use a sword, bayonet, and musket. The Grenadier Corps literally stood above the rest; all of its members were taller than five foot ten inches and shorter than six foot two inches, which was Henry's height. By June 8, 1772, the corps was ready to parade its colors before Boston. The men marched before admirers who were impressed by their military bearing. Knox, at the head of the parade, stood tall, broad-shouldered, and dashing.

Knox also kept up his military training through a careful study of books, determined to take an analytical approach in spite of his love for pomp and parade. Not only did he continue to order textbooks on military science, he asked questions of those British officers who frequented his shop.

Knox felt somewhat cloistered in the bookstore and spent his leisure in daily exercise and outdoor activities. He was close to his brother, and they often went hunting or fishing. Henry was a dedicated angler. The day before his twenty-third birthday, he boarded a small boat with his musket for a hunting expedition on Noodle Island in Boston Harbor. As he was exploring, his shotgun accidentally discharged, sending a blast of shot pellets through the fingers of his left hand. Knox winced in pain and gritted his teeth before summoning the strength to open his eyes to examine the wound, which was bleeding profusely. The pinky and ring fingers on his left hand were gone. His heart sank; one careless moment had left him with an irrevocable loss that could never be undone. He bound the wound and rowed back across the harbor to find two doctors to sew it up. Knox paid one of the physicians three guineas and the other five. He believed they had saved his life. He expressed his gratitude in a thank-you note, comparing himself to a mariner who had weathered a storm and who had emerged with "a firm respect and esteem for the means of his existence. So, Sir, gratitude obliges me to tender you my most sincere thanks for the attention and care you took of me in a late unlucky accident."[13]

He spent his birthday nursing the wound and trying to bear the pain. He was horrified to look at the injury and felt self-conscious about it. He took out a handkerchief and experimented with ways to hold it so as to veil his wound. For the rest of his life, Knox—even in portraits—would always be seen with a handkerchief wrapped around his left hand.

A few weeks after the accident, he appeared in another parade with the Boston Grenadier Corps as they marched through town in sharp military order to the staccato beat of drums. Henry's friend Burbeck noticed that "Lieutenant Knox appeared with the wound handsomely bandaged with a scarf, which of course excited the sympathy of all the ladies."[14]

Among those sympathetic was Lucy Flucker, one of the most fashionable young Tory women in Boston, who just days before had celebrated her seventeenth birthday. Watching the parade, she was transfixed by the tall, robust figure of Henry in uniform leading the column, and she immediately inquired about his identity.

Within days, Lucy showed up at Henry's shop and was delighted to find him kind, attentive, and all she had hoped for. He was equally smitten with her. She was a young woman of highly cultivated manners and tastes, blessed with beauty and, as a friend commented, a "bewitching face."[15] She had social charm and wit, was known for her intelligence and, as another friend put it, "very fond of books, and especially the books sold by Knox, to whose shelves she had frequent recourse."[16] She enjoyed social life, and because she was an eligible and attractive Tory lady, British officers vied for the attentions of her and her sisters at the frequent balls held around town.

Henry and Lucy were, however, from the opposite ends of Boston society. She was the daughter of Thomas Flucker, an affluent businessman who had served as the royally appointed secretary of Massachusetts since 1770. The fifty-four-year-old Flucker was a staunch, high-toned Tory with little patience for the radical element in Boston. He had served on the governor's council, the upper house of the legislature, which was patterned after the House of Lords, from 1761 to 1768 during the controversies over the Sugar Act, the Stamp Act, and the Townshend measures as resistance to Parliament grew.

But despite Henry and Lucy's social differences, a courtship developed, and soon both were expressing love to each other. She called him "Harry" and sympathized with his hard-luck past, the boy who supported his mother and brother at the age of nine, the loss of his father, the sacrifices he made in leaving school, and his dedicated effort to educate himself. She was not repelled by his mangled hand but instead viewed it as a war wound befitting a man of valor—even if it was only the result of a hunting accident.

Lucy also began to share Henry's political sympathies, which directly conflicted with the views of her own family. These differences became exacerbated as the gulf between Tories and Whigs widened in the late autumn of 1773, when news arrived that four ships transporting discount-priced tea that carried a three-pence-per-pound tax were being sent to America. This was an attempt by King George III and Parliament to tempt colonists to accept a British tax in which the cost was offset by the cheap price of the most popular drink in the colonies.

The first of these cargo vessels, the *Dartmouth*, arrived in Boston Harbor on November 28, 1773. By law, the ship had to be unloaded and the duty paid on its cargo at the end of twenty days, which in the case of the *Dartmouth*'s tea fell on December 16.

To prevent the crates of tea leaves from being unloaded at some quiet moment or in the dead of the night, radical leaders appointed a twenty-four-hour guard to watch the vessel while they tried to work out a resolution that would send the tea back to England. Knox's Boston Grenadiers volunteered to take their turn to prevent the cargo from landing on American soil. As Henry stood watch on Griffin's Wharf, he realized that he was in firing range of a fleet of British battleships that flanked the *Dartmouth*. By volunteering for the guard detail, Henry publicly identified himself with the colonial cause and was in open and defiant opposition to the convictions and politics of Lucy's family.

Shortly before six o'clock on Thursday, December 16, 1773, the captain of the *Dartmouth*, Francis Rotch, reported to a town meeting of about 8,000 residents at the Old South meetinghouse that the governor and customs officials refused to allow him to send the tea back to England without the duties being paid. The cargo would be unloaded by authorities the next morning. Within minutes a large group of young men disguised as Mohawk Indians marched to the three tea-laden ships (the fourth had been wrecked on the rocks of Cape Cod) at Griffin's Wharf. They boarded and began to remove the crates, splitting them with mock tomahawks so water would saturate the contents. It is not known whether Henry Knox took part in what became known as the Boston Tea Party. It had been engineered by Samuel Adams and the Sons of Liberty, and those who took part were sworn to secrecy and for the most part did not know the other participants under their disguises.

Massachusetts governor Hutchinson believed war between the colonists and the British was now inevitable and that the inhabitants had gone too far to recede. Yet despite the political polarization in Boston between loyalists and radicals, Lucy stood by Henry.

Her father was greatly concerned over Lucy's infatuation with a young man who was not only her inferior in social standing, but a possible rebel who sought to undermine the authority of King George III, Parliament, and royal officials such as himself. To dissuade his daughter from an ill-considered choice in her heart's desire, he bluntly laid the future before her. Britain was intent on extending its authority in America and settling the interior regions toward the Mississippi, he told her. Additional governors would be appointed and most likely given noble titles. British political and military power would overwhelm those who resisted, and rebels such as Henry faced certain ruin or even worse. If she married this humble bookbinder, she could anticipate a future of poverty or perhaps be reduced to begging from friends for support. The gulf in social standing would mean estrangement from her family, including her dear sisters. One day she would undoubtedly watch as her siblings traveled in fine carriages and attended elegant banquets and enjoyed all that a life of privilege had to offer. And she, living in need, would begin to rank the wants of her purse above the yearnings of her sentimental heart.

Her father told her that if rebels such as Henry resisted British authority to the point of war, she would be married to a traitor and unable to hold her head with dignity as she walked the streets of her hometown. Her husband would be fighting against her brother, who was enlisted in the British army. Lucy's friends were equally discouraging, explaining that her love for Henry could cost her everything, including their friendships.

Yet Lucy's devotion to Henry had grown beyond infatuation into a devoted love. She realized that despite the sacrifices, she could not live without him, and she would forsake her world if she must.

Knox was also going through agonizing turmoil. Because of her father's opposition to their courtship, they were forced to meet in secret and arrange times to run into each other, or to attend dances and public events where they could steal a private moment. They passed notes that revealed their true feelings while maintaining a façade of polite friendship in public. Thoughts of losing her amid all the complications swirling around their courtship gave him moments of grief-stricken panic. They discussed marriage and entertained the idea of eloping. Lucy tried to win over her father, to have him see Henry as she saw him and consent to their marriage.

Henry wrote to Lucy on Monday, March 7, 1774: "What news? Have you spoken to your father, or he to you, upon the subject? What appearance has this [to our] grand affair at your house at present? Do you go to the ball tomorrow evening? I am in a state of anxiety heretofore unknown. I wish the medium of our correspondence settled, in order to which I must endeavor to see you, when we will settle it."[17]

He expressed his faith in her love: "My only consolation is in you, and in order that it should be well grounded, permit me to beg two things of you with the greatest ardency: never distrust my affection for you without the most rational and convincing proof—if you do not hear from me in a reasonable time, do not lay it to my want of love, but want of opportunity; and do not, in consequence of such distrust, omit writing to me as often as possible."[18]

Confronted with Lucy's fervent pleas, Flucker gave in and consented to the marriage. Henry and Lucy set a date to exchange vows for Monday, June 20, 1774. Her father wondered whether Knox's radicalism stemmed more from military ambition than political ideals. Through his influence as royal secretary of Massachusetts, Flucker secured Henry a commission in the British army as a lieutenant and then a captain. Knox was flattered but said he had to refuse the offer, which made Flucker acknowledge that Knox's convictions ran deep.

Even before the wedding, the predictions that Henry's business prospects would plummet seemed prophetic. News arrived in Boston in early May that Parliament had retaliated for the Boston Tea Party by passing a coercive port bill that forbade any commercial trade ships in Boston Harbor. Residents approved another boycott of English goods on Thursday, May 12. This would mean a sharp drop in business at Knox's London Bookstore, which dealt almost exclusively in items shipped from England. Henry was left holding the debt for his inventory while being unable to sell the items and satisfy his creditors. The London bookselling firm of Wright & Gill notified him that 5 percent interest would be tacked on to his £350 debt. This debt was over two years past due, forcing the firm to write to him: "It really hurts us to be under the disagreeable necessity of thus writing you."[19] Yet despite the prospect of ruining his business, Knox spearheaded an "anti-consumption" league to help enforce the boycott.

The next day, Knox dressed in his militia uniform and marched with the Boston Grenadier Corps to the Long Wharf as British ships sailed into the harbor carrying four regiments of troops and General Thomas Gage, who was ordered to replace Hutchinson as the governor of Massachusetts.

As Gage disembarked, he noticed Knox's company marching in precise military movements and commented that he was impressed with their military bearing. The British troops set up camp on Boston Common and began daily exercises.

As Henry and Lucy prepared for their wedding, he had to arrange for his business to survive the boycott. Knox expected the tactic to be effective in forcing a repeal of the Boston Port Act, as similar tactics had been in defeating the Stamp Act and Townshend revenue measures. On Monday, May 30, the day before the Port Act was to go into effect, he wrote to Wright & Gill: "If the act to block up this harbor should continue in force any length of time, it must deeply affect every person in trade here, and consequently their correspondents on your side of the water. But it is expected the British merchants will see their own interest so clearly as to induce them to exert their whole influence in order to get so unjust and cruel an edict repealed."[20]

On June 1, Knox, along with colonists throughout America, fasted and prayed for Boston as well as for the repeal of the Port Act—and in the hope of avoiding a war. The call for a day of fasting had come from the Virginia House of Burgesses led by Thomas Jefferson and Richard Henry Lee. Jefferson said the result was "like a shock of electricity, arousing every man, and placing him erect and solidly on his center."[21]

Thomas Flucker worked closely with General Gage to enforce the ban on merchant shipping in Boston Harbor. He and other loyalists also kept a close watch on the defiant Massachusetts General Assembly. Gage had the power to close the legislature down if radicals passed any measures to undermine British authority.

On Friday, June 17, a panting messenger arrived at Gage's office to report that the assembly was passing proposals to send delegates to the upcoming Continental Congress, slated for September, to address the standoff between the colonies and England. Gage frantically drew up an order to shut down proceedings and handed it to Flucker, who raced to the legislature only to find the doors of the session chambers bolted shut. In his frustration, Flucker read the order aloud to the closed door, surrounded by fellow Tories. By the time the assemblymen emerged, they had approved a bill that chose delegates to attend the congress: Samuel Adams, John Adams, the Massachusetts Speaker of the House Thomas Cushing, and prosecuting attorney Robert Treat Paine.

Flucker returned to Gage seething with resentment over the actions of men he deemed rebels to both the king and Parliament. He could not help but feel wounded by the thought that in three days, his beloved daughter Lucy would marry a known rebel sympathizer.

On Monday, June 20, at the height of the swirling controversy, as colonists continued to sign on to the boycott, as British soldiers daily marched through Boston streets and militia companies throughout the region prepared for war, Henry Knox and Lucy Flucker exchanged wedding vows. About a month later, he would be twenty-four years old, and she would turn eighteen, their birthdays just eight days apart.

A friend composed lines of verse for the ceremony in praise of Lucy's decision to risk a promising future for the considerations of her heart:

> Blest tho' she is with ev'ry human grace,
> The mein engaging, and bewitching face,
> Yet still an higher beauty is her care,
> Virtue, the charm that most adorns the fair.[22]

The marriage sparked deep disappointment in Lucy's family and friends. By ignoring their pleas, by standing by Henry as his prospects declined and as he stood in opposition to the most powerful empire in the world, she showed a strong independent streak rare in her social circle.

Their wedded life began in the midst of financial crisis. Henry had to balance his political feelings with concerns for his business. The memory of his father's failed business and the turmoil it caused their family was still fresh in his mind. He tried to maintain cordial commercial relations with both loyalists and Tories. When James Rivington, the New York bookseller and publisher of *Rivington's Royal Gazette* in New York, sent him five chests of dutied tea on Thursday, July 28, Henry declined the commission. He wrote Rivington: "I forgot my politics—or rather, I have none to communicate at present. Things seem to be pretty much at a stand, since I wrote you."

He reported that the troops in Boston seemed disciplined and for the most part tried to avoid triggering confrontations with inhabitants, who also wanted to avoid another incident like the Boston Massacre. But he noted that militias were growing in ranks and the boycott had spread throughout the New England colonies, even though it had been prohibited by General Gage. Knox could not help but let his politics show in writing Rivington: "The new acts for regulating this government will, I perfectly believe, make great difficulties. The people are in no disposition to receive an act pregnant with so great evils. What mode of opposition will be adopted, I do not know; but it is the general opinion that it will be opposed; hence the key to the formidable force collecting here."[23]

To further his own military education, Knox often watched the British soldiers drill. He noticed another keen observer of the troops, a thirty-two-year-old Rhode Island Quaker by the name of Nathanael Greene, who was destined to be the closest male friend of his life. Despite the pacifism of Greene's religious upbringing, he harbored an almost overwhelming ambition for military glory. He looked like anything but a soldier, walking with a pronounced limp that was believed to be the result of an accident when, as a boy, he fell from a roof while sneaking to a dance. Quakers are forbidden to dance, and this would not be the last time Greene defied the restrictions of his denomination.

Greene grew up in Warwick, Rhode Island, where he worked in his father's ironworks. He had an early interest in military life. In 1770, he moved to Coventry, Rhode Island, a sixty-mile horseback ride from Boston, to take over a foundry, and soon was elected to the colonial legislature. Three years later, he again defied religious sanctions by attending a military parade and as a consequence was turned out of the Quaker meeting. Undeterred, he organized a stylish militia called the Kentish Guards. Yet Green was denied a commission because of his game knee.

Sharing similar military aspirations as well as political sentiments, Knox and Greene became quick friends and spent hours discussing military strategy and tactics at Henry's bookshop or at Nathanael's Boston lodging, the Bunch of Grapes, which had become a favorite hangout of Whig leaders. Henry suggested several books on military science to him and was not impressed with Greene's knowledge, thinking him "the rawest, most untutored being I ever met with."[24]

Gage knew of Knox's reputation as a skilled military engineer and grenadier, and he gave orders prohibiting him from leaving Boston. Aware that he was under surveillance, Knox became cautious about what he said and who was listening. Paul Revere's commitment to the colonial cause had not yet come to the attention of authorities. When he visited Knox's bookstore and loyalists or British soldiers were browsing the shelves, Revere pretended to quarrel with Knox over work that had been commissioned by Henry for engraving or silverwork. They had fun with the ruse and shouted insults at each other. Their apparent animosity fueled gossip, and it was widely held that they detested and distrusted each other. British spies approached Revere, seeking information about the rebel bookseller.

Knox sensed that a conflict was coming. He quietly advised the rest of the grenadiers to leave town while they could. Almost all of his company left. Colonists began to slip out of Boston smuggling gunpowder, munitions, and military supplies. Knox tried to gain information about activities outside of Boston and became part of a network of spies. He heard that inhabitants were building up military stocks in cities around the region such as Quarry Hill, between Cambridge and Medford, and at Charlestown, in preparation for the advent of war. The same information came to the attention of Gage, and Tories became alarmed that many of their radical neighbors had closed their homes and disappeared. Boston lay on a round peninsula that at the time was nearly an island, connected to the mainland only by a 120-yard-wide isthmus called Boston Neck. British troops fortified the neck, mounted twenty-eight cannons along its length, and monitored traffic in and out of the city.

Knox's anxiety grew. Although he still entertained military ambitions, if he left Boston, he would surely be tracked down and arrested by royal authorities on charges of treason. He also had his business to consider; he desperately did not want to fail like his father. He was deeply in debt to London booksellers and had to weigh the needs of his young wife and eighteen-year-old brother. If he joined the ranks of the militia, he would be abandoning his wife, his brother, and his business, just as his father had once forsaken his family.

On the first day of September, Gage commanded 260 soldiers to march from Boston to Cambridge before sunrise, and to seize the powder from the town's community gunpowder magazine, and confiscate two cannons. When news of this order spread, thousands of militiamen raced to Cambridge to protest the taking of the items. No shots were fired as the British troops quietly removed the military supplies and commandeered the two field pieces. Wild rumors spread throughout the colonies. According to one report, six colonists had been killed in a desperate battle with British soldiers. According to a report that reached the Continental Congress in Philadelphia a week later on September 8, Boston had been cannonaded through the night and the town lay in ashes and heaps.

In October, a meeting of town leaders throughout Massachusetts approved a provincial congress to operate outside of royal authority, collect taxes, and raise militia companies. This was the first nonroyally authorized state government in the colonies.

Knox was uncertain what he should do. His business was suffering badly from the boycott and the economic strain under the British Coercive Acts or intolerable acts, which were passed as punitive measures in the wake of the Boston Tea Party and included the closing of the town's harbor. In November 1774, he wrote his book distributor in London, Thomas Longman, that he would abide by the boycott and that he was unable to meet his payments for shipments already received. "I had the fairest prospect of entirely balancing our account this fall; but the almost total stagnation of trade, in consequence of the Boston Port Bill, has been the sole means of preventing it, and now the non-consumption agreement will stop that small circulation of business left by the Boston Port. It must be the wish of every good man that these unhappy differences between Great Britain and the Colonies be speedily and finally adjusted. The influence that the unlucky and unhappy mood of politics of the times has upon trade is my only excuse for writing concerning them."[25]

He asked Longman to lobby for colonial interests, which were closely aligned with the book distributor's own. "I cannot but hope every person who is concerned in American trade will most strenuously exert themselves, in their respective stations, for what so nearly concerns themselves."

The inhabitants around Boston suffered under severe economic hardships. They survived on a steady stream of donations from surrounding colonies of wheat, corn, flour, and other foodstock along with money. Provisions were smuggled in at night on small boats that crossed the Charles River and the back bay of Boston Harbor. Henry may have been broke, but he was not starving. Married life agreed with him, and his waist began to expand. He was still strong and energetic, but his physique became less athletic and more pear-shaped, and his weight began to rise to about 260 pounds, despite the boycott.

On the first day of February 1775, a Wednesday, a second Massachusetts provincial congress, which considered itself the legitimate constitutional government of the colony, convened in Cambridge and drew up plans to begin full preparations for war and build defenses to thwart British aggression. Dr. Joseph Warren, a prominent Boston physician and fiery patriot, was named to head the Committee of Safety. On Thursday, February 23, Warren was directed to ascertain the number of grenadiers from Paddock's old artillery company who could be "depended on to form an artillery company when the Constitutional Army of the Province should take the field, and that report be made without loss of time."[26]

Knox wondered if he should list himself among those who could be counted on. He considered abandoning his business and leaving it in the hands of his brother. He seemed to clutch at the hope that the boycott could work to prevent a war, as it had before. Knox also had to consider that British soldiers were no longer careful not to insult the colonists. The homes of patriots who had left Boston were looted and vandalized. Soldiers broke into the houses of noted radicals, shattered windows and destroyed furniture. Knox knew that his own business would be targeted. But his hope for peace diminished daily. News arrived that on Thursday, February 27, British forces landed at Salem and captured a colonial arsenal. No shots were fired.

The last advertisement for Knox's London Bookstore appeared in the *Boston Gazette* on Monday, March 20, 1775, touting copies of a pamphlet sent along by Rivington and written by a young student at King's College in New York named Alexander Hamilton. The ad said: "Just published and to be sold by Henry Knox in Cornhill, price 1 s. 6 d. *The Farmer refuted: Or a more impartial and comprehensive view of the dispute between Great Britain and the Colonies, intended as a further vindication of Congress.*"

Knox had refused to carry Tory pamphlets, but he promoted Hamilton's piece, which proclaimed "[t]hat all Americans are entitled to freedom is incontestable on every rational principle."[27]

On the evening of Tuesday, April 18, Knox and others around Boston noticed that many of the British troops were not at their usual posts. Dr. Warren walked through the streets trying to find out if they were preparing to march. He sent for Knox's friend Paul Revere to carry a warning to radical leaders outside of the city. Warren suspected that soldiers were being sent to arrest Samuel Adams and John Hancock, who were staying at the home of the Reverend Jonas Clark in Lexington, a town about twelve miles north of Boston. Perhaps their mission was to destroy the storehouse of munitions in Concord, eighteen miles to the north. Word spread that the army was collecting boats along the back bay of Boston Harbor. Knox and others watched closely to divine British intentions. By 11 P.M., 700 soldiers had marched to the west side of town, where they began to climb into boats to cross the harbor. Within a couple hours, the troops formed ranks and began the march from Cambridge. Church bells rang, guns were fired, and flares shot into the night sky as patriots tried to rouse the inhabitants along the road to Lexington.

Early that Wednesday morning, Knox watched the Forty-seventh and Thirty-eighth regiments of about 1,200 Welsh soldiers, carrying light muskets and carting two cannons, leave Boston to support the mission, marching to the tune of "Yankee Doodle" to mock the colonists. Then news arrived that shots had been fired at Lexington between British soldiers under Major Pitcairn and the patriot militiamen. Seven colonial soldiers were killed and nine others wounded.

Knox's heart sank. The war so long anticipated had begun. He could no longer stay out of the conflict. He would have to abandon his business and sacrifice everything he had built and all that he owned. Lucy wanted to accompany him if he left the city. William agreed to stay and watch the bookstore, to try to prevent looters and vandals from destroying the shop.

By Thursday morning, British troops, many wounded, straggled back into Boston. A significant battle had erupted the previous evening in Lexington and Concord as the troops destroyed munitions, spiking two field pieces and throwing 500 pounds of cannonballs and 60 barrels of flour into the river. Samuel Adams and John Hancock had escaped capture. Almost 500 militiamen rushed to Concord's defense and fired at the British soldiers from every direction. After two hours, the king's troops were forced to retreat. On the way back to Boston, they were ambushed by a group of 150 colonists from the line of trees flanking the road. The British suffered nearly 300 casualties. The American loss was 90 men, including 8 killed.

Shortly after the battles of Lexington and Concord, Henry and Lucy dressed in disguises and prepared to sneak out of the city. With his size, however, there was little that Henry could do to hide his identity. Lucy sewed his sword into her coat. The couple said good-bye to William and, under the cover of darkness, slipped out of their house and headed for the waterfront, carefully avoiding the posted guards. If detected, they would be arrested and would spend the war in a British prison. They could even be hanged under charges of treason.

They reached the water safely, and Henry helped Lucy climb into a small boat. They pushed slowly from shore, under agonizing tension so as not to make a sound.

As Lucy watched Boston disappear in the night air, she could not help but wonder if she would ever see her family again, her sisters Hannah and Sally and her brother Thomas. She had forsaken everything for Henry and was about to accompany him to the war. Knox wondered how long his business could last. He knew that it almost certainly would be a casualty of the conflict. Everything he had achieved, rising as a fatherless kid from the tough streets of Boston to become a respectable owner of a popular business, was gone. As he rowed the boat across the river, the couple soon became enveloped in darkness, unable to see Boston behind them or the future in front of them.

TWO

TICONDEROGA

H enry planned to visit the camp of colonial militiamen surrounding Boston and find a secure place for Lucy to live. She pleaded with Henry to allow her to accompany him, but he was concerned about her safety amid the thousands of rowdy young militia soldiers and backwoodsmen who filled the army's ranks. He accompanied her to nearby Worcester, where she was taken in by friends. Knox then walked to the Cambridge encampment, which was being called the "camp of liberty."[1] In the aftermath of Lexington and Concord, the Massachusetts Committee of Safety put out a call for other provincial militias to aid in the siege of Boston. The force quickly grew to 13,600 men. New Hampshire sent 1,200, and Connecticut provided 6,000. Rhode Island planned to send another 1,500.

Knox quickly saw that the "camp of liberty" was a chaotic collection of hunters, farmers, unemployed seamen, and tyros. Many had little if any military training and lacked discipline or order. He found his way to the headquarters of Artemas Ward, who had been named commander in chief of the hodgepodge of militias. The forty-eight-year-old Ward had made his mark as a lieutenant colonel of the Massachusetts militia during the French-Indian War and had been appointed brigadier general in charge of the province's militia in 1775. Ill during the battles of Lexington and Concord, he had risen to take command of the siege of Boston and was frantically trying to organize the army before the British marched out and attacked. Ward was ecstatic to see Knox. Among the thousands of troops under his command, almost no one had any skill as a military engineer. Henry declined a specific commission and instead suggested that he might be more useful in helping design fortifications throughout the army. Ward agreed.

As Knox surveyed the camp around Boston, he realized that the patriot army had erected few obstacles to bar the British from taking the offensive. His first concern was building a line of defenses at Roxbury, a small town along the road leading from Boston Neck, the only land route out of the town. Knox drafted plans for a redoubt on a hill overlooking Roxbury and put men to work digging entrenchments and building fortifications that could help repel a British attempt to leave Boston or prevent enemy troops from circling around and flanking rebel musket men.

Knox walked throughout the camp and noticed men coming and going as they pleased. When he tried to assess the number of men fit for battle, he found that company commanders could only guess at the figures of troops they could depend on. There was no system to channel food and no allowance for hygiene. The camp stunk from the lack of sanitation. Many men had no rifles, and others had only fowling pieces that discharged buckshot. Fights broke out from rivalries within the mosaic of militias.

News arrived in camp that an expedition headed by Ethan Allen, a militia leader from Vermont, and Benedict Arnold, a Connecticut militia captain, had on May 10 captured Fort Ticonderoga in upstate New York and its rich supply of munitions, which included 78 serviceable cannons, 6 mortars, 3 howitzers, and 30,000 musket flints. Knox thought that the patriots surrounding Gage's 6,500 men in Boston were sorely in need of those supplies. But Ticonderoga was almost 300 miles away, and the ground in between was rugged, hilly forest.

Dr. Warren and the Committee of Safety also were concerned about the lack of training and skill in the American force and on May 16 recommended that Knox "be applied to for supplying the Colony Army with military books."[2] Henry could do nothing to acquire books while Boston was occupied and could only recommend books from the library at Harvard College. When he could, he visited Lucy, who had moved into the crowded home of John Cook in Watertown, where the *Boston Gazette* publishers Benjamin Edes and John Gill also were staying. After the works at Fort Roxbury were complete, Knox helped train gunners. The American artillery received a boost when 12 cannons, 18-pound and 24-pound pieces, arrived with a company from Providence and four more large guns came with another Rhode Island unit.

Many of the soldiers were frustrated by inactivity. Patriot leaders had ordered Ward to attack only if the British fired first. On June 12, Gage posted an order declaring that all rebels who did not lay down their arms and swear an oath of allegiance to the crown would be deemed traitors. When it was learned that the British planned to take Bunker Hill, the strategic height overlooking Boston, the American commanders decided to seize the position first. Knox was sent to reconnoiter the sloping hill and the adjacent Breed Hill, which lay about 1,500 yards north of Boston across the Charles River on the Charlestown peninsula. As darkness fell on the evening of Friday, June 16, 1,200 militiamen marched to Breed's Hill to build a line of fortifications. The next day, the British crossed the harbor in 28 barges with about 3,000 men.

The battle opened when the British cannons on Boston Neck rained fire on the Knox-designed works at Roxbury. Knox responded with cannon fire and demonstrated his marksmanship with the heavy guns. Cannonballs came crashing around his men. It became quickly evident that the colonists were no match for the British firepower.

Knox was awed by the precision of the British gunners aboard the battleships, as the 68-gun *Somerset*, the 20-gun *Lively*, the 36-gun *Cerberus*, the 34-gun *Glasglow*, and other war vessels opened thundering fire on the Breed Hill redoubt. The redcoats mounted cannons on Copp's Hill, about a mile opposite of the American entrenchments, and sent accurate shots pounding the position. The patriot line atop the hill stubbornly held, however. Gage lost patience and ordered his gunners to level Charlestown. The English artillery from sea and land sent whistling shots against the buildings, which exploded into flying splinters. British soldiers lit the wooden structures on fire, and the town soon was aflame. The carnage was devastating.

Knox watched as the sea of red-clad troops formed a battle line and began the march up the green slope of Breed Hill. After the British neared the crest, a loud volley from colonial guns shredded their ranks and sent the British in retreat, stumbling among the tall grass and fallen bodies. The king's men made a second assault but were again repulsed by the muskets of colonials. On the verge of abandoning the battle, the British received news that the colonists were out of gunpowder. Gage saw his opportunity and ordered a bayonet charge. The Americans were not equipped with bayonets. The redcoats regained their composure to make one final attempt to take the hill. They raced to the top, stepping over their fallen comrades. The armies clashed in brutal hand-to-hand fighting, the British lunging their bayonets to spear the patriots. The Americans scattered in retreat, and the royal army gave up chase after a few hundred yards, too exhausted to pursue.

In what became known as the Battle of Bunker Hill, the British lost 1,150 men to 441 casualties for the Americans. Among the dead were many of Knox's friends, including Dr. Joseph Warren, who had received a commission as a general just four days earlier.

The defeat looked catastrophic for American hopes. Warren had been the most able of the American commanders, and the aging Ward was not up to the task of organizing the army. Optimism was renewed within a few weeks, however. General George Washington, whom the Continental Congress had named to replace Ward as commander in chief, arrived in the Cambridge camp on Monday, July 3, after a twelve-day journey from Philadelphia, accompanied by several New York militia companies and a troop of Philadelphia cavalry. Two days later, on Wednesday, July 5, as Knox walked on an errand to Cambridge, he met Washington and General Charles Lee, who asked him to accompany them to the Roxbury works. As they came upon the line of entrenchments and crescent-shaped batteries, Washington and Lee marveled at Knox's design and breathed a sigh of relief that someone in the disordered Continental Army knew how to build fortifications. Knox reported to Lucy in a letter the next morning: "When they viewed the works, they expressed the greatest pleasure and surprise at their situation and apparent utility, to say nothing of the plan, which did not escape their praise."[3]

Washington took an instant liking to Knox even though they came from very different worlds. The general, addressed as "Your Excellency," hailed from the pinnacle of hierarchical Virginia and was a wealthy planter with a large estate and hundreds of slaves. Knox came from the rough side of egalitarian Massachusetts. But they shared a rugged physical quality. Both were tall, energetic, active men. As Washington talked with Knox, he found that Henry possessed an analytical mind and sound judgment as well as a deep understanding of the army's shortcomings. The forty-three-year-old Washington, who was childless, surrounded himself with promising young men whom he treated as surrogate sons. Knox, who was just short of his twenty-fifth birthday, was pulled into this familial circle. From Watertown, Henry wrote in a July 9 letter to Lucy: "General Washington fills his place with vast ease and dignity." He added that he had to rush off to wait on the commander in chief. Two days later, he wrote: "The new generals are of infinite service in the army. They have to reduce order from almost perfect chaos."[4]

Washington believed that discipline and corporal punishment were needed to rein in the unruly troops. One soldier was given the penalty of twenty lashes for "abusive language to Colonel Gridley. The General confirms the sentence, and orders it to be executed after prayer time tomorrow."[5]

Another soldier received thirty-nine lashes for robbing the surgeon general of the army. After Colonel William Prescott was found guilty of "threatening and abusing a number of persons," a court-martial sentenced him to the humiliation of riding "the wooden Horse, fifteen minutes."[6] Knox heartily approved of the army crackdown: "I think they are in a fair way of doing it."[7]

Knox was pleased to see that Nathanael Greene, the commander of three Rhode Island regiments, had arrived in camp. On June 22, 1775, Congress appointed Greene one of seven brigadier generals in the quickly fashioned Continental Army, with Green being the youngest.[8] The record is unclear how Greene jumped from military novice to the youngest brigadier general in the patriot army in merely a year, and whether it was political connections or the result of his ardent study on field strategy, tactics, and engineering.

In Philadelphia, Massachusetts delegate to Congress John Adams believed the reorganization of the army did not include enough New England men among the officer ranks. He recommended to his colleagues that Knox, among others, should be appointed to a lucrative post such as quartermaster general, commissary of musters, or commissary of artillery. Some congressmen felt those appointments should be left up to Washington. Feeling a bout of regional pride, Adams wrote to the Massachusetts Committee of Safety on July 23 with a list of local men, headed with Knox's name, to support for promotion, who "are well qualified for places in the army, who have lost their all, by the outrages of tyranny, whom I wish to hear provided for. . . . They could be made Captains or Brigade Majors, or put into some little places at present I am very sure, their country would loose nothing by it, in reputation or otherwise."[9]

Washington, however, was already considering an appointment for Knox within the army. Henry regularly dined with him and generals Charles Lee, Israel Putnam, William Heath, Nathanael Greene, and Horatio Gates. Washington and Lee asked about Lucy and invited her to dine with them. On Friday, September 22, she attended a dinner at Washington's residence, where she displayed the charm and genteel manners that had once made her so popular among her Tory friends.

The next day, Knox was relieved that she had left the camp when the British artillery opened a cannonade on the American position. Henry was not impressed with these grenadiers, who were not as skilled as the gunners aboard the battleships who leveled Charlestown. He wrote to his brother on

September 25 with a sense of bravado: "Let it be remembered to the honor and skill of the British troops, that they fired 104 cannon-shot at [our] works, at not a greater distance than half point blank shot—and did what? Why, scratched a man's face with the splinters of a rail-fence! I have had the pleasure of dodging these heretofore engines of terror with great success; nor am I afraid they will [hit me] unless directed by the hand of Providence."

In Congress, Samuel Adams and John Adams continued to push for New England officers in Washington's army. Other delegates complained about the apparent lack of qualified military men in Massachusetts suitable for promotion. On September 26, Samuel Adams wrote to Elbridge Gerry, a patriot leader in a town about 15 miles up the Atlantic coast called Marblehead: "Until I visited headquarters at Cambridge, I had never heard of . . . the ingenuity of Knox and [Josiah] Waters in planning the celebrated works at Roxbury. We were told here that there were none in our camp who understood this business of an engineer, or anything more than the manual exercise of the gun. This we had from great authority, and for want of more certain intelligence were obliged at least to be silent."[10]

Samuel apparently gave his second cousin John Adams the same information, for on Thursday, October 5, 1775, Adams wrote to John Thomas, a brigadier general stationed at Roxbury: "I beg your opinion in confidence of two gentlemen, Mr. Henry Knox and Mr. [Josiah] Waters, whether they are qualified for engineers and whether they have studied the sublime art of war, I mean fortifications and gunnery whether they are sufficient masters of those sciences to hold any considerable employments in that branch of the service."[11]

Thomas wrote Adams praising Knox's qualifications and recommended him for a commission in the army. On October 23, a congressional committee recommended that Knox be appointed a lieutenant colonel rather than a full colonel. When this news arrived in Cambridge, Knox was hurt by the slight. He wrote to John Adams: "I have the most sacred regard for the liberty of my country and am fully determined to act as far as is in my power in opposition to the present tyranny attempted to be imposed upon it—but as an honor is comparative, I humbly hope that I have as good a pretension to the rank of colonel as many now in the service, the declining to confer which by the delegates not a little surprised me. If your respectable body should not incline to give the rank and pay of colonel, I must beg to decline it. But I will do every service in my power as a volunteer."[12]

Knox held out hope for a commission, writing Adams that the commander of the artillery, stricken with poor health, was unpopular with his men. Henry expected that the commander in chief would soon reorganize the regiment's command and that he was a likely replacement as its leader. To Adams, he confided: "[The] other field officers of the regiment wish it and I have great reasons to believe, the generals too. . . . It ever appears to me to detract from the merit of a person when he takes the liberty to recommend himself—nothing but the flattering idea of being in a small measure assisting to free my country would induce me to do it."[13]

Washington, who was trying to transform the variety of provincial militia units into regiments of the Continental Army, wanted Knox as a key commander. On November 2, the general acknowledged his impact on fortifications throughout the army in a letter to Connecticut governor John Trumbull, explaining: "Most of our works which have been thrown up for the defense of several encampments have been planned by a few of the principal officers of the army, assisted by Mr. Knox."[14]

Washington's other major concern was shoring up the sagging Continental artillery regiment, which was under the command of the aging Colonel Richard Gridley, a veteran of the French-Indian War who had been commissioned by Congress as colonel of artillery on September 20.[15]

Congress also urged Washington "that an attack upon Boston if practicable was much desired." At a war council of his top commanders, all eight generals present disapproved of an assault. British cannons kept the army at bay, and the Continental artillery was inferior to the British in skill as well as in firepower. Furthermore, Washington received intelligence from John Hancock, president of the Continental Congress, that an American spy in London reported that a large number of cannons were being prepared to be sent to Boston along with 400 artillery soldiers.

Washington needed an energetic and resourceful artillery leader to replace the infirm Gridley. David Mason, the man next in command under Gridley, agreed to serve as a lieutenant colonel of artillery of the regiment if Knox was appointed colonel. Several gunners from Paddock's old Grenadiers agreed to serve under Knox. On November 8, 1775, Washington wrote to Congress: "The council of officers are unanimously of the opinion, that the command of the artillery should no longer continue in Colonel Gridley, and knowing of no person better qualified to supply his place, or whose appointment will give more general satisfaction, have taken the liberty of recommending Henry Knox."[16]

Contingent on congressional approval, Knox was to be promoted to the rank of colonel to lead the army's artillery corps without ever having served a single day as a private in the army. When Washington informed Henry that he was to take over the army's artillery, Knox teasingly asked where the artillery was. Washington admitted that there was almost none to speak of. As flattering as the prospect of promotion certainly was, Knox knew that a monumental task lay before him. America did not even possess a foundry to produce cannons and had, under colonial rule, been prohibited from building one. For decades, the colonies had relied on England to supply its militia with field pieces. The American army had but one artillery regiment of about 635 men and only about a dozen heavy guns.

Within a few days, a letter from Congress dated October 23 arrived that authorized cannons at Fort Ticonderoga to be procured for service at Cambridge. This was much easier decreed than done. The fort was 300 miles away from Washington's army, separated not only by distance but rolling hills, winding rivers, and lakes. The roads along the way were seldom used and not worn solid by heavy traffic, much less the tonnage of cannons. Although most of Washington's generals thought this solution offered no help at all, Knox proposed that he make the trip and bring the cannons back to Massachusetts. The commander's circle advised against the plan. It almost certainly would fail, and at a time when embarrassment to the army would hurt enlistments and embolden the British and Tories. The expenditure would divert badly needed funds to a hopeless cause. But Washington overruled the objections. He saw something in Knox, his energy, his ingenuity, and his determination, that made him believe the young man could overcome seemingly impossible obstacles.

Perhaps Washington thought of himself at the beginning of his own military career, twenty years earlier, when he was sent on a mission through hostile Indian country to forward the British demand that the French vacate forts and land within the Ohio Territory claimed by England. Washington had made his name and reputation by the mission and his subsequent report, which was widely published and praised. He also had to consider that Knox was a native of Boston and would be highly motivated to rescue his hometown, regardless of the personal costs.

As Knox began his preparations for the mission, Lucy expressed her unhappiness about the prospect of being separated from her husband. Pregnant and without her family, she would struggle just to survive. But she also understood that a continent depended on him not to fail. Henry promised to write as often as he could as a reminder that she was constantly in his thoughts.

In Philadelphia, Washington's letter recommending that Knox be promoted to colonel had not yet arrived when John Adams wrote to Henry on November 11: "I have been impressed with an opinion of your knowledge and abilities in the military way for several years, and of late have endeavored, both at camp, at Watertown and at Philadelphia, by mentioning your name and character, to make you more known, and consequently in a better way for promotion. It was a sincere opinion of your merit and qualifications, which prompted me to act this part and therefore I am very happy to be able to inform you, that I believe you will very soon be provided for according to your wishes, at least you may depend upon this that nothing in my power shall be wanting to effect it."

Adams continued to be obsessed with the poor ratio of New England commanders in Washington's army, and apparently he was embarrassed by criticism from his colleagues that his area lacked men with military know-how and engineering skills.

Although, as he pointed out to Knox, Adams "held a place in the Great Council of America," he needed intelligence from the American army. He asked Henry to provide "the name, rank and character of every officer in the army, I mean every honest and able one, but more especially of every officer, who is best acquainted with the theory and practice of fortification and gunnery. What is comprehend[ed] within the term engineer? And whether it includes skill both in fortification and gunnery—and what skillful engineers you have in the army and whether any of them and who have seen service and when and where."[17] Adams also asked for a list of the best books on military science in the Harvard library.

Washington issued Knox orders on Thursday, November 16, to take stock of supplies in the artillery corps and to inventory its needs, then to proceed first to the New York Provincial Congress and then to Albany to procure and send supplies to Cambridge. He was then to go to Fort Ticonderoga in upstate New York or even as far as St. John's in Quebec, if needed, to gather as many cannons and as much munitions as he could cart back with him.

"The want of them is so great, that no trouble or expense must be spared to obtain them—I have wrote to General Schuyler, he will give every necessary assistance that they may be had and forwarded to this place, with the utmost dispatch," Washington wrote.[18] He also wrote out a expense requisition for Knox to receive $1,000 in Continental currency, which had recently been authorized by Congress. In an afterthought postscript, the general reminded him not to forget flints for the muskets. The commander also gave him letters of introduction and a formal request for the New York Congress to give Knox "all the assistance in your power."[19]

Knox was provided with letters to present to General Philip Schuyler (future father-in-law of Alexander Hamilton), stationed in New York, ordering him to send much-needed supplies to Cambridge, including "powder, lead, mortars, cannon, indeed of most sorts of military stores. For want of them, we really cannot carry on any sort of spirited operation." Washington also reported that a train of British artillery had recently arrived in Boston along with reinforcements of men from five Irish regiments.[20]

In these letters, Knox was introduced under the title of "esquire" and as "an experienced engineer." A private citizen was in charge of the artillery of the fledgling Continental Army. Knox had no way of knowing this fact, but a day after he received Washington's orders and letters, 300 miles away at the Continental Congress in Philadelphia, the general's recommendation for his promotion was read. With the urging of John Adams, Congress approved, and the body's journal noted: "Whereas it is become necessary to appoint another colonel of the regiment of artillery, in the room of Colonel Gridley, on account of his advanced age . . . Henry Knox, Esqr. was unanimously elected."[21]

After taking account of the artillery regiment's needs, Henry said good-bye to Lucy and set off. He and his nineteen-year-old brother, William, who had managed to slip out of Boston after Henry's business had been vandalized, traveled on horseback and headed for New York City in their first extended trip from home. Most of the trees had shed their leaves, and the cool autumn air surely reminded Henry of the onset of winter and the difficulties he would face during the expedition. While passing through Marlboro, Massachusetts, they were caught in the most violent northeastern storm he had ever seen. They bunkered down in the pouring rain and chilling wind. After drying out, they resumed their trip.

Henry and his brother reached the northern army in New York City on Saturday, November 25. He was waited on by Colonel Alexander McDougal of the First New York Regiment. Like Knox, McDougal had been a merchant and shopkeeper before the war. Knox presented his letters from Washington, and McDougal said he would meet with the New York Provincial Congress over the matter but had no doubt that the commander and chief could, for the most part, be accommodated. He could not agree to send some of the heavy cannons but promised to provide several smaller field pieces along with shells and other munitions to Cambridge. To Knox's surprise, he discovered that a foundry for casting cannons had been completed in New York, and guns could be produced cheaper than imports.

On Monday, November 27, Knox wrote Washington with the news of an accessible foundry: "I very sincerely wish your excellency had been acquainted with this circumstance and charged me with a commission to have a number cast for the camp. . . . If you should think proper to have some done and will give orders to Colonel McDougal or some other gentleman of this city—the foundry will execute one in two days after he shall receive the orders—and in any number in proportion. He can also cast brass mortars."[22]

Knox explained to Washington that McDougal "gave such reasons for not complying with the requisition for the heavy cannons as would not be prudent to put to paper." It was likely that stripping the city of big guns would make it vulnerable to attack. That meant, Knox told Washington, that the army at Cambridge would have to rely on the big guns he could drag from Ticonderoga. Washington needed the most powerful cannons against the British battleships in the harbor and to reach Boston from the surrounding shores of the harbor.

Knox and his brother left New York City on November 28 and headed north along the Hudson River. A bitter winter wind blew across their faces, and on Monday, December 4, a heavy snowstorm began as they reached Fort George. The outpost sat on the south end of Lake George, a long, narrow body of water that stretched north for more than twenty miles to meet Lake Champlain. His destination, Fort Ticonderoga, was at the confluence of the two lakes. By 2 P.M., they had reached Fort George.

Knox decided to spend the night there and to set sail early in the morning. He was given lodging in a one-room cabin, which, due to a lack of space, he shared with a captured British soldier, Lieutenant John Andre, who was being escorted south to Lancaster, Pennsylvania, with others to await a prisoner exchange between the two armies. As Knox and Andre sat before the crackling fire, they developed an instant liking for one another. Knox was careful not to reveal his purpose for traveling to the fort and, dressed as a private citizen, appeared to have no military connection. Andre said that he was a member of the British Seventh Regiment, stationed at Fort Chambly on the Sorel River in Canada. Knox found that Andre loved literature and, like Knox, was an ardent student with a variety of passions. Under different circumstances they might have become good friends, and Andre's personality and intelligence left a lasting impression on Henry.

Knox rose early the next morning, December 5, to set out on the trip across the lake. He needed to sail his cargo across the water before it became capped with ice. Yet he also depended on cold, snowy, winter weather to set in for the overland journey. "Without sledding, the roads are so much gullied that it will be impossible to move a step," he wrote in a dispatch to Washington.[23]

At Fort Ticonderoga, Knox found guns ranging from 12-inch howitzers to 11-foot cannon that weighed 5,000 pounds apiece. The total weight of the load that he expected to drag to Boston was almost 120,000 pounds. Knox ordered the men at the fort to drag the massive load to the shores of the lake, where they were shipped aboard gondolas, bargelike scows, and dugout canoes, and then portaged a short distance to the northern tip of Lake George.

By three o'clock Saturday, Knox left William in charge of the slow, heavy-laden vessels while he climbed into a canoe and pushed off from shore, intent on hastening to Fort George to check on the sleds and oxen for the land leg of the mission. Knox reached the opposite end of the lake and Fort George on Monday, December 11, and contracted a local militia captain to round up 40 sleds that could carry 5,400 pounds apiece and oxen teams to pull them.

Back in Cambridge, as he anxiously waited on news from Knox, on December 12 Washington received a letter, dated December 2, from John Hancock with Henry's commission as a full colonel enclosed.[24] Washington immediately issued a general order that day that read: "The Honorable Continental Congress having been pleased to appoint Henry Knox Esqr. Colonel of the Regiment of Artillery, upon the new establishment; he is to be obeyed as such."[25]

Henry, at the far outpost of Fort George, would not hear of the promotion for weeks. His more immediate worry was the dropping temperature as he scanned the horizon for any sign of the boats from Fort Ticonderoga. He tried to push thoughts of disaster from his mind as he viewed the ice beginning to form on the surface of the lake; it could become impassible at any time. If a deep freeze descended, the mission would be completely stalled until a spring thaw. At 2 P.M. on Wednesday, December 13, he sent the crew of an express boat back up the lake to inquire about the delay. He soon received the news that a strong wind had beaten against the sides of a scow, which then foundered and became engulfed with water and sank. His brother William was on that scow. But a note from William soon arrived that the craft had gone down close enough to shore, with its gunnel above water, for the crew to bail out the vessel. They only waited for the wind to pick up to resume their trip. By Saturday, December 16, all the boats, along with his brother aboard the resilient scow, had arrived at Fort George. The cannons were unloaded, the crews brought them within the stockade walls of the fort, and Knox paid off the boatmen.

He then turned his attention to the sleds and teams of oxen and horses that Schulyer and Squire were rounding up. With the cannons safely over the lake, Henry welcomed the onset of winter weather and prayed for snow. He wrote to Washington on December 17 that the lake crossing took ten days, as he had expected, and the mission was on schedule despite the setbacks: "It is not easy to conceive the difficulties we had in getting them over the lake, owning to the advanced season of the year and contrary winds; but the danger is now past, please God, they must go." He expected by Wednesday to have 42 strong sleds and more than 160 oxen, and 500 fathoms of sturdy three-inch rope to haul the 43 cannon and 16 mortars as far as Springfield, Massachusetts, where he planned to get fresh animals for the final leg of the journey. He told Washington that he planned to follow a route through Kinderhook, Great Barrington, and on to Springfield, but the mission could not continue without another snowfall to provide a sufficient base to "make the carriage easy." Knox sanguinely predicted that the caravan could cover twenty miles a day and would arrive in Cambridge by New Year's Day to "present to your Excellency a noble train of artillery."[26]

Henry's thoughts had constantly been with Lucy during the mission, and he wrote her that day: "Had I the power to transport myself to you, how eagerly rapid would be my flight."[27]

Knox soon realized that he had to scuttle his timetable. No snow fell, day after frustrating day. On Christmas Eve, he left the teams with instructions to move out to Albany, usually an eight-day trip, as soon as the weather permitted. He traveled south on foot to Fort Miller, where a local judge procured a carriage that took him near Glen Falls. He proceeded to Saratoga and, by the afternoon, he saw to his elation that it was "snowing exceeding fast."

Henry awoke on Christmas Day at Ensing's tavern to view what he must have regarded as a holiday gift from heaven: a two-foot blanket of pristine snow. He braced himself for the bitter temperatures and wind, and headed for Albany, where he reached General Schuyler's headquarters by 2 P.M. on Tuesday, December 26. "I almost perished with the cold," he wrote in his journal.[28]

He and Schuyler rounded up sleds and transports for the next sixty-two-mile leg of the mission, destination Springfield, putting out a call and offering to pay anyone who sent sleighs and horses twelve shillings per ton hauled for each day of the trip. To Henry's dismay, the temperature began to rise, the snow started to melt, and the rivers began to thaw. On January 2, a day after Knox had told Washington that he would arrive in Cambridge, he still had most of the journey before him. In desperation, he ordered soldiers to pour buckets of river water over the ford in the Hudson to reinforce the ice, an effort that proved useless.

On January 4, he wrote to Washington: "The want of snow detained us some days and now a cruel thaw, hinders [us] from crossing the [Hudson] River, which we are obliged to do four times from Lake George to this town."[29] He explained to Washington that "these inevitable delays pain me exceedingly as my mind is fully sensible of importance of the greatest expedition in this case." General Schuyler wrote Washington a letter in support of Knox, blaming the delay on "the uncommon mildness of the weather for several days past. One frosty night if not deferred too long, however, will put everything in order."[30]

To ease his anxiety, Henry wrote to Lucy late that evening. He had wanted to share so many sights along his journey with her. She would have appreciated the view of New York City, he thought, and he wished he could have shown it to her. "New York is a place where I think in general the houses are better built than in Boston," he wrote her. "They are generally of brick and three stories high, with the largest kind of windows. Their churches are grand, their college, workshop and hospitals most excellently situated and also exceedingly commodious; their principal streets much wider than ours. The people—why the people are magnificent; in their equipages, which are numerous; in their house furniture, which is fine; in their pride and conceit, which are inimitable; in their profaneness, which is intolerable; in the want of principle, which is prevalent; in their Toryism, which is insufferable, and for which they must repent in dust and ashes."[31]

Albany had only a third of the population of Boston, he wrote, about 5,000 to 8,000 people, whom he believed were "honest enough, and many sensible and polite." He closed the letter: "It is now past twelve o'clock, there I wish you a good night's repose, and will mention you in my prayers."[32]

The much-welcomed frost came on Saturday, January 6, and on Sunday the van of the procession of sleds headed out from Albany and crossed the Hudson, bound for Springfield. Schuyler jotted an excited note to Washington: "This morning I had the satisfaction to see the first division of sleds cross the river. Should there be snow all the way to Cambridge, they will probably arrive there about this day [next] week." Knox made a similar estimate of eight or nine days for the journey. He had inspected the ice and was careful not to test its strength too much. Almost all the cannons in the lead division were over when the last one crashed through the cracking surface, despite Knox's precautions. Ropes were secured to the cannon and it was rescued, with the assistance of many of the townspeople of Albany.

At 8 A.M. Monday, January 8, Knox was again at the river supervising each crossing. Along the shores, inhabitants and soldiers watched throughout the day, many holding their breath as each team inched across the precarious bridge of ice. Teamsters walked the animals slowly to prevent the hammering of hooves on the fragile ice, but they still needed to move with enough celerity and momentum to tow the weighty cargo. The teams had to work hard against the slippery surface. At the completion of each successful crossing to the east side of the Hudson, onlookers cheered, and heads shook almost in disbelief. Knox wrote thankfully in his journal that the teamsters had "proceeded so carefully that before night we got over twenty three sleds."

Thanks to a continued cold front, most of the sleds crossed the river the next morning, and at noon Knox rode on ahead, traveling south about fifteen miles on the Old Post Road to pass through Kinderhook and then continuing another nine miles to Claverack, on the edge of the Berkshire Mountains. He decided to ride to the snow-covered crest of one of the highest elevations and see if he could spot the teams behind him. He noted that he could "have almost seen all the kingdoms of the earth."

The next stretch of the trip was over a difficult twelve-mile stretch of mountainous passes through the Berkshires and a dense pine forest called Greenwoods. The animals quickly became exhausted. It seemed "almost a miracle that people with heavy loads should be able to get up and down such hills as are here," Knox noted in his diary. Many of the teamsters became discouraged. It took Henry "three hours of persuasion" and cajoling as he appealed to the teamsters' patriotism and stoked their desire for these guns to avenge the sufferings inflicted by the British before the teams were moving again.[33]

After emerging from the mountains and forest, the trekking was somewhat easier along an old American Indian trail. When Knox arrived at Westfield, Massachusetts, ten miles short of Springfield, inhabitants came out to see the curiosity, bring food, cider, and whiskey for the crews. Many local militia leaders turned out to meet Knox; in fact, they all seemed to boast of leading one company or another. Knox commented, "What a pity it is that our soldiers are not as numerous as our officers."[34] Knox agreed to unleash some fireworks and directed the men discharge an eleven-foot, twenty-four-pound cannon to entertain the local residents.

Knox rode ahead and reached Cambridge on Wednesday, January 24, to report to Washington, who was overjoyed to hear that the artillery would arrive in the next few days. Knox finally learned that his appointment as a full colonel had been approved by Congress and he would head the army's artillery corps of 635 men. His mission had taken twenty-four days longer than his prediction on December 15. Instead of fifteen days, the return trip took forty days, and the entire mission stretched for about fifty-six days. The rest of the train reached Framington, about ten miles from Washington's camp, on January 25. John Adams, who was dining nearby with Elbridge Gerry, heard about the procession and went to see it. He excitedly scribbled down an inventory of the load: "nine eighteen-pounders, ten twelves, six to nine pounders, three thirteen-inch mortars." He wrote in his diary that the sight made his dinner that night taste "very agreeably."[35] His support for Knox's promotion in the Continental Congress had not been misplaced, and Henry was already producing significant results. Washington's faith in Knox had been reaffirmed as well. As a token of his appreciation, Washington sent an invitation on Thursday, February 1, for Henry and Lucy to join him and Mrs. Washington for dinner the following day. Lucy had been bored and lonely during the two months of her husband's absence and was ecstatic over a social invitation. At 2 P.M., she and Henry were received by the Washingtons. Martha, who came from an affluent family atop the social hierarchy of Virginia, instantly took to the pregnant Lucy and was pleased at her vivacity and cultivated manners.

Knox had little time to recuperate from his exhausting mission and immediately went about putting the army's artillery in order. He decided that the forty-three cannons and sixteen mortars taken from Ticonderoga did not completely fill his needs. He wrote to General Charles Lee, who had headed to New York City, with a requisition for more guns. He was pleasantly surprised to learn that shortly after he had left camp on his mission, the American ship *Lee* captured the British transport *Nancy* outside of Boston. The vessel was laden with military supplies, including 3,000 shells for twelve-pound guns and 4,000 shells for the six-pounders. The spoils also provided the army with 10,500 flints, 2,000 muskets, and a supply of musket balls. But for all of Knox's efforts over the past two months, his artillery supplies lacked one critical component: powder. The cannons were useless without it.

Knox accompanied Washington and his staff on Sunday, February 11, as they rode beyond the Roxbury works and ventured up Boston Neck to get a glimpse of the enemy defenses. They dismounted and had walked about half a mile when they spotted a British officer riding hard in their direction. Cannon fire erupted from the British fortifications as the Americans raced back to their horses. No one was injured. Knox along with Washington and his men must have berated themselves for this reckless bit of daring. Had the commander in chief, his staff, and his top artillery commander been killed or captured, the damage to the American cause would have been catastrophic.

Washington felt tremendous pressure from Congress and many leaders around the country to order a strike at Boston. He also was desperate to attack and felt a golden opportunity was slipping away. Because of the small amount of powder on hand, he thought that an artillery bombardment would be ineffective and would destroy sections of the town without dislodging the British. Instead, he favored taking advantage of a strong track of ice that lay across the harbor between Dorchester Heights and Boston, where his soldiers could march into the city and avoid the fortifications and cannons at Boston neck. He believed they needed to strike quickly before the king's troops received reinforcements, which were expected any day, and estimated that he had a superior force of 8,797 men fit for duty and another 1,405 available against 5,000 British regulars in Boston. At a council of generals on Friday, February 16, Washington urged "that a stroke well-aimed at this critical juncture might put a final end to the war and restore peace and tranquility so much to be wished for."[36] But his generals disagreed and wanted to wait for powder for Knox's guns and additional militia troops from other states. Only half of the anticipated men promised by other colonies had arrived.

Washington wrote pleading letters to other colonies, such as Connecticut, that had not sent the amount of powder that had been pledged, along with an admonition to Congress to supply the deficiency of military supplies.

February 18, Washington told Knox that Connecticut was sending 3,000 pounds of powder, which Henry said would provide his guns with enough ammunition to force the king's men from the city. The critical point of his plan was for the army to take Dorchester Heights, which overlooked Boston Harbor. His aim was to mount his big guns on the heights to attack the royal battleships. By February 26, while the army waited for the powder, preparations were underway for a major attack. Knox readied his guns to fire on the city from three sides: Roxbury from the south, Lechmere's Point from the north, and Cobble Hill from the west. On Saturday, March 2, Knox ordered his men to begin a cannonade of his hometown. Shells whistled into the town, panicking inhabitants. Soldiers and townspeople scrambled for any kind of cover. "The shots and shells were heard to make a great crashing in the town," the *Pennsylvania Journal* reported.[37] The British opened fire from batteries at the neck and along the west side of Boston.

The American troops, meanwhile, watched from behind their entrenchments to see if the British would march out of Boston in an attempt to stop Knox's guns. The bombardment was a diversion, however; Knox planned to level a more serious blow. On Monday evening, March 4, as the cannons blazed uninterrupted, 2,000 men under the command of General John Thomas marched to Dorchester Heights. Under Knox's direction and with the help of 400 oxen, the heaviest guns from Ticonderoga were hauled up the hills and mounted in a position to strike at the city and the battleships in the harbor. Entrenchments were dug throughout the night, and by morning the guns were afforded secure spots from enemy fire. Washington wrote enthusiastically to Congress that this tactical victory was "equal to our most sanguine expectations." An American captain who slipped past the British posts to escape occupied Boston during the confusion of the attack reported that the "bombardment and cannonade caused much surprise in town as many of the soldiery said they never heard or thought we had mortars or shells."[38] The mission to Ticonderoga had been completely undetected by the British.

Knox's artillery corps continued to shell Boston on Tuesday, the missiles ripping through houses, sending chunks of brick and splintered wood flying. A British admiral spotted the new works on Dorchester Hills and immediately recognized the danger to the fleet and the royal army. He sent an urgent message to General William Howe, who had taken over command in Boston from Gage the previous October. Howe immediately ordered an attack on Dorchester Heights and sent men aboard marine transports to Castle William Island in preparation to launch the assault. But a furious wind sprang up and continued through Wednesday, preventing the British from landing troops on the shores surrounding Dorchester. During that time, Knox continued to direct the mounting of additional cannons on the works, and Washington sent thousands of troops to support the position. When the wind died down, Howe realized "that I could promise myself little success by attacking them under such disadvantages; wherefore I judged it most advisable to prepare for the evacuation of the town."[39] The troops on Castle William returned to Boston to pack for the retreat. Many felt bitter about the order to move out; throughout the siege, their commanders had promised that reinforcements would arrive and that they would destroy the American army and conquer Massachusetts in the spring. Now, just days before help was to arrive, the regulars were forced to accept defeat. Knox's Ticonderoga mission provided the Americans with punishing firepower. The British battleships could no longer remain safely in the harbor.

At eight o'clock on St. Patrick's Day, March 17, Knox watched a flotilla of small boats in the harbor loaded with soldiers heading for seventy-eight ships that appeared on the horizon. More than 8,900 soldiers and 1,100 loyalists left town to sail for Nova Scotia. Among the fleeing population was Henry's former teacher at the Boston Latin Grammar School, John Lovell. In recent years, Lovell and his patriot son had differed in their views on the Anglo-American conflict and had taught at separate ends of the one-room school, each proclaiming the justness of his side. His son had been imprisoned by the British during the occupation. Also among those leaving was Adino Paddock, who led Knox in the artillery company the Train and had remained a loyal Tory. Most disheartening for Lucy Knox was that her father, Thomas Flucker, who remained the royal secretary of Massachusetts, boarded a ship along with her mother and sisters, never to return to America.

Shortly after the last of the British soldiers left, American troops marched in and took possession of Boston "in the name of the 13 United Colonies of North America."[40]

In large part due to Henry Knox, Washington could claim his first victory of the American Revolution and report "with the greatest pleasure" to Congress the liberation of Boston.[41] No one played a more critical role in the triumph than Knox, who not only overcame remarkable obstacles in dragging the cannons from Ticonderoga to enable the success but also commanded the artillery corps that secured victory. The triumph remains one of the most significant military victories in U.S. history, for it boosted hopes for independence in that heady spring of 1776 at a time when provincial congresses were deciding whether to authorize their delegates to the Continental Congress to support a break with England; it quieted claims that the British military could not be defeated; and it came at a time when many delegates to the national Congress had not yet left for Philadelphia and were canvassing their constituents about their feelings toward independence. When he asked Virginians, Thomas Jefferson found that "I may safely say nine out of ten are for it."[42]

Without the victory at Boston, support for nationhood would have seemed a hollow cry based on unrealistic expectations. By forcing the British out of this stronghold, the Americans showed they could indeed fight against the world's most powerful army. The triumph gave them something to build their hopes on, and thoughts of defeat were pushed aside for the season. Henry Knox had not only played a leading role in liberating his hometown of Boston, but he had given the impetus for Americans to support liberating their land from British rule and push toward independence and nationhood.

THREE

RAGAMUFFINS

Despite the victory, Henry Knox had little reason to celebrate. As he reentered Boston for the first time in almost a year, he surveyed the damage that British regulars and vandals had inflicted on his once-fashionable bookstore. Volumes were scattered around the floor, thrown open to the weather, damaged, water-soaked, and destroyed. The windows had been shattered, and glass lay upon the floor. His shelves were broken up. All his hard work to build the business had been wasted. He still owed a considerable sum on the store's stock to merchants in England, which despite the present circumstances he hoped to repay.

While the homes and businesses of many of the patriot leaders in Boston had been vandalized, overall the town was in surprisingly good condition considering the military occupation and his incessant cannonading. The home of John Hancock, the president of the Continental Congress, suffered no damage to speak of. Fine portraits from masters such as Jonathan Singleton Copley still hung undisturbed on the walls of the mansion. Henry also found, as he had hoped, that the British had been forced to leave behind military supplies and their heavy guns. But many of the guns had been damaged, rendering them useless.

Henry and Lucy heard that the British fleet in which the Fluckers traveled had not gone to Nova Scotia, where loyalists who had remained in Boston said the ships were headed. Instead the vessels were just five miles south of Boston in Nantasket Roads. Washington suspected the real British intention was to land in New York City. On Sunday, March 24, he sent six regiments racing there and ordered the rest of the army to prepare to follow. It soon became apparent, however, that the fleet had merely stopped to arrange its cargo and take on water for the trip to Nova Scotia, a point from

which civilians could continue on to England. Henry spent the week arrang-
ing for the heavy guns to be loaded onto wagons and hiring drivers to transport the rest of the artillery while Lucy packed for the trip to New York.

On Sunday, March 31, Knox received orders for the artillery to move
out at dawn on Thursday and march with a regiment under the command
of Brigadier General Joseph Spencer. Lucy, who expected to give birth any
day, chose to accompany Henry. Knox was directed to follow the coast
while his regiment headed for Norwich, Connecticut, on the way to New
York. Washington was anxious about protecting the coasts, and he asked
Knox to inspect the fortifications at New London and Colonel Richard
Gridley to inspect those at Cape Ann. Congress shared his concerns and
approved a resolution ordering the commander in chief to send engineers
to secure New England harbors.[1]

The first of 300 wagon teams assembled on Boston Common on Sunday,
April 3, as soldiers strained to load cannon, musket balls, gunpowder, buckshot, shells, cannon cartridges, flints, fuses, and other munitions. Washington
knew there was very little he could tell Knox about moving cannons. Instead
of issuing his characteristic detailed orders, he simply penned to Henry:
"Trusting in your zeal, diligence and ability, I remain confident of every exertion, in your power, for the public service."[2]

Leaving the train under the direction of Lieutenant Colonel David
Mason, Knox and Lucy headed for Norwich, then proceeded to Fairfield.
Lucy felt that the delivery of their child was imminent, and they quickly
found lodgings. She gave birth to a daughter, whom they named Lucy. Knox
could not afford to spend time lingering with his wife and newborn, however
much he wanted to, and torn between his paternal and military duties, he left
for Providence, Rhode Island. There he was met by several of the town's leaders, who appealed to him to help shore up the defenses in Newport and its
harbor. Residents had recently driven away British ships that threatened the
towns. Knox designed five batteries from which "the advantageous situation
of the ground, must, when executed, render the harbor exceedingly secure,"
he wrote Washington on Sunday, April 21. He added that the harbor would
be a safe rendezvous for the fledgling Continental Navy, and its lee side would
protect vessels during even harsh storms.[3]

Three days later, he was in New London scouting the topography around
the harbor. He boarded the ship of Admiral Esek Hopkins, the commander in
chief of the Continental Navy, who seven weeks earlier had led eight ships in
the victorious capture of New Providence in Nassau of the Bahamas. The tri-

umph netted substantial supplies and munitions for the army. Knox was surprised that Hopkins was not a dashing, heroic-looking figure but a kindly old man with pleasant manners. "Though antiquated in figure, he is shrewd and sensible," he wrote in a letter to Lucy. "I, whom you think not a little enthusiastic, should have taken him for an angel, only he swore now and then."[4]

Knox continued to New York City, where the army was hurriedly building fortifications. News had reached the troops that Howe and the British fleet had finally reached Halifax, and Washington expected him to return with fresh British regiments. Planning adequate fortifications for New York City, surrounded on all sides by water, was especially difficult. The British could land troops at almost any point or attack several spots at once. Knox's artillery guns were mounted at Governor's Island, Red Hook, and Paulus Hook, and he marked out the ground for an artillery park on Monday, April 29, to erect the camp and storehouses for his regiment.

From New York's artillery company, Knox noticed a bright young captain by the name of Alexander Hamilton, who reported that he had sixty-nine men fit for duty.[5] During Knox's days as a bookseller in March 1775, he had advertised in the *Boston Gazette* the sale of a tract written by Hamilton, entitled *The Farmer Refuted*, which argued for colonial rights. Knox was pleased to find that Hamilton's talents were not confined to literary efforts and that he possessed remarkable organizational skills. His company of gunners was among the most disciplined in Knox's regiment. Like Knox, Hamilton had been abandoned by his father and had gone to work in a shop at a very early age. Both had developed business and accounting skills, and despite their mercantile upbringings, each had hungered for martial glory and become ardent military students.

Knox's time was spent organizing his regiment. He ferried back and forth to the various batteries around the city, directing platforms for cannons to be erected and guns to be moved into place to command the harbor and surrounding rivers. His artillerymen, along with their cannons, were posted with regiments throughout the army. Unlike most commanders, he had to take a view of the overall situation of defenses and troop dispositions just as the commander in chief was required to do. He placed the heaviest mortars in the batteries facing the sea and the light mortars near the fort encampments. He inventoried each battery to make sure the requisite amount of shot, rammers, spungets, and ladles were ready for battle. In assessing his corps, he found it had too few to man the 121 light and heavy cannons. His regiment had been reduced to 520 men, including 50 officers, and he needed 1,210.

As the soldiers worked, they scanned the horizon of the Atlantic looking for any signs of Howe's ships. Picket guards were sent out in the mornings and evenings to watch for a surprise attack if the British landed somewhere along the coast, and men were ordered at night to "lay upon their arms and be ready to turn out at a minute's notice."[6] In the case of an attack or the sighting of British ships, Knox's men were to fire two cannons from Fort George, at the south end of Manhattan near his headquarters, and a flag would be hoisted at General Washington's headquarters at a house on Pearl Street. If the attack came at night, a light would be raised instead of a flag.

In anticipation of the battle, the Continental Congress declared Friday, May 17, a day of "fasting, humiliation and prayer, humbly to supplicate the mercy of Almighty God, that it would please him to pardon all our manifold sins and transgressions, and to prosper the Arms of the United Colonies, and finally, establish the peace and freedom of America, upon a solid and lasting foundation."[7] Washington ordered the army to observe the declaration.

Tensions ran high not only in anticipation of the British fleet but out of suspicions of disloyalty within the patriot army. Knox heard rumors that Tories and spies had infiltrated its ranks. To prevent sabotage, orders were issued to post sentries at all batteries armed with cannons as Knox saw fit, and for the guards to be doubled at night. Only generals and men assigned to the batteries were permitted on the cannon platforms "or to approach the cannon, or to meddle with the rammers, spungets, or any of the artillery stores placed there. The Officers of every guard are to see that their men are particularly alert in executing this order."[8]

Knox, who was just twenty-six years old, was building an artillery corps virtually from scratch. He seemed to be the sole man in the Continental Army with both the expertise and authority to oversee a myriad of details, ranging from recruiting men to the minutia of casting cannons. He continued to press for more troops to man the gun posts and for additional cannons to guard the coastline. Meanwhile, Robert Treat Paine, a Massachusetts delegate to the Continental Congress, wrote him that the government's order for the casting of forty mortars on April 13 was still delayed due to the uncertainty of the proper weights for the guns: "The opinion I have of your understanding and zeal in these matters induces me to write thus freely to you hoping you will with all convenient speed inform me of those matters and favor me with such further observations as you may think of service in the affair."[9]

A letter from John Adams, dated June 2, arrived from Philadelphia, thanking Knox for his advice on military books to be obtained from Europe. Adams thought that Congress should pay for American editions of these texts and agreed with Knox's advice to establish military academies "for the education of young gentlemen in every branch of the military art: because I am fully of your sentiment, that we ought to lay foundations, and begin institutions, in the present circumstances of this country, for promoting every art, manufacture and science which is necessary for the support of an independent state."[10] Knox was already preparing for American nationhood by advocating a military school that could produce its own highly trained officers.

Adams wrote that the signs in Congress and across the continent seemed to be leaning toward independence. "The votes of the Congress and the proceedings of the colonies separately must before this time have convinced you, that this is the sense of America, with infinitely greater unanimity, than could have been credited by many people a few months ago."[11]

On Friday, June 14, Washington took Knox's advice to allocate more men to his artillery corps. Four men from every company in New York were to be assigned to Knox's command and report to him on Sunday. Knox and General Greene traveled to the northern tip of Manhattan to scout the terrain and plan fortifications overlooking the north Hudson. General Putnam wanted to build a fort at Kingsbridge to safeguard a possible retreat route. Knox and Greene disagreed and thought any defenses would be ineffectual unless a fort was built at Mount Washington, which overlooked both the Hudson and Harlem rivers. His excellency agreed and ordered Fort Washington to be built at the spot.

Lucy arrived with their child and stayed at Henry's artillery headquarters, which was at a comfortable home at the foot of Broadway, overlooking New York Harbor. With preparations for a major battle ongoing, she became increasingly concerned about her husband's safety. After losing her family to England, she worried about possibly losing her husband as well, and seeing him every day eased some of her anxieties. Knox wanted her to return to a safer part of the country. He was concerned that the British fleet might arrive at any moment, and in the midst of an attack, his wife and child might not have time to flee. He also had other apprehensions. Several of the soldiers had been stricken with smallpox, and many were being inoculated. Also, despite the threats and discipline from Washington, men continued to fire off their muskets without concern over where the shots landed. Several men had been killed by friends. Lucy promised him to leave soon.

The detection of a Tory plot on June 21 to assassinate Washington and his top commanders and then sabotage the American cannons exacerbated Lucy's worries. Gilbert Forbes, a gunsmith from Broadway, was arrested. After realizing he would be hanged, Forbes sought absolution and revealed that the plan was headed by one of Washington's guards, Thomas Hickey. The conspirators hoped to execute the scheme as the British launched their attack, and planned not only to kill the top commanders but to blow up the magazines and block the roads out of town. At a June 26 court-martial, Forbes said Hickey coaxed recruits by pointing out "the impossibility of this country standing against the power of Great Britain." News of the conspiracy led to immediate orders for the doubling of sentries at Knox's artillery park and its laboratory for making munitions. Knox undoubtedly was a prime target for assassination.

A total of thirty-four men, including the Tory mayor of New York City, David Matthews, were implicated in the plot and arrested. The court-martial found Hickey guilty of crimes of "[s]edition and mutiny, and also of holding a treacherous correspondence with the enemy, for the most horrid and detestable purposes," and sentenced him to death. Two days later, on Friday, June 28, 20,000 people attended his hanging at Bowery Lane.[12]

The following day, as Henry and Lucy were having a quiet breakfast and enjoying the view from a window overlooking the harbor, a fleet of British ships appeared in the distance with bright white sails billowing from a strong northwest wind, heading directly for the straits of the Hudson and East rivers. Knox was shocked. The enemy could be at his doorstep at the lower tip of Manhattan within a half hour. Alarm guns began to fire, and two cannons let out deafening roars calling the troops to battle stations. Soldiers raced to their posts. Lucy was overcome with distress not only for her own safety but for their child's. Henry, equally panic-stricken, masked his guilt over leaving Lucy by losing his temper. "Everything in the height of bustle; I not at liberty to attend her, as my country calls loudest. My God, may I never experience the like feelings again!" he wrote, describing the scene to his brother. "They were too much; but I found a way to disguise them, for I scolded like a fury at her for not having gone before."[13]

Rather than landing troops, however, Howe anchored off of Sandy Hook, and waited for the rest of the fleet to arrive to give him a total of 32,000 men.

Lucy departed to stay with friends near Stamford and Fairfield. "Indeed the circumstances of our parting were extremely disagreeable," Knox wrote his brother.[14] Within days, she was writing that she was very unhappy separated from him and wanted to return to New York City. But Henry discouraged her, reminding her of the danger and her recent flight.

By midafternoon of June 29, more than 100 ships had arrived. Knox spent June 30 directing the completion of artillery batteries and having his men familiarize themselves with routes to their alarm posts that would protect them from enemy fire. Fifty ships came into New York Harbor and anchored off the Staten Island side on Tuesday, July 2. More than 10,000 British soldiers landed there unopposed and began to set up defenses opposite the troops under General Nathanael Greene. The remaining ships began to surround the island, and American troops at posts along its shores were forced to evacuate to Manhattan to avoid being cut off from the rest of Washington's men. But instead of pushing ahead, the British waited and held their ground.

Knox read the newspapers and kept up with the debate over independence. Unless the colonies declared a break from England, he was a rebel. If captured, he would be deemed a criminal, not a member of a national army. He also knew that America could not supply its needs for artillery and would be required to import guns from France and the Netherlands. If the country was still dependent on Great Britain, no significant help could come from other nations. Knox had become a prominent figure in the army and was buoyed with the thought of helping build a nation. On July 9, news arrived in New York that the Continental Congress had given final approval for the Declaration of Independence on Thursday, July 4, 1776. The general orders to the army that day proclaimed: "The Honorable Continental Congress, impelled by the dictates of duty, policy and necessity, having been pleased to dissolve the connection which subsisted between this country, and Great Britain, and to declare the United Colonies of North America, free and independent States."[15]

Washington exhorted the army, telling the men: "This important event will serve as a fresh incentive to every officer, and soldier, to act with fidelity and courage, as knowing that now the peace and safety of his country depends (under God) solely on the success of our arms: And that he is now in the service of a state, possessed of sufficient power to reward his merit, and advance him to the highest honors of a free country."[16]

At 6 P.M., Knox gathered his men at the regimental parade ground at his artillery park to hear the Declaration of Independence read. Knox listened to Thomas Jefferson's memorable words: "We hold these truths to be self-evident, that all men are created equal, that they are endowed by their Creator with certain unalienable rights, that among these are life, liberty, and the pursuit of happiness." As he listened, Knox could take pride in his role in the victory in liberating Boston, which gave America the triumph needed to stake its support of independence. Loud cheers and shouts of joy went up. Soldiers vowed to cut down the enemy. Knox smiled at the bravado. He knew that his men faced a formidable army, and their courage was not yet tempered by the realities of war.

That night, the soldiers and citizens of New York City celebrated. The gilded, leaden statue of an equestrian King George III—located at Bowling Green at the foot of Broadway, not far from Knox's headquarters—was pulled down and decapitated, the lead taken to make musket balls for the army. Washington did not welcome the unbridled enthusiasm and issued orders to the soldiers: "Though the General doubts not the persons, who pulled down and mutilated the statue in the Broadway, last night, were actuated by zeal in the public cause; yet it has so much the appearance of riot, and want of order, in the army, that he disapproves the manner, and directs that in future these things shall be avoided by the soldiery."[17]

Much of that zeal was deflated three days later when a fleet of another 150 ships carrying 11,000 fresh troops was seen along the horizon. Drums beat to call men to their posts, but many were so awestruck by the sight of the massive sea power that they stood along the banks gazing in amazement, unable to move. One of the most impressive vessels flew the flag of St. George and was instantly recognized as that of Admiral Richard Howe, the commander of the British navy in North America, known popularly as Black Dick due to his swarthy complexion. He was the brother of General William Howe, commander of British forces on the continent. The other ships in the fleet immediately fired salutes in honor of the admiral. At 3:20 P.M., two British frigates, the *Phoenix* and the *Rose*, of forty and twenty guns respectively, sailed up the Hudson River to the Tappan Sea. Knox ordered his artillery to open fire on the ships, which skirted the opposite shore nearly out of reach of his guns. The guns belched furiously, and in the blinding, acrid smoke and deafening noise, Knox yelled for his men to keep firing without pause. In the excitement, his men misfired and cannons exploded, killing some and leaving others writhing in pain. Knox's heart sank. Despite the incessant cannonade, he could not force the ships to turn back, and his men seemed to have inflicted as much damage to themselves as the enemy. His only consolation was that Lucy was safely away from the danger. He wrote her the next day: "I thank Heaven you were not here yesterday. Two ships and three tenders of the enemy . . . weighed anchor, and in twenty-five minutes were before the town. We had a loud cannonade, but could not stop them, though I believe we damaged them much. They kept over on the Jersey side too far from our batteries. I was so unfortunate as to lose six men by accidents, and a number wounded. This affair will be of service to my people; it will teach them to moderate their fiery courage."

Although soldiers along the shore prevented the British from landing troops, the ships denied Washington access to a key water channel to Albany. Now communications and provisions could be sent only by land. The skirmish was a rude awakening for Knox, who had believed that New York could be defended by cannons. He quickly recognized that the plan to fill the ranks of the artillery regiment by borrowing unqualified men from other units would not work. He told Washington that he needed another battalion of men assigned specifically to his corps who could train and develop the necessary skills to duel with the British. The general asked him to draft a plan, which Knox provided and Washington sent to Congress with his recommendation.[18] Knox also faced another problem due to the return of the British. As Robert Treat Paine pointed out in a letter to Knox: "The approach of the enemy has rendered it necessary to find some other place to cast brass cannon [than New York]."[19]

Admiral Howe believed the show of British strength and the presence of 10,000 troops dug in on Staten Island would induce the Americans to seek a peace settlement. On Sunday, July 14, he sent a man-of-war with a flag of truce four miles from the city. Knox and another officer sailed to meet the British officers. The captain of the *Eagle* greeted them by rising, bowing, and removing his hat. "I have a letter, sir, from Lord Howe to Mr. Washington," he said, according to Knox in a letter to Lucy. The captain referred to the commander in chief of the American army merely as a private citizen, since the British did not recognize independence or the legitimacy of the rebel army. Under Washington's orders, Knox and Reed refused to accept the letter.

"Sir we have no person in our army with that address," Reed said. The British captain took the note out of his pocket, however, and handed it to them, asking them to look at the address, which read: "George Washington, Esq., &c., &c., New York."

"No sir," Colonel Reed said. "I cannot receive that letter." The captain expressed his deep regret. Knox, Reed, and the captain saluted and bowed to each other and parted. As the Americans sailed back to shore, Henry noticed that British captain had turned his boat around to meet them again and asked what particular title Washington would prefer. The American colonels said politely, while shouting across the water, that this was a ridiculous question not worthy of a response. Knox reported to Lucy that the British officer regretted that the divided parties did not come together just a few weeks earlier, which Henry interpreted as meaning before the signing of the Declaration of Independence.

In communicating a peace proposal to Washington, the British commanders were in an awkward position. They could not acknowledge Washington's title as the general of the American army without implying tacit recognition of independence. On Saturday, July 20, General Howe sent his adjutant general, a Lieutenant Colonel Paterson, to complain about the refusal to receive British letters. At a meeting at Knox's headquarters, Paterson was very civil. Knox wrote in a letter to Lucy: "In the course of his talk every other word was, 'May it please your Excellency, if your Excellency so please,' in short, no person could pay more respect than the said adjutant-general."[20] But Washington was not pacified by flattery; instead he wanted formal recognition of his country. Paterson tried to explain that the salutation of "&c., &c." addressed to him "implied everything." Washington nodded, saying, "It does so, and anything." The British officer again expressed regret over the impasse concerning the issue of titles and explained that Lord and General Howe had come with great power to negotiate a peace settlement. Washington responded that he had heard that Lord Howe had the power to grant pardons, but he believed the Americans had not offended and did not need pardons, and only defended their rights.

"This confused him," Knox wrote to Lucy. He told her, "General Washington was very handsomely dressed, and made a most elegant appearance." Henry noticed that the British officer was impressed by Washington's commanding presence, and "appeared awe-struck, as if he was before something supernatural. Indeed, I don't wonder at it. He was before a very great man indeed."[21]

After a half hour of meeting, the Americans brought in wine, and Henry "lamented exceedingly the absence of my Lucy" to grace the diplomatic nature of the occasion. Paterson excused himself and returned to the *Eagle* to report to the Howe brothers.

Behind the pleasantries lay the threat of the destruction of the American army. Knox knew that his artillery regiment was inadequate against hundreds of guns from the British battleships anchored around New York and that his guns were poorly manned. During the last week of the month, he learned, however, that the Continental Congress in Philadelphia had on July 24 approved his plan to raise another battalion of artillery and ordered it "carried into execution as soon as possible."[22] Robert Treat Paine, who served on the Congressional Cannon Committee, wrote Knox on July 27: "We have contracted with a man to cast eighteen-, twenty-four- and thirty-two-pounders, he has succeeded so well in long eighteen-pounders that we hope he will answer our desires in the rest."[23] As encouraging as these steps may have been, they offered no help for the battle for New York that appeared imminent.

Lucy, meanwhile, stuck in Connecticut, felt bored and lonely and began to wonder what Henry did to pass the time. She wrote asking about his daily schedule. He replied on Sunday, August 11, that he usually rose around sunrise and attended regimental prayers, sang a Psalm, and then read a chapter of the Bible at the main battery with General Putnam. "I dispatch a considerable deal of business before breakfast. From breakfast to dinner I am broiling in a sun hot enough to roast an egg." He usually dined with the American generals, Washington, Putnam Greene, and William Alexander, who styled himself Lord Stirling, claiming he descended from the Scottish Earl of Stirling. He told Lucy, "I am mortified that I haven't had them to dine with me in return. However, that cannot be. I go to bed at nine o'clock or before every night."[24]

Lucy was especially homesick for her family and the gaiety of her life of just a few years earlier. She felt out of place in Connecticut, where the people, she thought, lacked gentility and displayed coarse manners and unrefined behavior. Henry advised her: "Take care, my love of permitting your disgust to the Connecticut people to escape your lips. Indiscreet expressions are handed from town to town and a long while remembered by people not blessed with expanded minds. The want of that refinement which you seem to speak of is, or will be, the salvation of America; for refinement of manners introduces corruption and venality. . . . There is a kind of simplicity in young states as in young children which is quite pleasing to an attentive observer."[25]

The last of the ships of the British fleet arrived on Monday, August 12, giving General Howe a total of 32,000 men to oppose Washington's army of 19,000 soldiers fit for duty. "The Enemy's whole reinforcement is now arrived, so that an Attack must, and will soon be made," Washington admonished the next day. "Be ready for action at a moments call; and when called to it, remember that liberty, property, life and honor, are all at stake. . . . Their cause is bad; their men are conscious of it, and if opposed with firmness, and coolness, at their first onset, with our advantage of works, and knowledge of the ground; victory is most assuredly ours."

At the first sign of the British attack, Knox's men were to fire three guns from the artillery park on Bayard's Hill and hoist a flag or light when the attack came, to call men to their posts.[26] Gray clouds descended and rain poured down for the next several days, postponing any attack or the ability of the British to land more troops on Staten Island.

Congressional delegate Samuel Adams, who visited the army on his way home from Philadelphia to Boston, listened to concerns from men he trusted, such as Knox and Washington, that Congress should not rely on militia to win the war and that the short-term enlistments meant an annual dissolution of the army and the loss of veteran experience. Congress needed to upgrade inducements to enlist and for longer periods of service than a year. Adams immediately wrote to his second cousin, John Adams, on August 16: "I see now, more than ever I did, the importance of Congress attending immediately to enlistments for the next campaign. It would be a pity to lose your old soldiers. I am of opinion that a more generous bounty should be given, twenty dollars and one hundred acres of land for three years at least."[27]

A few days later, Knox received a letter from John Adams dated August 13, reiterating his concern that so few men from Massachusetts had been commissioned as generals in the army despite a recent spate of congressional promotions. "I wish I was better acquainted with the persons and characters of the colonels from that state. It will never do, for the Massachusetts to furnish so many men, and have so few generals while so many other states furnish so few men and have so many generals."[28] Knox continued to press Adams and Robert Treat Paine regarding the need for more cannons. Congress, which was finding it difficult even to obtain the necessary metals or find a suitable air furnace to cast cannons, resolved on Wednesday, August 21 "[t]hat Colonel Henry Knox be authorized to draw upon the pay master general for money sufficient to pay for any quantity of copper."[29]

That same day, Knox wrote to Adams that he feared the inadequacies in the artillery corps could cause the loss of New York or even the war itself. He urged Congress to increase the pay of enlisted soldiers rather than placing hope in untrained and amateur state militias. To build an experienced army, Congress could not afford to economize on the soldiery. "When their homes were invaded," Knox wrote Adams, "they fought for self-preservation. Now that they are moved away from these, they naturally consider that those who do not fight should pay."[30]

On August 21, local inhabitants crossed the East River with reports that the British attack was imminent. According to intelligence they had gathered, about 20,000 regulars were gearing up and in motion for an assault the next day. Seven battleships were to surround New York and pin the American army in, as the British had been pinned in Boston earlier in the year. At 7 P.M. that same day, Knox watched the most dreadful thunderstorm that many people could ever remember. He was jarred by terrific thunderclaps as the storm raged for three hours. Lightning struck a tent in the city, killing a captain and two lieutenants. The tips of the men's swords melted and twisted in the electric shock, along with silver dollars in their pockets. Another man was killed on Main Street, and ten others on Long Island died from lightning strikes. The sailors in the British fleet were tossed about in the ferment of the Atlantic.[31]

The storm abated by 10 P.M., at which time British and foreign troops boarded transports and began crossing the East River from Staten Island to Gravesend Bay at Utrecht on Long Island. By 10 A.M. on Thursday, August 22, 15,000 troops had landed and established a foothold within three miles of the American lines. On Friday, the British advance guard pushed north as far as Flatbush under heavy American fire from the nearby woods. Knox remained at Fort George, where Washington and his advisors believed the main attack would be against Manhattan. His men stayed on alert for three days, hoping that a timely cannonade might discourage British ships from approaching the city's shoreline. On Monday, August 26, Howe feigned an attack on Flatbush and the adjoining Bedford Pass to draw the patriot army while the bulk of his force moved farther north up Staten Island along the Jamaica Pass during the night. At two o'clock Tuesday morning, a force of Hessian mercenaries attacked the Americans in the woods with British field artillery. Knox's gunners returned fire from just a couple hundred yards away. British guns fired into the trees, splintering trunks and branches and ripping through fortifications where the Americans hoped to make their stand. A gunfight and cannon duel dragged on for seven exhausting hours. Rain fell again, leaving the soldiers drenched. Ammunition became soaked and ruined. By 9 A.M. on Wednesday, August 28, the patriots realized they had been outflanked. Surrounded by the British troops that had come up the Jamaica Pass, they had to make their retreat through British lines, which were posted on roads leading to the fortifications at Brooklyn Heights. Washington ordered six regiments from Manhattan to cross the East River to reinforce the position. Knox also arrived at the scene. Two generals, Sullivan and Lord Stirling, were taken prisoner on Long Island. Sullivan was commanding only because Nathanael Greene was severely ill. Henry wrote Lucy that "I met with some loss in my regiment: they behaved like heroes and are gone to glory."[32] Several British ships attempted to sail up the East River and cut off the army on Long Island, but wind from the northeast prevented their progress.

Washington ordered an evacuation of Brooklyn Heights on Thursday, August 29. Knox, in charge of one of the two embarkation points, was mortified when one of his cannons accidentally fired. Fortunately for the Americans, the blast did not reveal the troops' secret departure across the East River to enemy picket guards. A heavy wind blowing from the east caused a churning high tide that prevented the American departure as the British marched in their direction. In what must have seemed like a hand from providence, the wind changed at 11:30 P.M. and blew out to sea, and a heavy fog descended, providing cover for the 9,500 American troops attempting to cross the river. Knox was able to load almost all of the cannons onto barges, which were crewed by men from Massachusetts towns such as Beverly, Salem, Lynn, and Marblehead. Many of these soldiers had been fishermen and seamen before the war and were accustomed to the sea. They were led by a strict disciplinarian, Colonel John Glover, who had been a prosperous shipowner and a member of the close-knit "codfish aristocracy," which controlled the north shores of New England. Knox was able to tap the skills of the men from his home state to facilitate the crossing.[33]

Six heavy iron guns, however, were hoisted onto carriages, which immediately sank so deeply in the sodden ground that the spokes were buried up to the hubs and axles. The guns could not be moved and were abandoned. The troops rowed through the fog to safety in New York City. In the Battle of Long Island, 1,012 men of the Continental Army were killed, wounded, or taken prisoner. The loss of Brooklyn, overlooking Manhattan, meant the city could not be defended against British cannons.

The British moved up Long Island to Hell's Gate across from Kip's Bay and threatened to cut off Washington's land route out of New York. On Monday, September 2, a forty-gun battleship sailed up the Long Island Sound between Governor's and Long islands. Knox's artillerists opened fire from their batteries, but a strong wind allowed the vessel to reach Turtle Bay.

Knox quickly sent Major John Crane with two twelve-pound cannons and a howitzer to pound the ship, which took shelter behind an island. Several other British ships came into the sound and prepared to surround the Continental Army.

Knox, like Washington, was incensed that many of the state militia units suddenly found excuses to leave in the face of danger. "Apprehension and [despair]" characterized the army, Washington wrote to Congress.[34] Knox wrote in disgust to Lucy on Thursday, September 5: "We want great men, who when fortune frowns will not be discouraged. God will I trust in time give us these men. The Congress will ruin everything by their stupid parsimony, and they begin to see it. It is, as I always said, misfortunes that must raise us to the character of a great people. One or two drubbings will be of service to us; and one severe defeat to the enemy, ruin. We must have a standing army. The militia get sick, or think themselves so, and run home; and wherever they go they spread panic."[35]

★ ★ ★ ★

Knox spent several days moving military supplies out of New York City and farther up Manhattan Island, hoping to put them out of reach if the British forced the Continental Army into a retreat. The redcoats and Hessian soldiers entrenched themselves along the shores of Long Island and prepared to launch their assault. Knox's men at Hell's Gate stood watch with cannons ready, realizing they were in easy reach of enemy guns aboard the British battleships in Long Island Sound. Rather than following up their victories with a fatal blow to the American army, however, the British commanders sent out peace feelers, believing that their stunned opponents realized the inevitability of their defeat and would avoid a senseless slaughter. On Wednesday, September 11, Lord Howe met with congressional leaders John Adams, Benjamin Franklin, and Edward Rutledge for three hours on Staten Island to discuss his offer of reconciliation with Britain. But the delegates expressed an unwavering commitment to independence and said they could not rescind the July 4 Declaration.

The British landed more troops on Montresor's Island at the mouth of the Harlem River, causing Washington to split his force. On September 12, a war council of his generals reversed their decision of just five days earlier to defend lower Manhattan. Their force was spread thin and divided, and the British threatened to surround them. So the order was given to evacuate New York City and move eight miles north to Harlem Heights. Knox believed that, without the help of a navy, an island such as Manhattan could not be defended against an enemy blessed with a formidable fleet. He had been working to exhaustion for more than a month. In a letter to his brother, he wrote: "My constant fatigue and application to the business of my extensive department has been such that I have not had my clothes off once o'nights for more than forty days."[36]

Peering through their spyglasses, the British saw that the Americans were packing up to leave lower Manhattan. They launched their assault on Sunday, September 15, crossing the East River at Hell's Gate or Hook's Horn and landing along Kip's Bay under the cover of a heavy cannonade from British battleships. At the same time, the frigate *Asia* and two other ships sailed into the Hudson to prevent the Americans from evacuating across the river to New Jersey. Knox's artillery unleashed heavy fire from Paulus Hook. The Americans retreated north on land along the Hudson. Knox, weighed down with the task of moving cannons, was among the last to leave the city when British troops began to arrive. Cut off from the road leading to Harlem, he was forced to abandon many of the heavy cannons and a large supply of munitions along with his luggage. With some of his men, Knox climbed into a boat, pushed from the shore, and sailed north with only minutes to spare.

As evening set in, Knox still had not arrived at Harlem Heights to join Washington, who heard reports that Henry had been captured. Washington himself had nearly been captured that day, when a fleeing American brigade left him standing alone within eighty yards of the enemy. He had remained on his horse for forty-eight hours during the evacuation. Eventually Henry came straggling into camp, his strength completely sapped, to the relief and manifest joy of his comrades.

He could not afford time to rest, however, and had to ready his artillery regiment to defend Harlem. A British advance party neared the American lines the next day, September 16, but was repulsed with heavy losses due to a determination not demonstrated by the Americans the previous day. The Continental regiments chased the British for two miles before Washington ordered a retreat as enemy reinforcements advanced. As Knox suspected and preached to his fellow soldiers, the British were not invincible. "The affair of last Monday [the Battle of Harlem Heights] has had some good consequences towards raising the people's spirits," Knox wrote to his brother William. "They find that if they stick to these mighty men, they will run as fast as other people."

In the same letter, Knox reflected on a lack of direction that pervaded the ranks and hoped that the ongoing congressional reorganization of the army would include more officers and better pay and training for the troops. He wrote William again on Monday, September 23, commenting that Washington "is as worthy a man as breathes, but he cannot do everything nor be everywhere. He wants good assistants. There is a radical evil in our army— the lack of officers. We ought to have men of merit in the most extensive and unlimited sense of the word. Instead of which, the bulk of the officers of the army are a parcel of ignorant, stupid men, who might make tolerable soldiers, but [are] bad officers; and until Congress forms an establishment to induce men proper for the purpose to leave their usual employments and enter the service, it is ten to one they will be beat till they are heartily tired of it."

He admitted that he had been disgusted by much of what he had witnessed in the ranks. "As the army now stands, it is only a receptacle for ragamuffins." The remedy, he thought, was not only in attracting talent by better pay but in congressionally authorized military schools: "We ought to have academies, in which the whole theory of the art of war shall be taught, and every other encouragement possible given to draw persons into the army that may give a luster to our arms."[37]

Two days later, Knox wrote the same sentiments to John Adams, who replied that he had proposed in Congress on October 1 the formation of a committee to consider establishing a military academy. Adams, who was on the committee, wrote Knox, "Write me your sentiments upon the subject" and that "I wish we had a military academy, and should be obliged to you for a plan of such an Institution. The expense would be a trifle, no object at all with me."

Knox also had complained to Adams that by allowing state assemblies to appoint officers, many unqualified men would be given leading positions in the army; instead, the power of appointments should be given to Washington. Adams replied that politics must play a role in the appointment process in order that the army garner support throughout the country. "If you leave the appointment of officers to the General, or to the Congress, it will not be so well done, as if left to the assemblies. The true Cause of the want of good officers in the Army is not because the appointment is left to the assemblies, but because such officers in sufficient numbers are not in America."[38]

A letter from John Hancock arrived in camp by the end of September reporting that Congress was already addressing the concerns forwarded by Knox, Washington, and others. Hancock reported that on September 16, the legislature, realizing that short-term enlistments were crippling the army, agreed to enlist men for the duration of the war and provide as an inducement for privates a bounty of $20 and 100 acres of land, which would go to a soldier's family if he were killed in the war. To attract talented officers, Congress offered commissioned colonels 500 acres; lieutenant colonels, 450 acres; majors, 400 acres; captains, 300; lieutenants, 200; ensigns, 150; and each noncommissioned officer and soldier, 100. Congress provided quotas for each of the thirteen states in hopes of raising eighty-eight battalions. Each state would supply officers, who were to be commissioned by Congress.[39]

As hopeful as this news was, it offered no help for the present crisis, which threatened to destroy the Continental Army. The enlistments of most of the men currently in service, including Knox's artillerists, were set to expire at the end of the year.

Congress sent a committee to inspect the army in New York. Several members were concerned about reports of panic sweeping through the ranks, and they had questions about the recent defeats. Between September 24 and 27, Knox, Washington, and key commanders met with delegates Elbridge Gerry of Massachusetts, Francis Lewis of New York, and Roger Sherman of Connecticut. Knox told the commission that the army lacked sufficient qualified officers and reiterated the suggestions he had made to John Adams. He also proposed that the military laboratories, which produced such necessities as gunpowder, should not be located near the theater of war, but at a distant, safe place. Knox drafted a letter outlining his recommendations, which he politely placed under the heading "Hints for the improvement of the artillery." It was presented to Congress on October 3.[40]

The national legislature gave Knox almost everything he asked for. His call for a military academy, a more visionary proposal, could not yet be accommodated. But his persistent efforts would lead to the institution of West Point a quarter of a century later. Henry Knox would be seen as the founding spirit of the national military college.

As Knox daily surveyed his artillery batteries, he could see the extensive fleet of ships moving up the Hudson and East rivers on both sides of Manhattan Island. As the *New York Mercury* reported on Tuesday, October 8: "The multitude of masts carries the appearance of a wood."

At 8 A.M. on October 9, three British battleships sailed up the Hudson, overcoming the obstacles the Americans had placed in the river and the cannon fire from Knox's men. Henry realized that Washington's army would soon be surrounded.

On Wednesday, October 16, Knox was asked to attend the war council of Washington's generals. Henry was the only colonel included in the meeting;

the commander in chief found his input indispensable. Knox agreed with the prevailing feeling that Harlem Heights should be evacuated.

Knox reached White Plains by Tuesday, October 22, and quickly began to mount the artillery. The enemy attacked the following Monday at Chatterton's Hill. Knox and the army retreated about half a mile north to a series of hills on Friday, November 1. As frustrating as the successive retreats had been, Henry explained the underlying strategy to his brother: "The enemy are determined on something decisive, and we are determined to risk a general battle only on the most advantageous terms."[41]

The heavy iron guns that Knox and his men were forced to haul during each grueling, successive retreat slowed the pace of the Continental force. The nature of the war had changed since the earlier weeks when the Americans fought behind fortifications on Long Island and Manhattan. The hilly terrain had prevented the British from cannonading their position. But now troops were entering open country without mobile field guns. The redcoats could easily swing field guns into action and rip apart their ranks. Henry told Washington that since the American strategy was to keep the army mobile and avoid a pitched battle against the British troops, which were superior both in number and in discipline, the Continental artillery needed to be tailored to fit their needs. Instead of big iron siege guns, each battalion should be equipped with mobile, brass field artillery mounted on carriages. Knox pointed out that when an iron cannon burst, it was unusable, unlike brass, which could simply be melted down and recast. To make up a respectable artillery train that could duel on par with Howe's gunners, Knox calculated that Washington's army needed cannons in a variety of sizes: a hundred three-pounders, fifty six-pounders, fifty twelve-pounders, and as many eighteen- and twenty-four-pound guns.

This was a difficult order to fill, Knox acknowledged. America was virtually without the high-temperature air furnaces to cast strong-bronze cannons, and he recommended that help should be sought abroad, perhaps from France or the Netherlands. Washington agreed to forward Knox's advice to Congress as soon as he could afford moments away from battle preparations.

Rather than attack the American fortifications head-on at White Plains, the British began to march back toward the Hudson for an apparent attack on American troops at Fort Washington and at Fort Lee on the New Jersey side of the river. Washington decided to split his force and send reinforcements to prevent the redcoats from penetrating into New Jersey or, even worse, marching south through New Jersey to Philadelphia in an attempt to capture the

Continental Congress. Before leaving White Plains for Nathanael Greene's headquarters at Fort Lee on Sunday, November 10, Washington left orders for Knox to divide his field artillery and send whatever guns, men, and supplies he deemed necessary into New Jersey. Washington placed full confidence in Knox's discretion: "With respect to yourself, I shall leave it to your own choice to go over [to New Jersey] or stay . . . your own judgment will govern you, and I am persuaded sufficiently stimulate to the discharge of every act by which the public service can be benefited."[42]

Knox chose to accompany the army to New Jersey. Because the Hudson was blocked by British ships, he and his artillerymen had to haul guns and supplies more than ten miles north to Peekskill before crossing the river and turning south on a forty-five-mile trip overland to Fort Lee.

Washington took the time to write Congress with Knox's pleas for more mobile field artillery, penning on Thursday, November 14, "application should be immediately made to such powers, as can and may be willing to supply them. They cannot be obtained too early, if soon enough, and I am told they may be easily had from France and Holland."[43]

Knox was still on the road to Fort Lee when news arrived that Fort Washington, a post directly on the other side of the Hudson at the northern end of Manhattan Island, had been captured by the British along with a considerable amount of artillery and ammunition. Knox's heart sank, not only for the loss of men but for the critical military supplies. Washington had been indecisive over whether Fort Washington should be evacuated, first ordering that it be held to the last man and then rescinding the order and leaving the decision whether to pull out to Major General Greene.

Before a plan could be decided upon, the British captured Fort Washington. Greene, shattered by this blow to American hopes, poured out his anguish in a letter to Knox. "I feel mad, vexed, sick, and sorry," Greene confided. "Never did I need the consoling voice of a friend more than now. Happy should I be to see you. This is a most terrible event: its consequences are justly to be dreaded. Pray, what is said upon the occasion? A line from you will be very acceptable."[44]

Greene explained that with Howe's men posted near the fort, he, Washington, and General Putnam rowed from Fort Lee across the Hudson to determine if evacuation was wise. Before they reached the Manhattan shore at 10 A.M., British cannons boomed, signaling the start of the battle. Greene offered to stay in New York and fight, but Washington forbade it, and they rowed back across the Hudson to Fort Lee. The 3,000-man garrison at Fort Washington was quickly surrounded by 13,000 redcoats and Hessian mercenaries, and a pounding cannonade battered the position. The Americans returned fire from a line of men outside the fortification, and Knox's artillery sent shot and shell ripping through the enemy ranks, killing hundreds. After three hours of desperate fighting, the Americans retreated into the fort. Within an hour, a white flag was hoisted. More than 150 men from the Continental Army were killed and another 2,828 were taken prisoner; 458 British soldiers were killed. Knox lost more than 100 men and 43 cannons from the artillery regiment.

"I was afraid of the fort," Greene confessed to Knox, "the redoubt you and I advised, too, was not done, or little or nothing done to it. Had that been complete, I think the garrison might have defended themselves a long while, or been brought off."[45]

When Knox reached Fort Lee, he noticed that even Washington seemed dejected and forlorn. In the recent weeks, he watched the loss not only of New York but of 4,000 of his troops. His army was divided, half still in upper New York under General Lee. A large part of the American army's munitions was now in enemy hands.

Knox and the other commanders realized that without Fort Washington, Fort Lee was powerless to prevent ships from coming up the Hudson. That post would also have to be abandoned. Knox began to direct the evacuation of the artillery as the army was ordered to march south through New Jersey to Brunswick, Princeton, Springfield, and the Acquackanonk Bridge over the Passaic River.

The British followed close behind, crossing the Hudson on Monday, November 18, and the next day forcing a hasty withdrawal of Fort Lee and the loss of all its cannons except two twelve-pounders. Knox, wondering if these guns could ever be replaced, agonized over his dwindling weaponry. The whole American army seemed to be vanishing, and what remained appeared more "ragamuffin" than ever. Driven from their forts, Knox and the 3,500 remaining troops moved over flat, open ground that favored the British. Rumors floated that the enemy had landed cavalry that could swing in front of the Americans and ambush them. Knox urged his men to push through the fatigue during a trip to Newark, knowing Washington's army had no hope in an open battle against British troops. The redcoats, under the command of Major General Charles Cornwallis, were not far behind. Knox reached

Newark on Friday, November 22, when heavy rains began to pour and slow the British pursuit.

Knox and the rest of the army waited for the weather to improve and for General Lee to send help from his division, which had remained at Peekskill. Help never came. The army was on the move again by early Thursday, November 28, and reached New Brunswick that evening. Knox had no time to rest. With each stop, artillery had to be moved into position to guard against an attack. Picket guards were thrown out around the camp to keep watch for British in the distance. Many of the soldiers grumbled at the apparent hopelessness of their situation and the demoralizing effect of successive retreats. Several were without tents or blankets, which had been abandoned in the flight from Manhattan, and more than a few were clothed in rags. Some were literally naked and would be unable to fight if the British suddenly attacked.

By Sunday, December 1, Cornwallis's 10,000-man division came within a two-hour march of Knox and the main American army, having pushed as far as Woodbridge and Amboy. Washington received credible reports that the British planned to advance to Philadelphia and unseat the capital. Many of the militiamen had seen enough, and two regiments, one from Maryland and another from New Jersey, headed home. Knox was disgusted. Washington's force was reduced to just 3,000 men. The commander in chief had no choice but to order another retreat and keep his army between the British and the American capital. Knox moved his artillery regiment south through Princeton on Monday and on to Trenton, where he immediately began loading the cannons and munitions into boats to cross the Delaware River into Morrisville, Pennsylvania, where a camp was set up. American soldiers traveled along the river in a seventy-five-mile radius, commandeering or destroying every boat, flat-bottom barge, and shallop they could find in order to prevent the British from finding a way to cross. On December 5, reinforcements began to arrive, amounting to about 2,000 men from the regiments of the Pennsylvania Associaters along with Pennsylvania Germans and men from Maryland.

The redcoats arrived on Sunday, December 8, just as the American soldiers who had been stationed in Princeton retreated and crossed the river into Morrisville. Knox watched with cannons ready as the British searched in vain for boats. Troops were dispatched along the river to guard the fords. Knox, on constant duty, was a whirlwind of activity, sending artillery and men to every regiment stationed for a distance of twenty-five miles along the river since no one knew where the enemy might attempt to cross.

He heard that Philadelphia was in a state of panic as residents fled to the country. On Thursday, December 12, the Continental Congress headed for Baltimore, leaving Washington with almost dictatorial authority by resolving that "until the Congress shall otherwise order, General Washington be possessed of full power to order and direct all things relative to the department, and to the operations of war."[46]

General William Howe, who had joined Cornwallis, decided to wait for more favorable weather, and turned his army around and marched the men back to New York to build winter quarters. Knox knew they would return shortly and scanned the flowing waters of the river each day for signs that ice was forming. Once the river froze over, it would be an avenue for the British to cross and surround Washington's army. He thought about his beloved Lucy and the daughter whom he hardly knew, and he wondered if he would ever see them again. He had not written home very often lately because the news was invariably dispiriting. Henry had risked everything for the war, and the outcome seemed as inevitable as the coming winter. The river would freeze, the British would cross the ice, with perhaps 13,000 troops, and destroy the American ranks of 5,000 men.

FOUR

DELAWARE CROSSING

Foremost among Knox's frustrations was Congress's plodding efforts to supply the army's needs. His advice to delegates in October to beef up the Continental artillery by recruiting fresh battalions and procuring mobile field guns was still being debated and yet to be implemented in December of 1776. Knox was convinced that Congress had little understanding of military matters and was ignorant of the critical tools for victory or even survival, choosing instead to risk all to satisfy budget concerns. Knox pressed Washington to use the dictatorial powers granted to him to order battalions recruited immediately, a step the commander in chief took.

With Congress now in Baltimore, Knox believed that it was up to the army to organize the war effort. On Wednesday, December 18, he drew up "A plan for the Establishment of a Corps of Continental Artillery, Magazines, Laboratories" to submit to Washington and Congress.

In the report, he explained the dire need for an effective artillery corps, which the British fully realized:

> In the modern mode of carrying on a war, there is nothing which contributes more to make an army victorious than a well regulated and well disciplined artillery provided with a sufficiency of cannon and stores. The battles which have lately been fought in Europe have generally been with cannon, and that army which has had the most numerous and best appointed artillery has commonly been victorious. The experience of this campaign [demonstrates that] the enemy depends on a superiority of their artillery. They scarcely or ever detach a single regiment without two or three field pieces. The regulations of their artillery are founded upon the most convincing experience of their utility and we shall have no reason to blush by imitating them in this particular.[1]

He explained that an artillery corps relied on educated, skilled veterans, especially to run the laboratories that produced everything from powder to explosives. He believed his men, who were spread throughout the army, should be paid 25 percent more than regular troops because their costs were greater than those of men in a unified regiment, and the army did not pay for much of their supplies. Pay among artillerists "in the British and French services is double" to that of infantrymen, he pointed out. His plan proposed that five battalions be recruited and laid out a command structure from regimental colonels down to gunners and bombardiers and skilled craftsmen to build cannon carriages, platforms, and wagons, among other needs. He asked that someone be appointed to obtain 150 brass cannons and that "[t]he persons appointed for this purpose are to spare neither pains or expense in getting the cannon cast and mounted as soon as possible." He also requested the power to form magazines, laboratories, and construction crews immediately.[2]

In submitting his plan to Washington, Knox offered himself as a candidate to head the artillery corps and said he would resign if not promoted. Two days later, on Friday, December 20, the commander in chief wrote a sternly worded letter to Congress in forwarding Knox's plan with his full support: "I have waited with much impatience to know the determinations of Congress on the propositions made some time in October last for augmenting our Corps of Artillery." Under the powers recently granted to him by Congress, he reported that he had ordered three battalions of artillery immediately raised "at the repeated [insistence] of Colo. Knox."

Washington told the delegates that "the casting of cannon is a matter that ought not to be one moment delayed" and that he would soon send Knox to Connecticut and New York to accomplish this and set up laboratories and magazines. Washington also urged Henry's appointment to the rank of general: "Colo. Knox (at present at the head of that department, but [who] without promotion will resign) ought to be appointed to the command of it with the rank and pay of brigadier."[3]

Washington apologized for the tone of the letter as well as his decision to raise artillery battalions and take other measures usually reserved for Congress, but that absolute necessity and the possible destruction of his army and American hopes were his greater concerns. He wrote, "A character to lose, an estate to forfeit, the inestimable blessing of liberty at stake, and a life devoted, must be my excuse."[4]

These acts would not, however, relieve the Continental Army of its immediate danger. Chunks of ice were forming in the Delaware and Howe's troops would soon be able to march across the river. The enlistments for many of the men in camp at Morrisville would expire by January 1, and Washington could do little to convince them to stay without offering them hope for success. A letter intercepted from the enemy revealed that Howe planned to launch his attack as soon as the American army enlistments expired and the Delaware had frozen. Even though he felt his force insufficient to launch an offensive strike, he decided he had no choice. "Necessity, dire necessity, will, nay must, justify my attack," Howe wrote to his adjutant general, Joseph Reed, in confidence on Monday, December 23.[5]

Early on Christmas morning, as the sun rose over the glistening snow, Washington issued orders for an assault of the 1,900-man Hessian regiment and British cavalry stationed across the Delaware in Trenton, New Jersey. The watchword for the mission was "Victory or Death." Knox was to supervise the crossing of the main body of the army over the river and was to send several gunners to march without their cannons with the lead divisions to either spike the enemy's six field guns or turn them to their use in the battle. These men were given spikes and hammers along with ropes for dragging off the cannons. The remaining part of Knox's artillery crew readied eighteen field pieces for the river crossing.

Christmas Day was clear and bright at 3 P.M. when Knox and the vanguard of troops began the nine-mile march north to McKonkey's Ferry, where they hoped to cross the 800-foot-wide Delaware undetected. Each man carried three days' rations, forty rounds of ammunition, and a blanket. Knox arrived at sunset and waited with Washington for the 2,400-man force to reach McKonkey's Inn, a two-story brick house that looked especially inviting to the men shivering in the cold. Some of the troops were guided to the site by the trail of blood left in the snow by men who marched without shoes. At 6 P.M., a messenger arrived from General John Cadwalader, who had been sent downstream of Trenton to Dunk's Ferry to cross the river and cut off the enemy's retreat route. Cadwalader reported that the rising tide was throwing up chunks of ice in the swift current and neither horses nor artillery could be rowed to the Jersey shore. He and the men around him were certain that Washington would also be unable to cross and that the mission would be canceled. Brigadier General James Ewing, who was ordered to cross the Delaware directly below Trenton with 700 men, also gave up the attempt.

Knox, however, was not dissuaded and told Washington that he believed he could get the force at McKonkey's Ferry across. As Washington sat on a frozen beehive along the bank, Knox's booming baritone was soon shouting out orders. Horses were led onto flat-bottom barges and the eighteen field guns, fifty horses, and ammunition weighing more than 350 tons were loaded on board. Knox had planned the crossing carefully. He had obtained a number of renowned Durham boats, long barges with running boards on the outside for men to stand and propel the craft forward by pushing poles against the ice. The boats were forty feet long but just two feet deep with narrowed, canoelike ends that had adjustable oars, front and back, to use as rudders and two masts for sails. The larger boats could carry fifteen tons while only drawing twenty inches in the river. Knox also knew where to look for pilots. He recruited Marblehead, Massachusetts seafaring fishermen and sailors from Colonel John Glover's regiment to lead the way. These were the same men who had ferried them across the East River after the evacuation of Brooklyn Heights.

An hour before midnight, a blinding snow mixed with rain, sleet, and pelting hail began to fall, and a cold wind blew down the length of the river, funneled by the riverbanks. Thomas Rodney, a soldier on the mission, remembered, "The night was as severe a night as ever I saw."[6]

Washington had hoped to be over the river by midnight, which would give the troops four or five hours to make the nine-mile march to Trenton before sunrise. But the weather and ice slowed the loading of men and weapons, and the delays endangered the mission.

With the cargo finally in the boats, Knox rode with Washington. According to legend, James Monroe, the future U.S. president, was aboard the same boat, and Alexander Hamilton was among the troops crossing the river. The Marblehead men chopped at the thin ice to forge a path in the current, then struck their poles against the floating chunks of ice and pushed from shore. Halfway across, ice slowed the convoy and put them in danger of being stranded midstream. Washington considered canceling the mission but realized there was no turning back. The setback would destroy any faith remaining in the army or his command.

The snow and hail rained down on the men in the open boats. They huddled together and wrapped blankets around their shoulders, wondering if they would die of exposure before ever reaching the New Jersey shore.

Knox labored to break up the ice, fighting the cold as well as exhausted muscles. "Perseverance accomplished what first seemed impossible," Knox admitted in a letter to Lucy.[7]

"The force of the current, the sharpness of the frost, the darkness of the night, the ice which made during the operation, and a high wind, rendered the passage of the river extremely difficult, but for the stentorian lungs and extraordinary exertions of Colonel Knox," Major James Wilkinson would still vividly remember 40 years later.[8]

Knox later praised the mariners guiding the boats. When Washington wondered aloud "[w]ho will lead us on," Knox said that "the men of Marblehead and Marblehead alone, [stood] forth to lead the army along the perilous path."[9]

By 2 A.M. on Thursday, December 26, the first of the boats carrying General Adam Stephen's vanguard brigade of Virginians reached the opposite bank, followed by troops from Connecticut, Maryland, and Massachusetts. Knox reached land and spent the next hour directing the embarkation of men and the unloading of cannons and horses. By then, "it hailed with great violence," he wrote. It was not until 4 A.M., the time Washington had hoped the force would arrive in a sleepy Trenton, that the troops were ready to leave the river. Now the force could not arrive until after sunrise, when much of the element of surprise would be lost. But recrossing the river in daylight would be suicidal, Washington knew; they would be discovered and be easy targets for the enemy. They had no choice but to move ahead. "I determined to push on at all events," Washington later told Congress.[10]

Knox had horses hitched to the artillery carriages and munitions wagons, and he assigned men with four field guns to lead each column and three pieces at the head of each supporting division as well as two cannons to accompany the reserves. As the blizzard continued, the troops moved out under orders not to utter a sound and with the warning that any man who deserted the ranks would be put to death.

For the first mile and a half, the road led up a rather steep hill that ran along the shore. The horses struggled to maintain their footing. Ropes had to be tied to trees and attached to the multi-ton cannons, and men grabbed hold of the lines in an effort to hoist the guns up the incline. The challenge must have reminded Knox of the trip from Ticonderoga. Upon reaching the crest at Bear Tavern, the men resumed the march along flat ground the rest of the way to Trenton. Knox was thankful that the snow now fell to their backs and they no longer had to fight the wind. Legs ached as the men trudged through the freshly fallen base of snow, pushing forward along the winding road that cut through a forest of hickory, ash, and black oaks. When they arrived at Birmingham, three miles from Bear Tavern and four and a half miles from Trenton, Washington split his force. Major General John Sullivan was to lead his brigade on the road along the river to arrive below Trenton, while Major General Greene was to lead his men on Pennington's Road, which ran to the north side of the town. Knox and Washington accompanied General Greene's column. Sullivan, with the shorter route, paused a mile outside of Trenton to wait for signs of Greene's force. Checking their weapons and powder, his men found that the weather had spoiled much of their ammunition. Sullivan immediately sent an aide to Washington, but before the commander in chief's orders to prepare for a bayonet assault arrived, the men had already fastened the blades to their guns.

Knox knew that the army could not afford any more delays or the Hessians would be awake when they arrived. Watching closely as the sky brightened and the sun began to rise, he noticed an unmistakable determination in the eyes of the men despite the discouraging conditions and the fatigue from a fifteen-mile march in freezing rain. It was evident that they desperately wanted to strike a blow after suffering the humiliation of so many retreats and the scorn of many of their countrymen. They seemed less concerned about their frozen fingers and numbed feet or the danger from the elements or the enemy in light of the chance to finally claim victory.

A half hour after daybreak, at 8 A.M., Knox and Greene's column were a mile from Trenton, where the lead regiment surprised the scrambling enemy pickets. "The storm continued with great violence," Henry wrote to Lucy, "but was in our backs, and consequently in the faces of our enemy."[11] Advancing American troops chased the advance guard of Hessians back into town. From River Road, Sullivan's men spotted the column along Pennington Road, then let out three cheers and chased the pickets along the river back toward Trenton. A Hessian company pouring out of their barracks to help the guards were stunned by the ferocity of the American charge and scampered across the bridge over the Assunpink River, which divided the town and ran at a right angle from the Delaware. The British cavalrymen were able to mount their horses but were not eager to join the fight; instead they joined the flight across the sixteen-foot-wide Assunpink bridge.

On the north side of the city, Knox's artillerymen raced to seize the enemy cannons with spikes, hammers, and ropes in hand, flanked by an escort of soldiers. The rest of the column followed and, in Washington's words, "each [corps] seemed to vie with the other in pressing forward."[12] Knox and Washington entered Trenton near the head of King and Queen streets, which ran parallel north and south, perpendicular to the river. Knox directed field guns and howitzers to be placed at the heads of the streets to prevent an enemy charge. Dr. Benjamin Rush, the surgeon for the American army, later wrote to Congressmen Richard Henry Lee that "I saw [Knox's] behavior in the Battle of Trenton; he was cool, cheerful and was present everywhere."[13] Hessian soldiers rushed into the streets, clutching their muskets, but could not form ranks between the shouting and confusion and the flight of the men. A few mercenaries were able to man two cannons posted near the Hessian headquarters of Colonel Johann Gottlieb Rahl. Washington charged on his chestnut horse with a company of infantrymen to seize the guns, which continued to fire.

Rahl emerged to mount his horse, screaming for his men to form a line of battle: "Forward, march; advance, advance!" His men fired up the street, shooting Washington's horse beneath him and wounding James Monroe. Just then, Knox's artillery from Captain Thomas Forrest's company opened fire from the head of the street with six cannons a mere 300 yards away. The shots ripped through the Hessian line, tearing soldiers apart. Knox was stunned at the destructive power of cannons in such close-range fighting. "Here succeeded a scene of war of which I had often conceived, but never saw before," he would write his wife. "The hurry, fright, and confusion of the enemy was not unlike that which will be when the last trump shall sound. They endeavored to form in streets, the heads of which we had previously the possession of with cannon and howitzers; these, in the twinkling of an eye, cleared the streets."[14]

The booming cannons disheartened the Hessians, who abandoned hopes of breaking the American lines and instead took cover. Continental troops circled around the barracks. Those with good powder fired at the crouched soldiers, and others menaced with bayonets. Rahl's men found an open lane in the American line and raced to an orchard east of the town near the road to Princeton. Knox had posted cannons on all the routes leading out of town, however. "It was impossible for them to get away," he relayed to Lucy.[15]

Washington was concerned that the Hessians would assemble and try to attack his men on the north side of town and push the Americans toward the river.

Rahl ordered a charge to retake the town. Knox recalled: "The poor fellows after they were formed on the plain saw themselves completely surrounded, the only resource left was to force their way through numbers unknown to them. The Hessians lost part of their cannon in the town; they did not relish the project of forcing [a charge]." American muskets fired, sending up a cloud of smoke as shots pelted the Hessians. Rahl was hit and fell from his horse, mortally wounded. The Continental troops, almost delirious with fury, charged with bayonets. The beleaguered Hessians "were obliged to surrender upon the spot."[16] With Knox's cannons sweeping the field, Washington thought that the enemy realized they must surrender or "they must inevitably be cut to pieces."[17]

A total of 23 officers and 886 men were taken prisoner, and 6 field guns and 1,200 small arms were captured. About 25 Hessian soldiers were killed and 7 were wounded. Among the Americans, 4 were killed and 8 wounded. Two other men froze to death. A sizable number of Hessians escaped with the British light horse along the river because the American commanders Cadwalader and Ewing had been unable to cross the Delaware the previous night and cut off the retreat route.

For Knox, the victory demonstrated how effective the use of mobile field guns could be in leading an assault. He had proven to Washington and the rest of the army that he knew how to fight a modern war with guns ahead of columns rather than dragged behind them in support and that his military knowledge was not idle theory but practical on the battlefield. This strategy was the same one that Napoleon, who also began his career in an artillery unit, would later use to great advantage in Europe.

Knox and his men had hauled eighteen cannons under the most difficult conditions imaginable—snow, sleet, hail, and freezing temperatures, across an ice-packed river—and yet were able to place guns with the vanguard of the army in a surprise, quick-strike attack.

The soldiers found two hogsheads of rum, which they broke open and drank, in hopes of taking the chill out of their bodies. Washington realized the Hessian and British soldiers who had escaped would soon sound the alarm to the British posted at Princeton and the surrounding area. Not wanting to risk being trapped against the river, he ordered his troops to return to Morrisville. As exhausted as Knox was, he directed the loading of the artillery along with the captured Hessian guns aboard the flat-bottom barges for another arduous crossing of the Delaware.

That same day, Knox's plan for a Continental artillery corps and Washington's letter of support reached Baltimore and was read in Congress, causing a stir among the delegates. Francis Lewis, who had been appointed to the Cannon Committee just two days earlier, rushed a letter to fellow delegate Robert Morris, a financially astute businessman known as the financier of the American Revolution, who was rounding up critically needed money and supplies for Washington's army. "Congress has this moment received letters from the General recommending in the most pressing terms the necessity of having a number of brass and iron cannon provided as early as possible for the next campaign on which he seems to say the fate of America in a great measure depends," Lewis told Morris. "He also strongly recommends an augmentation of the Continental battalions to 110—with five battalions of artillery."[18]

A committee of three was immediately appointed, which included Samuel Adams, who had known Knox for years, along with Virginia's Richard Henry Lee and James Wilson of Pennsylvania, to consider the implications of the plan. The following morning, Friday, December 27, before news of the Trenton victory had arrived, Adams recommended that Knox be given the power to augment the artillery, and Congress resolved that "a brigadier general of artillery be appointed; and, the ballots being taken, Colonel Henry Knox was elected."[19] It was also resolved to authorize the building of two magazines, one in Carlisle, Pennsylvania, and the other in Brookfield, Massachusetts, each to hold 10,000 stand of arms and 200 tons of gunpowder, as well as a powder factory. Congress also expanded Washington's dictatorial powers for six months, granting him the authority to raise the artillery battalions along with his other needs, which included sixteen battalions of infantry, 3,000 cavalrymen, and a corps of engineers.

Back in Trenton on Saturday, December 28, Henry wrote Lucy, who had returned to Boston, with an account of the triumph at Trenton. After avoiding writing her for weeks during the discouraging retreats through New Jersey, he proudly proclaimed victorious news: "My Dearly Beloved Friend, you will before this have heard of our success on the morning of the 26th." He gave her a full account of the battle, from the difficulties of the crossing to the harrowing scenes of destruction. "His Excellency the General has done me the unmerited great honor of thanking me in public orders in terms strong and polite. This I should blush to mention to any other than to you, my dear Lucy; and I am fearful that even my Lucy may think her Harry possesses a species of little vanity in doing [it] at all."[20]

The Americans discovered that the British troops had evacuated the surrounding area after the Battle of Trenton, and Washington ordered his men to make yet another crossing on Monday, December 30. General Cadwalader took possession of nearby Bordentown, Mount Holly, and Burlington. Knox spent two days getting the artillery across the river, which was completely congested with ice. The following day, many of the troops packed up their gear for the trip home, as their enlistments expired December 31. Washington, Knox, and the brigadier and regimental leaders tried to convince them to extend their duty. Thomas Mifflin, a former delegate to Congress from Pennsylvania who served as quartermaster general for the army, rode before the troops, wrapped in a rose-colored coat that had been patched together from pieces of blanket. He told his men that they could follow up the victory at Trenton by retaking much of New Jersey, as Washington planned, and by protecting Philadelphia, and bask in the credit of having saved the American cause. But many men had not received their pay in several weeks, and the paymaster had no funds. In Philadelphia, delegate Robert Morris was going door to door in an effort to raise $50,000 to send to the army. The 6,000 American troops paraded, many for the last time, and stood at attention to hear an appeal from Washington, who rode before the men. His force would dwindle to a mere 1,500 men once the enlistments expired in the next few hours, unless they could be persuaded to remain. Drummers beat a cadence to signal volunteers to step forward and pledge to stay six weeks longer with the army. Not one single man heeded the call. Washington called off the drums and directed his horse to the center of the line. "My brave fellows," he exhorted in an affectionate tone, "[y]ou have done all that I have ever asked you to do, and more than could be expected; but your country is at stake, your wives, your houses, and all that you hold dear." Washington promised them $10 of pay for an additional six weeks of service, which by that time he hoped fresh enlistments would invigorate the force. He felt it was a high price, but at the height of the alarm in Philadelphia, Pennsylvania had offered that amount to its militia. The commander in chief believed he must offer the going rate. To guarantee the offer, Washington told the men that he would pledge his own fortune to make certain they received the pay.

Knox believed that Washington was demonstrating remarkable leadership skills, and as he listened to the general's appeal, he felt a surge of patriotic inspiration. Many of the men realized that they could not leave with so much at stake. Washington preserved a force of about 3,300 men who agreed to stay for another short stint.[21]

Henry was greatly relieved that the army had not been reduced to a skeletal force. "Our people have exerted great fortitude, and stayed beyond the time of their enlistment, in high spirits, but want rum and clothing," he wrote to Lucy three days later.[22] Washington justified the offer to Congress by pointing out that "[t]he troops feel their importance and would have their price. Indeed as their aid is so essential and not to be dispensed with, it is to be wondered, they had not estimated it at a higher rate."[23]

The Americans spread out a camp in and around Trenton and posted picket troops a mile to the north to watch for an attack. Knox stationed most of his guns in a strong defensive position on the east side of Trenton across the Assunpink, a tributary that during the summer was a small creek but by winter became a swollen, ice-jammed river. A sixteen-foot-wide wooden bridge extended over it. Between the hill and the Assunpink, the Americans built a line of fortifications and tried to construct entrenchments in the frozen ground. Knox strengthened the position with forty cannons at the base of the hill and two field guns on its crest. On the first day of the year, 3,600 soldiers arrived to reinforce the Americans, swelling the force to about 6,800 men. The army received intelligence that Major General Cornwallis had advanced to Princeton, just twelve miles away, with 8,000 men and was eager for battle, believing that expired enlistments had decimated the Continental Army and that the Delaware River could no longer offer protection for the remaining American troops.

On Thursday, January 2, news of Knox's promotion arrived from Baltimore. He excitedly wrote to Lucy that day, uncertain whether his wife would prefer that he quit the service and return to her rather than become even more wedded to the army: "Will it give you satisfaction or pleasure in being informed that the Congress have created me a general officer—a brigadier— with the entire command of the artillery? If so, I shall be happy." Henry failed to tell her that he had threatened to resign if not promoted and somewhat disingenuously reported: "It was unsolicited on my part, though I cannot say unexpected. People are more lavish in their praises of my poor endeavors than they deserve. All the merit I can claim is industry. I wish to render my devoted country every service in my power."

In preparing for another attack, however, he was still troubled by the bloodshed he had witnessed a few days before. To his wife he confided, "The attack of Trenton was a most horrid scene to the poor inhabitants. War, my Lucy, is not a humane trade, and the man who follows [it] as such will meet with his proper demerits in another world."[24]

Shortly after Knox finished the letter, a British column attacked, the vanguard of 6,000 troops under Cornwallis. At three o'clock, the redcoats pushed back the pickets and outlying troops, and drove them back into Trenton. The American troops retreated across the Assunpink Bridge, seeking refuge behind Knox's artillery guns. The two field guns on the hill afforded a sweeping command of Trenton and provided the men cover as the British rushed forward and began a heavy musket fire. "The enemy advanced within reach of our cannon, who saluted them with great vociferation and some execution," Knox later wrote Lucy. The redcoats were able to bring cannons into place and fire at the fortifications, but in the descending darkness they did little damage.

Knox kept up sporadic cannon fire. "A few shells we now and then chucked into town to prevent their enjoying their new quarters securely," he wrote to his wife.[25]

Knox realized, however, that the Americans could not hold their position for long. They were pinned with the Assunpink to their front and the Delaware, which was now completely impassable by boats, on their left. If the British overwhelmed their right, they would be trapped and destroyed. Knox and the other generals agreed that the army should evacuate. Washington decided to send the army to the rear of Cornwallis's force. By cutting off his supply lines and communication with the rest of the British forces in New York, the Americans would be able to take back New Jersey.

Washington ordered the army to move out and march to Princeton to attack the British Seventeenth, Fortieth, and Fifty-fifth regiments, believed to consist of 1,200 men. About 400 troops were assigned to keep the campfires burning with rail fences and posts to make it appear that the army was bivouacking for the night. Before dawn, these men were to slip away and join the rest of the army. Men also were left to maintain the mock noise of engineers building fortifications to add to the ruse; they too were to escape in the early-morning darkness. Knox left men to continue to shell Trenton to disrupt the enemy's sleep.

At 1 A.M. on Friday, January 3, the army moved out. After several warm days, the temperature fell that night and the ground became hard and better suited for travel with heavy guns and carriages. "Our troops marched with great silence and order," Knox reported to Lucy.[26] They marched a roundabout route to Princeton, which was twelve miles to the north, in order to avoid detection, traveling east through Sand Town and from thence north along Quaker Road. The march went smoothly with no major delays. The men reached Stony Creek, about two miles short of Princeton, shortly after daybreak, when they encountered 800 British troops marching to Trenton to join Cornwallis. The redcoats believed Washington's main force was still at Trenton and that these troops must only be a small detachment. "You may judge of their surprise when they discovered such large columns marching up," Knox relayed to Lucy. "I believe they were as much astonished as if an army had dropped perpendicularly upon them."[27]

Knox ordered cannons moved into place, and Washington sent 350 troops under General Hugh Mercer to cut off the road to Trenton. The British attacked Mercer, whose men gathered in a patch of woods and were already exhausted by the long march, the incessant cold, and lack of sleep over several days. Mercer's men fired a volley of muskets at the enemy, who returned shots darting around them among the trees. Several men fell wounded, crying out in pain.

Then the redcoats let out a yell and charged with bayonets thrust forward. Mercer's men lost heart and fled, leaving the general unprotected. The British soldiers thrust the blades from their guns into his body and left him mortally wounded. Knox saw several of his comrades brutally attacked with bayonets, savage thrusts goring their bodies. The Pennsylvania militia tried to repulse the British, but they too had little strength left. Washington arrived and rallied the men as the rest of his force approached. Knox's artillery guns fired, signaling the full line of the Continental force to rush into place.

Suddenly the British realized that they were facing Washington's main force as well as Knox's artillery guns. The field guns blasted holes in the enemy line. In desperation, the British commander led a bayonet charge through the American line near the road to Trenton and was able to flee south. Continental troops chased them for several miles, rounding up hundreds of prisoners before Washington called off the pursuit and ordered his men to push toward Princeton. By the time they arrived, the remaining 200 British troops had fled east and had barricaded themselves behind the thick stone walls of Nasssau Hall, a building at Princeton University. Knox ordered Captain Alexander Hamilton and the New York artillery to attack the position. Hamilton's men wheeled a four-pounder into position and ignited the touchhole. A booming shot sent a cannonball shrieking into Prayer Hall, where it punctured a portrait of King George III, decapitating him. The British must have viewed this as an ominous sign. A second shot hit the cornice of Nassau Hall and ricocheted to kill the horse ridden by Major James Wilkinson. Then Hamilton ordered a charge, which convinced the remaining British soldiers to surrender. In the battle for Princeton, the British had 28 men killed, 58 others were wounded, and 323 soldiers captured along with 2 field guns and hundreds of blankets, shoes, and other provisions. The Americans suffered 23 killed and 20 wounded.

Washington wanted to push farther north to New Brunswick, where the British had left much of their munitions and supplies, but his commanders told him that the men were too exhausted for another extended march and then another battle. "Our men having been without either rest, rum, or provisions for two nights and days, were unequal to the task of marching seventeen miles further," Knox wrote to his wife. "If we could have secured one thousand fresh men at Princeton to have pushed for Brunswick, we should have struck one of the most brilliant strokes in all history." Knox and the other commanders felt the capture of New Brunswick could have ended the war. He was jubilant, nevertheless, over the Princeton victory. "The enemy [was] within nineteen miles of Philadelphia, they are now sixty miles. We have driven them from almost the whole west Jersey."

The Continental Army had been at Princeton just two hours when word arrived that Cornwallis was moving from Trenton and racing to protect their munitions at New Brunswick. "This they did, as we have since been informed, in a most infernal sweat—running, puffing, and blowing, and swearing at being so outwitted," Henry reported to Lucy.[28]

Washington needed to find shelter for his troops. Knox told him that during the army's retreat through New Jersey in November, he had reconnoitered the area for a favorable site to build winter quarters. He suggested Morristown, New Jersey, which was flanked by defensible hills and within striking distance of New York City. The Morristown site would also help the American army to protect the roads leading to Philadelphia. Having full confidence in Henry's judgment, the commander in chief immediately ordered the men to march to Pluckemin, New Jersey, and then on to Morristown to lay up for the winter.

The army arrived at Morristown on Monday, January 6, and Knox, still flush with the reversal of fortune over the past two weeks, wrote his wife the next day: "For my part, my Lucy, I look up to heaven and most devoutly thank the Governor of the Universe for producing this turn in our affairs; and the sentiment I hope will so prevail in the hearts of the people as to induce them to be a people chosen of Heaven, not to give way to despair, but at all times and under all circumstances never to despair of the Commonwealth."[29] He spent the next two weeks designing fortifications and barracks while also considering the needs of the artillery corps for the coming summer campaign. He was unhappy with the congressional choice of sites to locate the Continental arsenals, believing the decisions were based on political rather than military considerations. He recommended that Washington use his authority to relocate the magazines to sites more favorable to the army's needs.

On Monday, January 16, Washington gave Knox orders to establish the arsenals where he thought best. Knox was to travel to Hartford and hire contractors, rent buildings, and establish cannon foundries and gunpowder laboratories, keeping careful track of his expenses. Knox also provided Washington with detailed orders to pass on to Colonel Benjamin Flower, a skilled builder in the artillery regiment; Flower was to establish a similar arsenal in Yorktown, Pennsylvania. Unlike an artillery commander in any other army, Knox had to understand not only how to use cannons in battle but the intricacies of casting guns. His orders to Colonel Flower demonstrated his deep knowledge of the subject and included an itemized inventory for the arsenal, which included the construction of an air furnace and a mill for boring cannon after the barrels were cast. He ordered that Flower offer one-year enlistments to forty carpenters, forty blacksmiths, and twenty wheelwrights. The powder laboratories would employ turners and tin men and twelve harness-makers. Craftsmen were needed to make cannon carriages, wheels, and other parts to transport the guns.

The cannon foundry should be equipped to cast sixty guns in various sizes, six-pounders first and then three-pounders and howitzers along with ten twelve-pounders. The arsenal was to produce all kinds of ammunition for the army.

Knox ordered that sixty workmen be employed at the arsenal, each enlisted for the duration of the war and given various ranks with the artillery corps. He also provided Flower with a list of workmen needed to accompany the artillery corps in the field.[30]

The next day, Washington wrote to Congress: "Upon communicating this resolve to General Knox, who will have the principal direction of these matters, he was of opinion, that Hartford in Connecticut [and Yorktown in Pennsylvania] would be, on many accounts, more convenient for that purpose than Brookfield [and Carlisle], particularly in respect to buildings, which are already erected. . . . I should be glad, that you would, by a new resolve, permit me to direct the works to be carried on at the places last mentioned."[31]

For reasons never made clear, John Hancock, president of the Congress, was irritated with the alteration to its plans. Writing on behalf of Congress on Wednesday, January 29, 1777, he told Washington, "As some steps have been taken with respect to the magazines at Brookfield and Carlisle, the Congress judge it best they should be erected there in preference to the other places mentioned by General Knox."

But by then Knox had already arrived at Hartford, which was not as well suited for an arsenal as he had thought. At the point where the Connecticut River ran by the town, it became narrow and shallow, and Knox believed the river would be difficult for transports to navigate. He proceeded twenty miles up the river to Springfield, Massachusetts, where the river widened and deepened. The site would be ideal for sending supplies north to upstate New York, which was the primary purpose of the proposed arsenal. Springfield also possessed several buildings that could be easily converted into laboratories and magazine warehouses, and the site was safely removed from the reach of the British. The materials necessary for casting cannons—copper, tin, and brass—

also were available. Knox rounded up workmen from almost every manufacturing trade in the area and began to negotiate with blacksmiths, wheelwrights, coppers and tin men, carpenters and smiths, nail-makers and others. He made arrangements for an air furnace to be built and a foundry to be established. This was the beginning of the famous United States Arsenal in Springfield, which later produced many technical advances in weaponry, including the repeating Springfield rifles used to such advantage in the Civil War. The armory did not close until 1968.

Knox then returned to his hometown of Boston for a long-awaited reunion with Lucy and a chance to see his daughter. He spent several days with his family while carrying on business. His brother William was trying to resurrect the bookstore. He had rented the old shop and was ordering volumes and repairing the damage. He peppered Henry with questions on how to proceed.

Spurred by the recent American victories, recruitment in Knox's home state and town proceeded under the direction of Jeremiah Gridley and was "exceeding rapid," he wrote Washington on Saturday, February 1. The state was trying to fill its quota of raising three infantry regiments and one of artillery. But to Knox's dismay, Massachusetts was offering recruits $86.67 to enlist for the duration of the war—more than four times the amount of other states. The state was having difficulty attracting skilled soldiers, who felt there was little need to join the army with the threat removed from Boston. The exorbitant rate threatened to disrupt recruitment throughout America, he wrote. Knox wanted more Massachusetts men in his artillery corps and sent a memorial to the Massachusetts Provincial Congress, asking if a second regiment of gunners could be recruited.[32]

He also told Washington that he had decided to establish the munitions depot and foundry in Springfield and needed $20,000 to cover the costs. "If Congress should still adhere to Brookfield in preference to Springfield, it will delay everything for three or four months. I wrote General Greene from Springfield that it was the best place in all the four New England states for a laboratory, cannon foundry, &c., and I hope your Excellency will order it there."[33]

Washington responded in a letter dated February 11, conveying Congress's insistence that the magazines and laboratories be established in Carlisle and Brookfield, but he gave Knox permission to use his judgment. "I will inform Congress of the necessity of this variation from their resolve."[34] Three days later, Washington wrote to John Hancock that he placed "weight, particularly in this instance" in Knox's opinion and had "ventured to order the works to be begun [in Springfield]." Washington asked that Congress give its approbation to Knox's change in plans.[35]

The congressional Board of War recommended that the arsenal be located at Springfield, but John Hancock refused to give up on the Brookfield site and the proposal was tabled for future consideration. Hancock, a wealthy Boston merchant with ties in Connecticut, remembered Knox's humble status as a merchant. On Friday, February 21, the same day that Congress voted to leave Baltimore and return to Philadelphia, John Adams recorded in his diary that Hancock sent him a note "expressing great resentment about fixing the magazine at Brookfield, against the book binder [Knox]."[36]

Knox spent several weeks in Boston attending to the Springfield arsenal and helping recruit as many artillerymen as he could find. Washington, meanwhile, believed that the British were collecting a force in New Brunswick and would soon attack. He was growing anxious for Knox's return to lead the artillery. The enlistments of most men in Henry's corps had expired, and Washington was eager for Knox to arrive with fresh recruits with long-term enlistments. On Friday, March 14, he sent an express dispatch to Henry in Boston: "I have for some time past most earnestly expected you, to arrange matters in the artillery department, which has in a manner lain still since you went away. . . . As you see how necessary your presence is here, I hope you will make as much haste as possible to join."[37]

Knox was back in Morristown a few days later, accompanied by a regiment of men he began to train for the artillery corps. Alexander Hamilton had been reassigned from Knox's artillery corps to become Washington's aide. The army was suffering another smallpox epidemic, more serious than the previous year, and the whole army was being inoculated. Most of the men whom Washington had persuaded in January to agree to a six-week enlistment had returned home, reducing the force in Morristown to just 3,000 soldiers. Although Congress had authorized the recruitment of 75,000 men, enlistments were lagging. To make his army seem larger than it actually was in British eyes, Washington sent out parties to attack enemy sentinels and foraging parties to several towns.

The effort to raise arms was proving more successful. France promised Silas Deane, an American diplomat in Paris, that it would send 200 brass cannons, 30,000 muskets, 100 tons of gunpowder, and money. On Monday, March 31, Knox wrote ecstatically to Lucy: "The enemy and we are laying upon our oars. What think you of the care of Providence to Americans in bringing in so many ammunitions, notwithstanding the care of our very malignant enemies? For my own part, I bow with gratitude to that High Power who putteth up and putteth down. America, under his smiles shall win."[38]

To boost enlistments, Washington recommended that each state institute a draft. On April 14, 1777, Congress resolved that the provincial legislatures compel citizens "to furnish such a number of able-bodied soldiers" and that if quotas for regiments could not be reached by May 15 to "cause indiscriminate draughts to be made from their respective militia without regard to rank, sect of religion or other privilege whatsoever."[39]

John Adams decided that it was time to push Congress to give official approval to Knox's decision to establish a Springfield arsenal, which was already being built. Writing to General Greene on Sunday, April 13, Adams said, "Gentlemen will oppose it, particularly the President [John Hancock], I believe, thinking Brookfield the best Place. I am not very clear myself, that it is the best, but from a greater confidence in the opinion of General Washington and General Knox, than in my own, I voted for it, and shall continue to do so." The next day, Congress repealed its order from the previous December and passed a resolution relocating the arsenal to Springfield in compliance with Knox's plan.[40]

Knox received further encouraging news that a French ship, the *Amphitrite*, had arrived at Portsmouth, Massachusetts, bringing fifty-three brass four-pound field pieces, cannonballs, musket balls, entrenching tools, and more than six thousand muskets along with gunpowder.

Washington was uncertain of the British plans for a spring military campaign. He suspected Howe would either attempt to march to Philadelphia again or try to send ships up the Hudson and cut off New England from the lower states, thus dividing America into two smaller and more conquerable regions. Washington decided to send his two most trusted generals, Henry Knox and Nathanael Greene, to the highlands in Peekskill to inspect fortifications and devise defenses. They received their orders for the mission on Monday, May 12, and set out from Morristown. The spring weather was warm, and the two friends enjoyed the time together. They visited friends of Greene's, including Abraham Lott, who lodged them for a night at his home. At Peekskill, they were received by Colonel Alexander McDougal, whom Knox had met on his mission to Ticonderoga. Knox and Greene inspected Fort Montgomery, which guarded the narrows of the Hudson near Bear Mountain, and Fort Constitution and Fishkill, farther up the river. Knox and Greene recommended that a line of floating timbers connected by cables be extended from Fort Montgomery across the river as well as an iron chain to impede enemy ships. Two ships and two long, low oar boats equipped with cannons should wait behind the chain to fire on approaching enemy vessels. They thought that the highlands and its passes could be defended by about 5,000 men for a short period until reinforcements could arrive. On Saturday, May 17, they crossed the Hudson to New Windsor and inspected and evaluated the terrain at West Point. Both men felt the site was vital to the control not only of the region, but perhaps of the entire continent because it stood at the confluence of critical waters and lines of communication. Knox and Greene then headed back to Morristown. Greene fell from his horse on a rocky mountain trail, cutting his lip and leaving him bruised but otherwise unhurt.

When the men arrived back in Washington's camp, Knox received letters from Lucy, who was already overcome with loneliness. Her family in England had cut her from their lives. She spent time with General Heath's wife, whose restrained, austere personality was very different from Lucy's. Lucy described her as "so stiff it is impossible to be sociable with her."[41] Smallpox also was sweeping Boston. Lucy and her children went to Sewell's Point (now Brookline) to be inoculated. She feared being disfigured by the infection and wrote: "You will want to know if I look as I did or whether there is danger of you not liking me as well as you did when you saw me last." Feeling insecure, she continued: "My dearest friend, my all, my Harry—where are you—are you safe—are you well? Would to heaven I could see you for one-half hour. Do you wish for your Lucy? Do you think of me? Do you ever shed a tear for me? 'Tis very hard thus to be parted. Will it last long, my love, or is the day at hand that shall re-unite us?"[42]

Knox wrote her sympathetically on May 20: "Though your parents are on the opposite side from your Harry, yet it's very strange it should divest them of humanity. Not a line! My God! What stuff is the human heart made of? Although father, mother, sister and brother have forgotten you, yet, my love, your Harry will ever esteem you the best boon of Heaven."[43]

Henry told his wife that the Continental Army was much more prepared for the summer military season in terms of men and arms than the previous year. Washington's force had swelled to 9,000 men, and the munitions from France had been sent to Morristown, providing the army with 12,000 muskets, 1,000 barrels of powder, 11,000 flints, and clothing. "But, I am sorry to say it, we seem to be increasing most rapidly in impiety. This is a bad omen, but I hope we shall mend, thou I see no immediate prospect of it."[44] Professional gamblers had set their sights on the bored soldiers. Washington had recently banned the playing of cards, dice, or any games, except those designed for physical exercise, because it was impossible to distinguish "between innocent play, for amusement, and criminal gaming, for pecuniary and sordid purposes."[45]

Lucy, who was well informed of the news in Boston, was surprised to learn through her social connections that France had sent, along with its cannons, an officer to lead the American artillery corps, Phillipe Charles Jean Baptiste Tronson Du Coudray. An adjutant general in the French army, Du Coudray had signed an agreement with Silas Deane in Paris the previous September that promised a commission as major general of artillery and engineers. He was a man of proven ability and impressive credentials with powerful connections reaching the French throne. Lucy was uncertain what to make of the news and seemed torn between her desire for Henry's return to private life and the manifest pride she took in his service. She wrote her husband in May: "A French general, who styles himself commander-in-chief of the Continental artillery, is now in town. He says his appointment is from Mr. Deane, that he is going immediately to headquarters to take command, that he is a major-general, and a deal of it. Who knows but I may have my Harry again? This I am sure of, he will never suffer any one to command him in that department. If he does, he has not the soul which I now think him possessed of."[46]

Knox told Washington that he would resign if replaced or compelled to serve as second in command of the artillery corps. The general realized that Du Coudray's appointment was a delicate matter. American diplomats as well as congressmen were wooing the French, and rejecting one of their top officers could offend the court in Paris as well as the country's minister of war, who had hand-picked Du Coudray to aid the Continental Army.

Nevertheless, he was not about to lose Knox without protest. He wrote Congress on Saturday, May 31, asking that Du Coudray be given another assignment in the army, or the artillery corps risked becoming "unhinged." He wrote in praise: "General Knox, who has deservedly acquired the character of one of the most valuable officers in the service, and who, combating almost innumerable difficulties in the department he fills, has placed the artillery upon a footing, that does him the greatest Honor. He, I am persuaded, would consider himself injured by an appointment superceding his command, and would not think himself at liberty to continue in the service."[47]

The following day, he also wrote his friend and fellow Virginian, Congressman Richard Henry Lee, "by putting Monsieur D'Coudray at the head of the artillery, you will lose a very valuable officer in General Knox, who is a man of great military reading, sound judgment, and clear conceptions. He has conducted the affairs of that department with honor to himself, and advantage to the public, and will resign if any one is put over him."[48]

Generals Greene and Sullivan each threatened to resign if Du Coudray's contract with Deane was honored. John Adams vowed to Greene in a June 2 letter that he would never consent to appoint the Frenchmen as head of the Continental artillery and thought there was little support in Congress to do so: "I hope none," he wrote.[49]

But Adams quickly realized that Du Coudray could not be dismissed lightly because of his political connections. On Tuesday, June 3, the French general attended on Congress to await ratification of his contract with Deane. He presented his credentials, which included recommendation from three successive French ministers of war, along with letters from the American ministers in Paris, Benjamin Franklin and Deane. He impressed the delegates as a man of letters with proven military ability and knowledge and, in John Adams's words, was "esteemed the most learned officer in France."[50] Congressmen were flattered to learn that Du Coudray had been entrusted to oversee the casting of cannons in the French artillery and had personally picked out 200 cannons and escorted them to America. He was so subtle in his praise of the American militia that the delegates were encouraged by his pronouncement that it was the best he had ever seen. Believing the Frenchman did not hand out compliments lightly, they trusted his opinion all the more. On his trip from Boston, Du Coudray had reviewed the Springfield arsenal, and now he offered his advice for improvements to Congress. Delegate Charles Carroll wrote his father on June 13 with glowing praise of the French general: "I really am pleased with this gentleman, his address, though a Frenchman, is not elegant and easy, yet you may plainly see he has frequented and even been intimate with the polite and great. He seems to have studied more the arts and sciences than the graces; yet his plain and unaffected manner, his good sense and sweetness of temper gains upon us daily."[51]

Adams saw that finding a way to accommodate both Knox and Du Coudray was fraught with international complications. Massachusetts congressman James Lovell believed the American troops fighting British monarchy would "have a hard struggle in reconciling themselves to that monarchical devotion which is necessary in the adoption of Du Coudray's command."[52]

Carroll, however, believed that Du Coudray's contract needed to be ratified, even if it caused dissention in the army, for the sake of the hoped-for alliance with France and American credibility abroad. Even John Adams, who thought that "all the sages and heroes of France" were on their way across the Atlantic to take command of the Continental Army, was forced to concede that because Du Coudray's "interest is so great and so near the throne, that it would be impolitic not to avail ourselves of him."[53]

On Saturday, June 14, Howe's army began to march. Apparently the summer military campaign had begun. Knox noted that the British commander had been gathering troops from Rhode Island, New York City, Staten Island, and the surrounding region along with more than 1,000 wagons, many transporting all kinds of boats for the crossing of the Delaware River. Henry was mildly amused that this caravan seemed "a great encumbrance to an army not very numerous." He and Washington's other generals in the army, which had moved from Morristown to Middlebrook, New Jersey, hoped the British would attack their strong defensive position. Knox felt the army was prepared better than ever. He wrote in a letter to Lucy on Saturday, June 21: "We have the most respectable body of Continental troops that America ever had, no going home tomorrow to suck—hardy, brave fellows, who are as willing to go to heaven by the way of a bayonet or sword as any other mode. With the blessing of Heaven, I have great hopes in the course of this campaign that we shall do something clever."[54]

On June 28, the congressional Board of War sent orders to Washington that all the French cannons that arrived aboard the *Amphitrite* should be placed under the direction of Du Coudray and the newly arrived French officers. Knox was crestfallen. He believed that he had done everything in his power to build a formidable artillery corps from scratch and that all his efforts meant little to Congress. He was being cast aside for a political appointment. Equally insulting, he had not been notified that he had been discarded. On July 1, he submitted a conditional letter of resignation to congressional president John Hancock: "From the information I have received I am induced to believe that Congress has appointed a Mr. Du Coudray, a French gentleman, to command of the artillery. I wish to know of Congress whether this information be true: if it is, I beg the favor of a permission to retire, and that a proper certificate for that purpose be sent immediately."[55] His fellow generals Greene and Sullivan also sent letters submitting their prospective resignations in protest of the Frenchman's appointment.

Congress began to have doubts about Du Coudray when three French engineers arrived in Philadelphia with contracts from Franklin and Deane. They refused to serve under Du Coudray and told delegates that it was not appropriate that artillery and engineer corps be grouped together. These officers made it appear that Deane was a child in the hands of the savvy French artillery officer, who negotiated a contract uniting two separate corps in order to place much of the Continental Army under his control. Under the terms of the contract, Du Coudray had the sole power to fill every vacancy under his command throughout the war and would be answerable only to Congress and the commander in chief of the army.

On Thursday, July 3, General Sullivan's letter to resign if Knox was replaced by Du Coudray was read in Congress. Delegates viewed it as an unwarranted attempt to "control" the legislature. In a sharp rebuke, they immediately resolved to accept his resignation if it were formally tendered.[56]

Lovell remained Knox's staunchest defender in Congress. To Benjamin Franklin, he wrote on the first anniversary of Independence Day that foreign officers could not be allowed to take positions from Americans who had fought since the beginning of the war without injuring their honor. "The merit of Brigadier General Knox is great, and he is beloved by his Corps. How then could it be conceived that Mr. Du Coudray's treaty should not create the greatest confusion among our officers of artillery?"[57]

Knox's and Greene's letters threatening resignation were read in Congress on Saturday, July 5. Members viewed these as ultimatums directly affronting their authority. Two days later, they denounced the letters as "an attempt to influence their decisions, and an invasion of the liberties of the people, and indicating a want of confidence in the justice of Congress." They directed Washington to accept the generals' resignations if they could not serve their country under the authority of Congress, and acknowledge their improper attempts to subvert the will of the national legislature.[58]

That same day, July 7, John Adams also wrote a forceful letter to Greene demanding an apology from the three generals and scolding that the military was not to interfere with the civil government in a democratic government. Adams explained that Du Coudray's appointment had not yet been settled because of complicated considerations, including the possible insult to France and the discredit to American diplomats abroad. "It is in truth one of the most delicate and perplexing transactions that has ever fallen in our way: but those three letters instead of relieving us has only increased our mortification."

Adams chastised the three generals for lodging protests even before Congress made a final decision—and in formal addresses to Congress rather than private letters to individual members. "I must needs freely say, that there is more of rashness, passion and even wantonness in this proceeding than I ever expected to see in my friend Greene and Knox in whose judgment and discretion I had the utmost confidence."[59]

On Saturday, July 12, Washington conveyed Congress's resolution and its demand for apologies acknowledging "so singular an impropriety" from Knox, Greene, and Sullivan. All three refused. Knox, clearly hurt by the rebuke, wrote Lucy on Sunday: "Conscious of the rectitude of my intention and of the contents of my letter, I shall make no acknowledgments whatever though my country is too much pressed at present to resign, yet perhaps this campaign will be the last. I am determined to contribute my might to the defense of the country, in spite of every obstacle."[60]

Washington was privately supportive of the positions taken by his generals. On July 13, he wrote a letter to Du Coudray in a disdainful tone explaining that the Frenchman apparently did not understand the artillery suited for America's "mountainous and woody country." The commander in chief rejected his advice on how to use the newly arrived cannons from France, using dismissive phrases such as "you are even mistaken as to the fact" and "you also misconceived," and ordered the recasting of several of the large French cannons to produce lighter, more transportable guns. Washington no doubt consulted Knox in writing the letter, which was transcribed and perhaps partially written by artillerist-turned-aide Alexander Hamilton. Washington went into condescending detail to Du Coudray on the strategies for using artillery. His unmistakable message was that he was not impressed with the Frenchman. Washington stated bluntly, "It would be irregular to interfere with any arrangements General Knox has made with my approbation, in compliance with those you propose . . . every thing seems to me to be already in a very good train."[61]

For all the sharp admonishments coming from Congress over the matter, the delegates realized they could not ratify Du Coudray's contract without causing a revolt in the army not only from Knox, Greene, and Sullivan but many other officers. With more French commanders arriving daily, American soldiers throughout the ranks would be demoralized and feel insecure about their positions. On Tuesday, July 15, the delegates resolved to inform Du Coudray that "Congress cannot comply with the agreement he has entered into with Mr. Deane."[62] As a compromise, the Frenchman was commissioned on Monday, July 21, as a major general in the Continental Army and given an artillery train and a command separate from Knox.[63]

Whatever rivalry that sprang up between the two artillery generals ended on September 17, 1777, when Du Coudray drowned in the Schuylkill River. His horse was thrown from a ferry, plunging both animal and rider to their watery deaths.

FIVE

THE BATTLE FOR PHILADELPHIA

K nox was frustrated by the military stalemate that was prolonging the war. In the waning days of spring in 1777, Washington's army remained in New Jersey, guarding forest roads between Howe's army and Philadelphia. After a disastrous failed attempt in June, the British decided that marching to Philadelphia by land was no longer possible. The Continental Army was too well entrenched, and inhabitants who had been cooperative with the British a year before were now embittered by redcoat pillaging. Many locals had joined the swelling ranks of militia ready to take up the fight alongside the American army. On Tuesday, July 23, Howe's army of 18,000 men set sail aboard 260 ships from New York toward Chesapeake Bay. Washington was uncertain whether the British target was Philadelphia or if the enemy would swing north and join the troops under Major General John Burgoyne, who had begun an invasion of upstate New York from Canada. The Americans intercepted a British letter that detailed plans for Howe to attack Boston, but Knox and the other generals felt that the letter was a ruse to hide the enemy's true intentions. The commander in chief wrote his generals in New York, New Jersey, Boston, and Philadelphia to remain on high alert. He advised Congress to have lookouts posted at the Delaware Capes to sound the alarm in Philadelphia if the enemy fleet appeared on the horizon. Knox prepared his corps for the army's march to Philadelphia.

Washington's troops moved out on Friday, July 25—the day that Knox marked his twenty-seventh birthday—with the artillery train followed by the army's rearguard. Henry wrote Lucy the next day from Beverhout, eight miles from Morristown, reporting that the army was four days from Philadelphia: "We suppose he [Washington] will be at Philadelphia near as soon as we."[1]

But the whereabouts of Howe's fleet remained a mystery, and Washington halted his force on Tuesday, July 29, at Coryells Ferry, New Jersey, along the Delaware River, about thirty-three miles north of Philadelphia. The next day, American general Caesar Rodney, stationed in Dover, Delaware, spotted the fleet sailing behind a strong wind for the Delaware Capes leading to Philadelphia. Knox immediately directed his gunners to begin loading wagons and hitching horses to the cannon carriages for the march into the city. Washington left for Philadelphia with a cavalry regiment, followed by General Sullivan's division and two other brigades. But the wind became unfavorable for the warships, and to the American's astonishment, the fleet headed out to sea again at 8 A.M. Thursday.

Knox was immediately sent to the forts along the Delaware River to inspect their fortifications against enemy ships. He was unfamiliar with the landscape, and the myriad of inlets and islands along the twisting river presented a challenge for erecting a secure line of defense for the nation's capital. Working quickly, he traveled up- and downriver while wondering if the British ships would reappear before he had a chance to finish his critical mission. Washington understood that Knox possessed a keen eye for taking advantage of terrain. Although he had never served in a navy, Henry understood the needs of the British captains and put cannons at spots where vessels would need to moor to find protection from the punishing waves of the Atlantic and the hard, rocky coast. At the battery at Fort Island, he ordered the building of an additional redoubt, moved twelve heavy cannons into position, and assigned 150 gunners, 75 assistants along with 500 infantrymen to guard the waterway. He recommended an additional six cannons at the Red Bank battery and twelve big guns at Billingsport along with more men to man the post and the building of another 500-man fortification at Fort Island. He ordered riverboats to be built and armed with guns that could be repositioned along the river.

While Knox was busy securing the Delaware, a twenty-year-old Frenchmen arrived in Philadelphia seeking a place in the American army, the marquis de Lafayette. Seized, as he said, with "the love of liberty and glory" and stirred with a romantic idealism inspired by the writings of Rousseau, he fitted out a ship with supplies in direct disobedience of orders from the French government and sailed from Spain to America with eleven companions, including Baron de Kalb (who was not actually a baron but who had served with honor in the French army). Their vessel, poorly armed with two broken-down cannons, had to avoid the British ships to land in South Carolina in June, where Lafayette was charmed by the Americans' "simplicity of manners, kindness, love of country and of liberty, and [where] a delightful equality everywhere prevail," he wrote in a letter to his wife on June 19, 1777. He believed his political ideals were realized in the new nation. "In America, there are no poor, nor even what we call peasantry. Each individual has his own honest property, and the same rights as the most wealthy landed proprietor."[2] But he also was confronted with many suspicions during his 700-mile trip from Charleston to Philadelphia. Many Americans were wary of French adventurers, whom they often found to be arrogant and pretentious, and had begun to view democratic zeal from European mercenaries as masked ambition. Claims of military talent were often treated as abject quackery.

Lafayette arrived in the nation's capital in Philadelphia and received a cold reception from Congress, which was still dealing with the Du Coudray problem and was daily besieged with foreign soldiers sent by Silas Deane with signed promises in hand granting high rank in the army. Delegates finally decided to ignore all prospective European officers and rein in Deane. Lafayette was turned away but not dissuaded. He sent a note to Congress: "After the sacrifices I have made, I have the right to exact two favors: one is, to serve at my own expense; the other is, to serve at first as volunteer."[3]

Congressmen were intrigued by the note. They were aware that Lafayette hailed from one of the most powerful noble families at court in France and yet offered his services without regard to rank. The young Frenchman was received before Congress on Thursday, July 31, to address the delegates. With considerable charm, Lafayette spoke of his love for liberty and his thirst for glory and the honor to serve beside Washington. He had outfitted a ship during the discouraging days when the Continental Army was retreating from Long Island, New York, White Plains, and New Jersey. He had left a young, beautiful wife in Paris to undergo a hazardous trip and was willing to risk his life in battle or, if Congress preferred, to champion their cause at Versailles.

The delegates were so impressed with Lafayette's candor, enthusiasm, and willingness to risk his life for the cause that Congress resolved "that his service be accepted, and that, in consideration of his zeal, illustrious family and connections, he have the rank and commission of major general in the army of the United States."[4] The title was honorary, and his assignment was left up to Washington.

In the evening, the marquis dined with several members of Congress and Washington, who despite the recent troubles with French officers formed an immediate fondness for Lafayette and offered him lodging at his headquarters.

The next day, Washington invited Lafayette to review his 11,000-man army. Although his position had recently been threatened by a French officer, Henry was impressed with the marquis. Knox had taught himself to speak and write French during his youth, and Lafayette was delighted that an American commander could address him in his native tongue. The two came from distinctly different backgrounds, yet they had a sympathetic bond beyond their politics. Both had grown up without a father. The marquis wanted to fight the British not only for liberty's sake but to avenge his father's death in the Seven Years' War. Knox and the young man could not have been more different physically. Under the stress of his command, Knox's weight had ballooned to more than 280 pounds. Lafayette was diminutive, slender, and graceful.

As Washington, Knox, Greene, and Lord Stirling inspected the troops, the marquis was touched by their spirit and what he described as "a strange spectacle." The soldiers lined up in two rows with taller men in the second file. Their clothes were tattered and shredded. Some soldiers were almost naked; many were barefoot. There was no uniformity of dress among the enlisted men. Some wore hunting shirts, and others gray linen coats. Lafayette would later write of seeing the troops that day in his memoirs: "In spite of these disadvantages, the soldiers were fine, and the officers zealous; virtue stood in place of science." Washington, in a moment of self-consciousness, said, "We must feel embarrassed to exhibit ourselves before an officer who has just quitted French troops." Lafayette replied, "It is to learn, and not to teach, that I come hither."[5]

That same day, word arrived that the British fleet had turned away from the Delaware Capes and sailed out to sea at 8 A.M. Washington thought that the armada was headed back to New York and that Howe's army would join Burgoyne's advance from Canada against the northern army of Continental troops. On Monday, August 4, Congress appointed General Horatio Gates to lead the 4,500 troops facing Burgoyne. Knox returned to the Delaware to continue construction of the river fortifications, not knowing if the fleet had merely feigned a departure and would return suddenly. A series of chevaux de frize, or sharp wooden spikes, designed to rake open the hulls of approaching ships, was sunk in the river. On Saturday, August 9, Henry sent his plan and recommendations on the Delaware Cape defenses and troop dispersals in its series of forts to Washington, who wrote a lengthy note to Congress incorporating Knox's ideas.

The commander in chief was uncertain where to send his army and was frantically trying to obtain intelligence on the landing of Howe's fleet. On Sunday, the army had returned to Coryell's Ferry, about forty miles north of Philadelphia. Washington received word that Burgoyne had begun to cross the Hudson River in New York on Wednesday, August 13, and was heading for Saratoga. Knox wrote to Washington a week later that he believed Howe would not venture up the Delaware to Philadelphia and did not have the supplies to sail back to New York. Henry urged the commander to send the army to defeat Burgoyne and level a crushing blow to British hopes. He was especially concerned by recent attacks by American Indians engaged by the enemy in New York. "This power ought to be crushed at all hazards immediately—or the whole frontiers will be deluged in blood."[6]

At a council of generals on August 21, Knox stated these views, which were also held by Washington's other commanders, who were eager for battle. They believed that Howe could be targeting Charleston, South Carolina, 700 miles to the south. If so, the troops outside Philadelphia could offer little help, and a march in the muggy Carolinas would be unhealthy during the season when diseases spread through the waters. They were all in agreement; their army should march north to New York. But Washington had to wait for Congress to approve the mission since his command would supersede that of General Gates, who now headed the northern Continental troops.

While waiting for Congress's decision, Knox and Greene asked Washington if they could take a trip to Bethlehem, a day's ride from Philadelphia. Henry wanted to shop for gifts to send Lucy, who was recovering from an illness back in Boston. They set out at four o'clock on an excessively hot afternoon.

Lucy, meanwhile, had recovered and by Saturday, August 23, had the strength to write Henry, addressing him as "My dearest friend." He had asked her to relate the routine of her usual day. She would rise at 8 A.M. and after breakfast would read and take a cup of tea. Then family matters needed attending to, and she would work until a solitary, lonely dinner at 2 P.M. She reflected, "I used to sit at the window watching for my Harry, and when I saw him coming my heart would leap for joy when he was at my own side and never happy apart from me when the bare thought of six months absence would have shook him."

She took joy in watching her child grow yet regretted that Henry was not there. In the afternoon, she would take a carriage ride in the country or visit one of her few friends for tea. "But when I return home, how [to] describe my feelings to find myself entirely alone, to reflect that the only friend I have in the world is such an immense distance from me to think that he may be sick and I cannot assist him. My poor heart is ready to burst, you who know what a trifle would make me unhappy can conceive what I suffer now."

She lamented the loss of her family to Britain and pored over Henry's letters looking for any invitation to join him. In fleeting moments of doubt, she wondered if she had lost him. "'Tis hard my Harry indeed it is. I love you with the tenderest the purest affection. I would undergo any hardship to be near you and you will not let me."

In her anxiety, she was plagued with thoughts that other women would test his fidelity: "I sometimes fear that a long absence the force of bad example may lead you to forget me at sometimes. To know that it ever gave you pleasure to be in company with the finest woman in the world, would be worse than death to me."[7]

When Knox and Greene arrived in Bethlehem at 9 A.M. on Sunday, August 24, an express rider sent by Washington was waiting with orders to return immediately as the army was on the move south. The British fleet had bypassed the Delaware River fortifications and instead sailed up the Chesapeake Bay to Elk River, about twenty miles from Wilmington, Delaware. The two generals caught up with the army an hour after the troops had left the capital. They had ridden almost 100 miles in two days. Knox was disappointed that he had missed the march through town, he wrote in a letter the next day to Lucy.

Howe disembarked 15,000 men on Monday to begin a campaign against Philadelphia. His troops occupied a piece of high ground called Grey's Hill, about two miles past the city of Elkton. Knox and the rest of the Continental Army arrived in Wilmington on Tuesday and began to prepare for the long-awaited battle. Clouds gathered overhead, and steady rain began to fall, delaying action and heightening the tensions among the soldiers. The British also needed time to replace their horses, many of which had died, had starved, or had been injured during the six-week sea passage.

On Sunday, August 31, Knox was appointed as president of a court-martial that was to try a British lieutenant for recruiting soldiers for Howe's army in New Jersey. He then was off to set up an artillery park and drill his men. His gunners were to fire two field guns to sound the alarm for the troops to rush to battle stations. The armies were nine miles apart, and skirmishes erupted daily between pickets and advance troops. But the main body of the British army remained idle. Deserters from Howe's army reported on Sunday, September 7, that the enemy had sent away its baggage, even tents, and troops carrying only blankets and light gear had begun to march from Kennett Square seven miles to the Brandywine Creek, a tributary of the Delaware. The next day the redcoats came within two miles of the American post at Newport on the right of the Continental line but did not attack. Knox and Washington's other generals thought this was only a diversion. As the commander in chief put it in a letter to Congress, it was "only meant to amuse us in front, while their real intent was to march by our right and by suddenly passing the Brandywine and gaining the heights on the north side of that River, get between us and Philadelphia and cut us off from that city."[8] At 2 A.M. on Tuesday, September 9, Washington ordered the army to march six miles to Chad's Ford on the banks of Brandywine Creek, where Knox set up his main artillery force. American troops were posted at the fords along the river. The British marched within three miles of the river on Wednesday.

Knox was up before dawn Thursday morning, checking the guns and directing his men. By eight o'clock he saw a large force of redcoats appear through the morning fog on the opposite side of the creek. British field guns were moved into position and began a cannonade. Knox shouted for his gunners to return fire. An explosion of thundering cannon blasts erupted, and smoke filled the air on both sides of the creek. Knox's men kept up hot fire, unsure exactly where the enemy was digging in or where their shots were landing, aiming merely into the haze of acrid clouds. For two hours the cannons kept up a deafening roar as British guns tried to match shot for shot. The American general William Maxwell crossed the creek with his light corps and attacked the advancing redcoats with a pelting line of musket shots. Thirty British soldiers fell on the spot where they were trying to erect a battery. A body of 300 Hessian troops charged forward, supported by British infantry, but their lines were shredded in the fire. The Americans saw about 300 enemy soldiers hit amid the shots and wafting smoke, along with 50 of their own. Hundreds of British soldiers rushed to the scene, and Maxwell pulled his men back and quickly recrossed the Brandywine.

Howe, meanwhile, rushed a 3,000-man column of British infantry, artillerists with sixteen field guns, and Hessians led by General Cornwallis to circle around the Continental line on its right. These men found Jeffrie's Ford, six miles up the creek at a fork in the Brandywine, unguarded. In the confusion of the battle, Washington received contradictory and faulty reports from General Sullivan on the size of Cornwallis's column and possible fords along the river, and was uncertain of the enemy's destination until it had crossed the water and a dust cloud was visible. When the enemy's intentions were discovered at 2 P.M., Washington threw divisions led by generals Sullivan, Lord Stirling, and Stephen to race to stop the advance.

At 4 P.M., the two forces met halfway, about three miles from Chad's Ford with a hill between them. The redcoats fired on General Sullivan's men. Both columns tried to reach the high ground, and the soldiers came close enough to open fire on each other at point-blank range. For an hour and a half, the Americans and British kept up a desperate fight, with musket balls raining like hail. Hundreds of men were struck and lay in agony on the bloodstained field. The patriots soon realized they were running out of cartridges and could not keep up the fight much longer. An order was given to withdraw. Washington, who had galloped to the scene, sent back orders for General Greene's division and a brigade led by Francis Nash to pull out from the left side of the American line and provide cover for the troops, as the British field guns blasted shots in their direction.

"They formed and were of the utmost service in covering the retreat of the other divisions," Knox wrote in a letter to the Massachusetts Council, the upper body of its legislature.[9]

Henry, meanwhile, was engaged in an artillery duel on the opposite side of the American line that began shortly before 5 P.M. He pulled his horse up to the gun battery manned by Captain David Allen's company and found his gunners, several of whom were from Boston, wide-eyed. "They seemed in high spirits," Knox thought.[10]

"The enemy opened a battery on the left of seven pieces of cannon opposite to one of ours of the same number," Knox recounted. "The enemy's batteries and ours kept up an incessant cannonade, and formed such a column of smoke that the British troops passed the creek unperceived on the right of the battery, on the ground, which was left unoccupied by the withdrawal of Nash's brigade."[11]

American general Anthony Wayne's division raced to repulse the British momentum, and a gunfight erupted. The enemy troops were able to push to the top of a hill, which provided cover, and level their muskets at Wayne's men, who tried to cross the low ground to reach them. In unison, British muskets aimed and fired a whistling line of musket balls, cutting down the Americans. Wayne's men took cover and then rose to make a second charge. But again the British unleashed overwhelming fire and pushed back the Americans, then charged to their line. Knox ordered his men to retreat, and they had to abandon ten precious field pieces, a British howitzer, and several munitions wagons as the British pushed forward. With night setting in, Washington ordered a retreat of his entire army to Chester. Howe's army was too crippled by the day's losses to pursue, and the British commander again paused and failed to capitalize on the victory and destroy the Continental Army. At midnight, Washington sent a hasty note to Congress, who waited just twenty-five miles away: "Notwithstanding the misfortune of the day, I am happy to find the troops in good spirits." He said he believed the British had suffered greater losses than his army.[12]

Knox estimated that as many as 800 Americans had been killed or wounded or were missing. The official total pegged the Continental Army loss at 780 and the British casualties at about 600.

The American army retreated north toward Philadelphia on Saturday, September 13, crossing the Schuylkill River, as the British remained near Dilworth Town to bury their dead and tend to their wounded. Knox found time that day to write Lucy: "My dear girl will be happy to hear of her Harry's safety; for, my Lucy, Heaven, who is our guide, has protected him in the day of battle. You will hear with this letter of the most severe action that has been fought this war between our army and the enemy. Our people behaved well, but Heaven frowned on us in a degree. We were obliged to retire after very considerable slaughter of the enemy: they dared not pursue a single step. If they advance, we shall fight them again before they get possession of Philadelphia; but of this they will be cautious. My corps did me great honor: they behaved like men contending for everything that's valuable."[13]

Knox and the rest of the American generals received word that General Gates's northern army was entrenching to meet the advancing British army under Burgoyne at Saratoga, New York. The two main American armies were now facing the two main bodies of British troops. It seemed that the war could be decided in days. Knox moved with the rest of Washington's force to the White Horse Tavern, about twenty miles west of Philadelphia, to guard the fords of the Schuylkill. British troops led by General Cornwallis followed.

The two armies faced each other on Tuesday, September 16, and Knox drew his guns in line for battle. The British did not attack, however, and a torrential downpour erupted in what became known as a battle of the clouds. Knox was forced to move the field guns as the army tried to find a better position. The rain soaked the ammunition and dampened the gunpowder. Because of poorly made cartouche boxes, 400,000 cartridges became saturated. The men, without tents, had no shelter and had nowhere to protect their provisions. "This was a most terrible stroke to us, and owning entirely to the badness of the cartouch-boxes which had been provided for the army," Knox wrote Lucy. "This unfortunate event obliged us to retire."[14]

Knox moved with the army three miles north to Yellow Springs the next day and then on to nearby Warwick Furnace, where he and his men frantically tried to clean the guns and find fresh gunpowder. Meanwhile, Washington had to guard miles of the river along the Schuylkill in an attempt to prevent the British from crossing and marching to Philadelphia. Without provisions, his men could do little to bar the enemy's way. Cavalry riders reported that the royal troops had pushed toward Swede's Ford along the river. Washington sent Alexander Hamilton, Captain Henry "Light-Horse Harry" Lee (father of Robert E. Lee), and eight light horsemen to burn flour mills on the Schuylkill that might provide critical supplies for Howe's army, which was already strained for provisions. As Hamilton worked along the river at Valley Forge on Thursday, September 18, the advance troops of British soldiers appeared. He escaped with three other soldiers to a flat-bottom boat but was unable to destroy another ferry that could carry fifty men. All he could do was leave it adrift. As Hamilton and the soldiers battled a swift current, the redcoats raked the boat with musket fire. One of the oarsmen was killed and another wounded. When Hamilton reached the opposite shore, he wrote a frantic message to John Hancock in Philadelphia: "SIR: If Congress have not left Philadelphia they ought to do it immediately without fail; for the enemy have the means of throwing a party this night into the city."[15] The message arrived in the capital by midnight, and congressmen were awakened and warned to take flight before morning, when the British were expected to arrive. Delegates quickly packed their belongings and critical papers and began streaming out of the city, each choosing their own route of escape, beginning around 3 A.M. on Friday, September 19. They headed north to Trenton, bound for Lancaster, Pennsylvania.

That same morning, Knox moved his guns with the rest of the army, which recrossed the Schuylkill to the east to stay between Howe's army and Philadelphia, guarding the fords. Most of the men waded into the river and then remained wet up to their chests as they marched throughout the morning darkness to take up positions along the banks. Howe tried to divert Washington's army before trying to cross the Schuylkill. On Sunday afternoon, September 21, the British marched twelve miles to the right of the

American line. Knox moved with the army to meet them. When night fell, the redcoats kindled large fires, then countermarched and crossed unopposed at Swede's Ford. General Wayne's division was near the rear of the British at Paoli, where he hoped to attack the king's soldiers as they tried to cross the river. His division was discovered, and the redcoats ambushed his force on September 21. The British removed the flints from their muskets to prevent any accidental firing from signaling their approach as they crept though the woods. They were undetected until they launched their bayonet assault. In brutal hand-to-hand fighting, fifty-three Americans were killed with bayonet wounds and a hundred were wounded, compared to just eleven British casualties.

Knox realized that the British could march unopposed into Philadelphia. At a war council on Tuesday, September 23, at Pottsgrove, about twelve miles from the national seat, he agreed with the unanimous opinion of Washington's commanders that it was useless to attack the redcoats, given the shortage of ammunition and the need for reinforcements. "We fought one battle for it [at Brandywine]," he wrote Lucy on Wednesday, "and it was no deficiency in bravery that lost us the day. Philadelphia, it seems, has been their favorite object."[16]

He was disappointed but not without optimism, seeing the loss of the city as merely a temporary setback and less of a challenge than liberating Boston had been the previous year. He thought Philadelphia would be difficult to defend. What bore him up was the realization that the Continental Army was becoming battle-hardened and the men were enduring the trials of war like veterans. "The troops in this excursion of ten days without baggage suffered excessive hardships—without tents in the rain, several marches of all night, and often without sufficient provision. This they endured with the perseverance and patience of good soldiers."[17]

The royal troops crossed the creek at Schuylkill Falls, only five miles from Philadelphia. On Friday, September 26, the British, led by General Cornwallis, marched triumphantly into the city. They paraded up Second Street and posted guards around the city before setting up camp on the south side of town. The Tory *Rivington's Gazette*, owned by Knox's old business connection James Rivington, reported: "The fine appearance of the soldiery, the strictness of their discipline, the politeness of the officers, and the orderly behavior of the whole body, immediately dispelled every apprehension of the inhabitants, kindled joy in the countenances of the well affected, and has given the most convincing refutation of the scandalous falsehoods which evil and

designing men have been long spreading to terrify the peaceable and innocent. A perfect tranquility now prevails in the city."[18]

Howe believed his best supply route was the Delaware River. He sent
men to destroy the fortifications and obstacles that Knox had helped design
and to build three batteries of their own. On Saturday, September 27, the
crew of an American frigate in the river ran the vessel ashore after firing only
one shot at a British battery. Knox wrote a letter to Colonel Henry Jackson on
Thursday, October 2, calling the crew's actions "scandalous."[19]

A siege of Philadelphia began. Knox and Washington's other counselors
believed that the British could not hold the city unless they destroyed the
American fortifications guarding the Delaware River, which Henry had
helped plan. Howe needed free passage on the river to open supply lines with
the British navy before the Delaware froze. Without open river channels, the
British would starve. For the Americans, the key was maintaining the river defenses for just a few more weeks until the cold weather and ice forced British
ships to set out to sea.

With the British forces dividing their attention between Philadelphia and
the Delaware Capes, Washington decided on Friday, October 3, to order a
march to attack the enemy north of the city at Germantown, Pennsylvania.
That same day, he announced to his men the victory by General Gates over
Burgoyne at Freeman's Farm near Saratoga, New York, on September 19.
After the series of defeats and missteps around Philadelphia, Knox was hoping
for similar success "before we go into winter quarters."[20]

At 6 P.M., the army moved out in four columns for the thirteen-mile
march to Germantown, each man carrying forty rounds of ammunition. By
dawn Saturday morning, General Sullivan's division drove back the British
pickets and rushed forward. The surprised royal troops fled, leaving their
baggage behind, and the Americans gave chase through the enemy camp,
capturing several cannons before pushing on with victory within their
grasp. Knox was riding with Washington with the rear troops under General Lord Stirling. As the redcoats retreated, about 200 took protection in a
stone mansion owned by Benjamin Chew, a former chief justice of the
Pennsylvania Supreme Court. The redcoats barricaded the windows, creating a formidable fortress. Washington paused as musket fire opened from
the mansion. Several of his staff, including Adjutant General Timothy
Pickering and aide Alexander Hamilton, thought the army should keep
marching to meet up with the lead columns and ignore the barricaded
troops. Some recommended storming the house if the redcoats did not

quickly surrender, or leaving a regiment to keep them hemmed in during the battle.

Knox disagreed, however, and told Washington that it was against conventional military wisdom to bypass a fortification and leave enemy troops in a position to attack from behind. Washington agreed. Henry ordered his field guns to target the house. His men riddled the stone walls with grape and shot for an hour as riflemen pelted it with musket balls while the reserve troops halted on the road to Germantown. But the light three- and six-pound cannons caused only minor damage. The redcoats fired from windows at the American troops and the men trying to storm the house. Knox felt shots dart around him, and several of his gunners were hit. In desperation, troops began to call for the house to be set on fire. One man tried to approach the house with a torch but was shot. Knox's aide, Major Chevalier de Mauduit Du Plessis of France, and Washington's aide, Colonel John Laurens of South Carolina, volunteered to try. They crept up to the mansion and crawled to a window. Knox's aide climbed to the sill and forced open a shutter. A British soldier from inside screamed at him and pointed a pistol in his direction. Du Plessis responded sarcastically that he was taking a walk. A British officer demanded that he surrender or die, upon which another redcoat shot at the Frenchman and hit his own officer instead. The two aides raced back toward their troops under cover of American musket fire, and the British sent a line of shot in their direction. Laurens was hit in the shoulder, but Du Plessis was unharmed.

The delay at the Chew House cost the rear of the army a precious hour, when every moment was needed to reinforce the battlefront.

To add to the problems created by the cannon smoke, a heavy fog rolled in. Soon visibility was reduced to just twenty to thirty yards. At the vanguard of the American advance, an intoxicated General Adam Stephen became confused by cannon fire coming from the direction of the Chew House and believed the British were attacking the rear. He ordered his men to march in the direction of the booming guns, and coming upon their comrades under General Wayne's command in the heavy mist, they mistook them for hostile troops and fired. Wayne's men returned fire, believing the British were upon them.

The American lead columns were unable to see the enemy. Under the veil of murky fog, the British scrambled to re-form their lines and began to fire, forcing the American line to retreat and chasing them ten miles. The attempt to capture the Chew House by Knox and the reserve troops proved costly; the reserves were unable to help the front-line Continentals as they were pushed back by the royal troops. The initial hopeful signs of an American victory soon gave way to the realization of another crushing defeat. Washington ordered his troops to fall back. Knox's men were able to bring off all the artillery except for one gun. The Americans had 1,000 men killed, wounded, or captured in the Battle of Germantown from the 10,000-man force, while the British lost half that number from 9,000 men. The drunken General Stephen was cashiered out of the service and his division was given to the Marquis de Lafayette.

Three days later, from Perkiomy Creek, about twenty-seven miles from Philadelphia, Knox wrote a report of the battle to the Massachusetts Council. He blamed the fog for the defeat and failed to mention his advice to attack the Chew House. "In this unusual fog it was impossible to know how to support, or what part to push," he wrote. But he was nevertheless upbeat. "This is the first attack made during this war by the American troops on the main body of the enemy; and had it not been [for] the unlucky circumstance of the fog, Philadelphia would probably have been in our hands. It is matter worthy of observation that in most countries which have been invaded one or two battles have decided their fate; but America rises after a defeat!"

But in a letter to Lucy, he acknowledged that the failure at the mansion played a part in stealing victory: "To this cause, in conjunction with enemy's taking possession of some stone buildings in Germantown, is to be ascribed the loss of the victory."[21]

Knox had lost several men in the recent battles and had been fortunate to avoid being wounded. He tried to fill his ranks with men from other battalions, but these troops were inexperienced in the use of artillery. Washington wrote Congress, which had reconvened in Yorktown, Pennsylvania, asking that artillery units from other areas be assigned to join the fight there.

The Continental Army settled into a siege of Philadelphia, as Howe's men continued to try to capture patriot forts along the Delaware to open an avenue for their ships. Henry sent his aide, Du Plessis, who had distinguished himself at the battles of Brandywine and Germantown, to head the artillery at the Delaware forts. During the day, Knox could hear cannon fire and could only wonder whose arms they were.

News arrived that Fort Montgomery, along the banks of the Hudson in New York, had fallen. Henry wrote Lucy on Monday, October 13, expressing exasperation that the inhabitants had not done more to support the post. "America almost deserves to be made slaves for her non-exertions in so important an affair."

Lucy was having troubles of her own. She had doubts if she had enough money or provisions to make it through the coming winter. Henry tried to console her in a letter: "I trust the same Divine Being who brought us together will support us. . . . I have sanguine hopes of being able to live this winter in sweet fellowship with the dearest friend of my heart." He assured her that the prospects around Philadelphia looked promising, and Gates's early success against Burgoyne in New York bode well for the cause. "For my own part I have not yet seen so bright a dawn as the prospect, and am as perfectly convinced in my own mind of the kindness of Providence towards us as I am of my own existence."[22]

His optimism found justification when news arrived at camp on Wednesday, October 15, of Gates's stunning victory at Bemis Heights in a second battle of Saratoga on October 7 over General Burgoyne's 5,800-man army. The triumphs raised hopes that European nations would formally recognize American independence. As part of the celebration over Gates's success, Knox's men fired thirteen cannons from the artillery park at camp. Tories in the area scoffed at the almost unbelievable reports of Gates's victory and dismissed the celebrations as a delusional hoax. Howe issued a statement that the rumors were untrue and that, in fact, the British and Burgoyne had actually defeated the Americans. Henry wrote to Lucy: "They have been very angry for our feux de joie, which we have fired on several victories over Burgoyne, and say that by and by [we] shall bring ourselves into contempt with our own army for propagating such known falsehood. Poor fellows! Nothing but Britain must triumph."[23]

An express arrived on Saturday, October 18, announcing that Burgoyne's men had laid down their arms at Saratoga and had negotiated a surrender agreement with the victorious American general, Horatio Gates. Knox's men again fired thirteen cannons in salute at a five o'clock parade to mark the occasion. Burgoyne formally surrendered at 2 P.M. on Friday, October 17, as his army paraded from its fortifications to the beat of somber drums. After laying down their weapons, the king's troops were escorted to Boston and boarded ships bound for England. Under an agreement of honor, they swore not to serve again in the war against America.

In Pennsylvania, Howe abandoned Germantown on Sunday, October 19, and concentrated his efforts on the American river fortifications. Three days later, a force of 1,200 Hessians attacked the shoreline of Fort Mercer at Red Bank in the afternoon but suffered heavy losses. The fort had been strengthened with artillery under the direction of Knox's aide, Du Plessis.

On Thursday, October 23, six British ships maneuvered past the spikes of the chevaux de frize in the river and opened fire on Fort Mifflin on Mud Island and the American warships. Knox's artillerymen struck back with an unrelenting fusillade, sending shots crashing into the enemy hulls. The crews of the sixty-four-gun *Augusta* and eighteen-gun *Merlin* ran their ships aground and set them ablaze.

Washington wanted to attack the British troops in Philadelphia and liberate the city. At a war council on Wednesday, October 29, Knox advised against it, arguing that the troops were without blankets or provisions and that a setback would destroy the growing faith in America's chances that flowed from Gates's victory at Saratoga. He reminded Washington that this was a defensive war on their part, and their chances were much greater if the British were forced to attack their fortifications. "My opinion is to draw our whole force together, take post at, and fortify Germantown, considering it as our winter quarters." He stressed that "if they should come out, fight, and defeat us, we have a secure retreat and winter quarters."[24] The rest of Washington's generals agreed.

The success of Gates left many congressmen and military leaders wondering openly if the wrong man was leading the army. General Stirling wrote the commander in chief on November 3 with news that Washington's reputation was under attack by the ambitious Irish-born French brigadier general Thomas Conway, whom Washington had recently rejected for promotion. Two weeks earlier, Stirling had written to delegate Richard Henry Lee that "General Conway's merit . . . as an officer, and his importance in this Army, exists more in his own imagination, than in reality."[25]

Knox attended another war council on Saturday, November 8, in which Conway was present. Tensions were high. Washington again wanted to attack Philadelphia, especially if the British concentrated much of their force on Fort Mifflin on the Delaware River. But Knox and the other generals again unanimously advised against the plan and gave their previous objections. Much of the army was still without adequate clothing, shoes, stockings, and blankets as the weather grew frigid. Two days later, the British found that the swift current of the Delaware had opened a deep channel that allowed them to sail past the guns on Mud Island with a floating battery armed with twenty-two twenty-four-pound cannons. The king's troops positioned the vessel within forty yards of Fort Mifflin and began a furious cannonade. The British came close enough to the fort to lob grenades within its walls, which soon were reduced to ruins. After five days of shelling, the garrison evacuated on

Saturday night, November 15, taking with them all of the cannons. Two days later, Knox and two engineers were sent to Fort Mercer, farther up the river at Red Bank, to strengthen its defenses.

Meanwhile, General Conway decided to send a letter of resignation to Congress, saying that his lack of promotion endangered his rank in the French army and that his criticism of Washington had led to friction in the Continental force. He also asked the commander in chief for a leave of absence, which Washington denied until permission was granted by the government.

Congressmen also were wondering why Washington refrained from attacking Philadelphia. In a November 15 letter, Henry Laurens (father of Washington's aide John Laurens), who had replaced John Hancock as the president of the Continental Congress, acknowledged the criticism among delegates and the whispers that Washington placed too much faith in the judgment of Knox and Greene. Writing to his friend Major Benjamin Huger, a member of the Fifth South Carolina Regiment, Laurens warned: "You may be told Our General is under a pernicious influence of two General Officers [Knox and Greene]. Suspend judgment. I have seen the General's sentiments very fully and freely written to a friend on that subject. I will not believe a word of the whispers."[26]

Some of the criticism was coming from within Washington's own force. Major General Thomas Mifflin told congressmen that Gates should be appointed president of a Board of War to reorganize the army. Frustrated by his failure to be promoted, Mifflin accused Washington of surrounding himself with fawning advisors such as Knox. To Gates, Mifflin wrote bitterly in a letter on November 15, complaining of a "deep-rooted system of favoritism which began to shoot forth at New York and which has now arrived to its full growth and maturity."[27]

Knox returned from Fort Mercer to Washington's camp at White Marsh, about fourteen miles from Philadelphia, on Wednesday, November 19, and told the commander that it was critical that the fort be held. General Greene was sent with reinforcements, but British general Howe threw 2,000 troops, led by Cornwallis, over to the New Jersey side of the Delaware to strike the fort from land, a move that made the fortification untenable for its 350-man garrison. The fort was given up without firing a shot on Thursday, November 20. During the evacuation, the Americans torched everything useful: barracks, buildings, and food and military supplies.

The British now had control of the Delaware River and open supply channels to replenish the Royal Army.

Washington felt under tremendous pressure to attack. His reputation was at stake, and perhaps even his command of the army. Knox remained against an offensive strike, however, during a November 24 war council in which Washington's generals were divided. Ten thought it inadvisable to launch an attack and five supported a strike. Lord Stirling believed that with Cornwallis in New Jersey, an opportunity to crush Howe had arrived.[28] Washington decided against "the impracticability of answering the expectations of the world without running hazards which no military principles can justify."[29]

Congress, which was still convening in Yorktown, expected action. Rather than accepting the resignation of Thomas Conway, they sought a way to accommodate him despite his criticism of the commander in chief.[30] While most of Congress supported Washington, a faction wanted Gates to head the army, including Representative James Lovell of Massachusetts, former delegate and army surgeon Dr. Benjamin Rush of Philadelphia, delegate Jonathan Dickinson Sergeant of New Jersey, and, of course, former delegate turned brigadier general Thomas Mifflin.

Washington asked his generals to put their advice on whether to attack Philadelphia in writing to appease Congress. Knox wrote on Wednesday, November 26, advising against a rash move to satisfy politicians. Speaking frankly, he said that although many pointed to the sagging reputation of the army, in truth, the Americans had no military tradition and were still learning to fight. When the war began, "we were contending for our all, for everything dear to humanity," Henry wrote. "Now it seems otherwise with many persons, whose anxiety for military fame seems to absorb every consideration." He realized that Washington's honor suffered by inaction, but he believed that most Americans still thought of him "as their Father, and into your hands they entrust their all."

Knox laid down several tactical reasons for advising against an attack of the city and urged Washington not to risk everything in one single, decisive battle. Given the inexperience of the American army, it was unwise to fight when the disciplined British troops had equal numbers—and extremely hazardous to attack them with a comparable force when they had the protections of entrenchments, redoubts, and batteries. He estimated the Continental strength to be about 8,000 men and the redcoats to be about 10,000 strong. Even a small group of soldiers who were well fortified could defeat an assault from a much larger army. "I believe there is not a single maxim in war that will justify a number of undisciplined troops attacking an equal number of disciplined troops, strongly posted in redoubts, and having a strong city in their rear, such as Philadelphia."[31]

Probably recalling the difficulty at the Chew House, Knox pointed out that the enemy had a daunting series of expertly engineered redoubts, which would have to be overcome one at a time before the Americans could even engage the main force of the royal troops. He reminded Washington of the well-deserved reputation of the British army, which learned at Bunker Hill the bloody consequences of storming a redoubt with unprotected troops. He thought the army would do better to fortify Germantown and build winter quarters, and invite the enemy to come out and attack their entrenched position. Knox stated unequivocally: "From the experience derived from reading, and some little service, and the knowledge of the strength of the enemies works, my opinion is clearly, pointedly, and positively, against an attack on the enemies redoubts, because I am fully convinced a defeat would be certain and inevitable."[32]

Congress, however, desperately wanted Washington to liberate Philadelphia. On Thursday, November 27, Representative Lovell wrote to Gates: "We want you most near Germantown. . . . You will be astonished when you come to know accurately what numbers have at one time and another been collected near Philadelphia to wear out stockings, shoes and breeches. Depend upon it, for every ten soldiers placed under the Command of our Fabius [Washington], five recruits will be wanted annually during the war."[33] That same day, Congress appointed a new Board of War that included nondelegates and named General Gates as its president, granting him the power to reorganize the army.[34] The act seemed to be a direct rebuff of Washington and his generals. Delegates also unanimously resolved on Friday, November 28, to appoint a three-man committee of congressmen Robert Morris, Elbridge Gerry, and the Virginian Joseph Jones to consult with Washington on an offensive campaign and to recommend against the army retiring to winter quarters. They also formed an inquiry to investigate why Fort Mercer had been abandoned.[35]

Knox remained steadfast in his belief that the army should restore itself in winter quarters, preferably somewhere along the Schuylkill about thirty miles from Philadelphia. The troops did not have adequate clothing and food to withstand a winter campaign, he wrote Washington on December 1 and 5, nor did they possess the proper cannons to batter enemy fortifications.[36]

Lucy continued to write with urgent pleas to be with him in Philadelphia. She wondered how he could love her and yet insist on their separation, which by now had persisted for almost a year. He responded in a letter on Tuesday, December 2: "No man on earth, separated from all he holds dear on earth, has every suffered more than I have in being absent from you whom I hold dearer than any other object." He explained that many of the troops were going days without food, lacked adequate clothing or even shelter, and the strain of all these hardships was borne under the constant anxiety that the British could attack at any minute. At that very moment, news arrived in camp that Howe's army was on the move. The battlefront was no place for his wife and daughter.[37] The current alarm proved to be false; the redcoats failed to strike that day.

The congressional committee arrived at the White Marsh camp at noon on Wednesday, December 3. Morris, nicknamed the "financier of the revolution," had worked closely with Washington to raise funds for the army. Gerry was from Marblehead, Massachusetts, and had been a successful merchant before the war. He supported Conway and Gates. Jones was from Washington's home state of Virginia and was the uncle of James Monroe. The commander met with the delegates and ran down the litany of reasons why his generals opposed an attack on the enemy's front lines. The next day he supplied them with the written arguments of Knox, Greene, and the rest of the war council. Before the committee could come to an understanding, the British appeared about three miles from the right side of the American line on Chestnut Hill. Knox moved fifty-two cannons into place and prepared for battle. The armies skirmished for four days with the British moving to the American left on Friday. On Monday, December 8, the British gave up the fight and retreated to Philadelphia.

The congressional committee in camp agreed that an attack on Philadelphia and a winter campaign were not advisable and that Washington's army needed reinforcements, reorganization, and greater pay for officers to relieve some of the discontent and the almost-daily resignations of commissions. Knox had reason to be concerned about his position; General Conway's credibility in Congress was clearly rising, and the Frenchman was publicly critical of Knox's advice to Washington. On Saturday, December 13, 1777, delegates appointed Conway to the coveted rank of major general and unanimously named him inspector general of the army.[38]

Knox moved with the army to set up winter quarters. The troops arrived on Friday, December 19, at Valley Forge, along the Schuylkill about nineteen miles from Philadelphia. Knox favored the position because it allowed the army to prevent Howe's men from venturing farther into Pennsylvania to gather supplies. The site was a forest valley between two rolling hills and naturally protected on two sides by a river and a creek. The surrounding trees provided lumber for cabins, and roads could be cut beneath a protective canopy of pine. The men had few tents or blankets and needed to build barracks quickly. Knox took up headquarters in a small stone home owned by John Brown, which sat alongside the Valley Creek, a short distance along the same stream that ran by Washington's headquarters and a short walk from Lafayette's. While the troops built log-cabin quarters, Knox's regiment set up an artillery park outside the stockade fences that were erected. He received the news on December 20 that France was backing up its support for America. The French ship *Flamond* had arrived at Portsmouth, New Hampshire, loaded with 48 four-pound brass cannons complete with carriages, along with nineteen-inch mortars, 2,500 nine-inch bombs, and 2,000 four-pound cannon balls. The shipment also included 4,100 stands of arms, gunpowder, and provisions.

Washington began to believe that criticism against both he and his top commanders was now amounting to a concerted movement to replace him, which became known as the Conway Cabal. Knox heard the criticism leveled against his judgment. Gates's supporters tried unsuccessfully to woo the Marquis de Lafayette, who reported back to the commander in chief. Lafayette wrote of the abuse of his excellency's circle that "The Tories fomented all these dissensions. Greene, Hamilton, and Knox, his best friends, were slandered."[39]

Washington was wounded by the betrayal, but defiant. He sent for his wife, Martha, to visit him at Valley Forge and told his generals, "I have not sought for this place. If I am displeasing to the nation I will retire; but until then I will oppose all intrigues."[40]

Henry wanted to return to Boston to visit Lucy while the army remained inactive, but Washington was reluctant to part with his trusted aides during the most serious political crisis of his military career.

Henry and eight other brigadier generals signed a memorial headed "Protest of General Officers to Congress" opposing Conway's promotion and pledging their support of Washington.[41] Knox also wrote to Massachusetts congressman Elbridge Gerry on January 4, 1778, saying that the majority of the army was faithful to the commander in chief: "The prepossessions of the army in favor of the character [Washington] hinted at are founded upon a thorough experience of his ability, judgment, courage and attachment—and they would infinitely prefer him before a Turrenne or Conde. Every military character on this continent, taken collectively vanished before him, and he is not only a soldier but a patriot in the fullest sense of the word. As it is impossible truly to describe a living character, it must be left to posterity to do him justice." Knox explained that there were many jealousies in the army. Some wanted fame and glory; others were driven by financial concerns and the prestige and the power of high rank, in contrast to Washington's noble motives. "Something must be attributed to a rational, manly desire to be instrumental in the defense of the liberties of this country."[42]

Knox was already formulating a plan for a summer campaign. He wrote to Washington that the British were confined to two harbors, New York and Philadelphia. Of these, New York was more valuable because of its central location, accessible ports, and waterways to supply the Continental Army. Knox recommended that Washington concentrate on liberating the northern city using New England militia along with 5,000 men from the main army and reinforcements from the two brigades already along the Hudson River.

Knox's desires to see his family and fulfill his duty were usually at cross-purposes, but now they came to a confluence. Washington agreed that Knox should return to New England to check on the arsenals. Henry was given orders on Thursday, January 8, 1778, to prepare for the spring military campaign. As the head of the ordnance department, he had to assess the coming needs of the army. Washington told him to visit the arsenals at Springfield and Carlisle, to hire more workers for the gear-up, and to form additional magazines. He also had to arrange for artillery wagons and teamsters to haul the heavy guns from Albany to Valley Forge.[43]

While these duties were pressing and extensive, for Henry the mission was also a chance to return to Lucy and the long-awaited reunion with his family.

SIX

TURNING OF THE TIDE

hree hundred miles of snow-swept roads lay between Henry and Lucy. He set out from Valley Forge in mid-January 1778, bracing against the weather and accompanied by one of his artillery commanders, Captain Thomas Vose, a fellow native of Massachusetts. They rode north in a carriage until the snow became too thick for the wheels, then found a tracked sleigh to take them the rest of the way. As they coasted along the white-frosted landscape, the trace connecting the harness to the horses snapped in two. Vose climbed from the sleigh, pulled out a knife, and carved two holes in each of the severed pieces, then bound them together with a silk handkerchief. To the men's surprise, the trace held together until they could find someplace to make repairs.

As they traveled, Knox's thoughts remained on the threat to his career and Washington's in the wake of the Conway Cabal. When he reached Poughkeepsie, New York, on January 18, he took time to write his friend General Benjamin Lincoln, who was recovering from a minor wound suffered during the American victory at Saratoga. Knox mixed congratulations with an explanation of the inertia of Washington's army: "We at the Southward are quite put out of countenance by the brilliancy of your success, not that any exertions have been wanting on the part of the army; but at least we ought to have equal numbers with our opponent, which was not the case."[1]

When he reached Boston, Lucy was overjoyed to see him. He assured her that his love remained unabated and that he still cherished her above all else. He had longed to see his daughter, young Lucy. While he spent his evenings and nights with his family, his days in Boston were committed to military business. He was not on leave.

The town showed the battle scars from the British occupation as well as his own cannonading in 1776 in the battle to liberate it. After the Battle of Saratoga, Burgoyne's defeated, paroled British soldiers wandered the Boston streets, waiting for ships to transport them back to England. Knox visited the arsenals, met with the commissaries, hired workers, and inventoried the stock of arms. He sent Washington a list of the ordnance and estimates of the army's needs for the coming campaign. According to his estimates, Springfield and Boston had 7,000 arms, of which 4,000 would be sent to Pennsylvania to supply fresh enlistments.

He also saw that the recruiting efforts in his home state were progressing slowly. Inducements and bounties of land and money were not providing adequate incentive for men to join the ranks. Although he advised the Massachusetts Legislature to institute a draft, many of the assemblymen balked, believing their constituents would not abide conscription. Knox wrote to Washington on Wednesday, February 4, 1778, criticizing the state legislators' reasoning and recommending a Continental draft. Leaders in each state were hesitant to fill the national needs, many believing other states had not done enough, that their state had already done too much, and that local needs were a higher priority than the Continental Army. Knox believed the only way every state would fully comply with its quota would be if congressional legislation spelled out the expectations from each state. Relying on the states to spearhead enlistment was unreliable, Knox pointed out: "This is a debilitated way of thinking and I have no doubt were Congress to press the matter and leave no alternative, that your Excellency would in April find yourself at the head of a powerful body of forces fully equal to all exigencies."[2]

Because of the high wartime inflation—the cost of imports was six times higher than usual—Henry found it difficult to fill the civilian jobs at the arsenals despite offering exorbitant wages of $30 a month along with a suit of clothes and another suit every year along with the usual army rations. He wrote Washington that he would add an allotment of half a pint of rum per day to sweeten the deal. The contracts for many of the workers ended in March.

Knox traveled the surrounding country trying to procure lead. Here, too, wartime inflation drove up the price. Every dollar spent by the army was precious because the soldiers back at Valley Forge were starving. The choice was between bread and bullets.

Much of Knox's frustration lay with the Continental Congress, which appeared unwilling or unable to relieve the deprivations and suffering of the

army. Massachusetts delegate Elbridge Gerry, who supported Thomas Conway, wrote Knox on Saturday, February 7, responding to Henry's earlier letter
in praise of Washington. Instead of addressing the needs of the army, Gerry's
letter focused on the politics within the army. He insisted that Congress was
not trying to replace the commander in chief: "I have not yet been able to
make any discoveries that can justify a suspicion of a plan being formed to in-
jure the reputation of, or remove from office, the gentleman hinted at in your
favor of January the 4th. And the alarms that have been spread and jealousies
that are excited relative to this matter appear to be calculated rather to answer
mischievous than useful purposes."[3] Gerry reminded Knox that opposition by
officers to Congress's appointments only made the delegates more resolute
and furthered factions. "What has been the consequence of every appointment of general officers made by Congress? If it did not suit the whole army,
opposition has taken place, and reduced Congress to the necessity of asserting
the rights of themselves and their constituents, or consenting to give them up
in a manner that would sap the foundation of liberty."[4]

Knox felt that he did not need to be lectured on liberty. Of the delegates
in Congress, Gerry knew better than most the hardships the army suffered.
He had been a member of the committee that visited the army and witnessed
the hungry, ill-clothed soldiers. Knox wrote Washington on Monday, February 16, that he found a clothier who could produce 5,000 suits in just a couple
of weeks if he only had the money to complete the work. Knox reiterated his
support for a Continental draft: "The legislature of this state [is] willing to do
everything in their power to fill the army. It appears to me that a decisive resolve of Congress that every state should draft a certain number of men by
some day in March free of expense to the continent, and admit of no alternative, will be the only proper measure that can be adopted. It is certain the
money will not induce people to enter the service—there must be some other
excitement to their duty."[5]

Knox traveled to Albany and arranged for much of the area's artillery to
be sent to the theater of action near Philadelphia. He wrote Washington that
it would be better to wait until the rivers were thawed and the heavy guns
could be transported by boats. The commander in chief agreed and wrote
Knox on Saturday, February 21, to return to Valley Forge as soon as possible:
"I dare say you will, in your absence, be very usefully employed; but your
presence here, to superintend your department at large, is so extremely requisite, that I flatter myself you will make a point of rejoining the army as expeditiously as circumstances will admit."[6]

Washington needed his closest allies back in Valley Forge. Aside from the apparent Conway-Mifflin movement to replace him, conditions in camp were becoming unbearable for the men. Henry received a February 26 letter from Nathanael Greene, who had just returned from an eleven-day foraging expedition around Valley Forge. He detailed the startling conditions. "The army has been in great distress since you left it," Greene wrote. "The troops are getting naked; they were seven days without meat, and several days without bread. Such patience and moderation as they manifested under their sufferings does the highest honor to the magnanimity of the American soldiers."[7]

Many of the men went before their superior officers, saying that it was impossible for them to remain in camp much longer. They needed food. Greene noted that the men "told their sufferings in as respectful terms as if they had been humble petitioners for special favors." Washington had ordered Greene to lead the expedition to take what they needed from local residents, despite the bitterness it would certainly cause. Washington felt the army had little choice. Inhabitants became alarmed at the sight of soldiers roaming farms and commandeering property and animals. Many residents hid their livestock, wagons, and harnesses. Greene's men searched the woods and swamps and rounded up fifty head of cattle. Greene told Knox that his "collections" had prevented the army from totally disbanding, and he expressed bitterness over Congress's inability to provide relief. "We are still in danger of starving. Hundreds of our horses have already starved to death. The committee of Congress have seen all these things with their own eyes."

Part of the problem was ineptness in the department of quartermaster. Major General Thomas Mifflin, a former congressional delegate and severe critic of Washington, had resigned from the post after being denied promotion. Congress and Washington both wanted Greene to take over the job. Not only was Washington confident that Greene could greatly improve conditions in the army; he also wanted a loyal friend serving in such a vital position. Greene, however, was torn between his desire to retain a field command and the opportunity to help the army in an administrative position. He coveted fame and was painfully aware that no one in history had been celebrated for service as a quartermaster. "I hate the place [the quartermaster department]," he wrote Knox, "but hardly know what to do. I wish for your advice in the affair, but obliged to determine immediately."[8]

Greene knew he could not turn down the quartermaster job. Every day men were dying, and their gaunt bodies were wrapped up and stored to await burial when the ground thawed. As many as 2,500 men succumbed. Others felt they had no option but to desert and risk the penalty of death. By remaining in camp, they risked the same fate by starvation. The quartermaster was a vital link in transporting supplies from the commissary general to the men, whether in camp or on the march. If he took the post, Greene would have to establish supply posts over a vast amount of territory, and understand the terrain and the strategies of both the Continental and British armies and overcome the complex logistics of transporting provisions during a war.

He reluctantly took the job, commenting to General McDougal, "All of you will be immortalizing yourselves in the golden pages of history while I am confined to a series of [administrative tasks] to pave the way for it."[9]

Washington agreed with Knox that only a draft would fill the army's needs and had explained its critical importance to another congressional committee that had recently arrived at Valley Forge. The commander in chief wrote Knox on Thursday, March 5, 1778: "I do not know what steps Congress intend to recommend to the States for filling their regiments, but I am certain that nothing short of the measure you mention will prove effectual. . . . I very much fear that the States will each proceed in different ways, most of them feeble and ineffectual.[10]

The first week of March, Knox packed his bags for the return trip to Valley Forge. He and Lucy decided that she and their daughter would follow him to camp when the winter weather abated. Several wives of generals had made a home in camp, including Nathanael Greene's wife, Kitty, a close friend of Lucy's, Martha Washington, and General Lord Stirling's wife. As they parted, Henry and Lucy reminded each other that their separation would be short this time.

After an uneventful trip, Knox immediately went about organizing the artillery and directing the cannons and arms that were daily arriving at Valley Forge. On April 18, Congress directed Washington to convene a war council of his generals to plot out a military campaign for the spring, and the commander asked for written opinions from his key advisors. The generals had already discussed three plans. The first was to remain in a defensive posture while training and instilling discipline in the army and new recruits in order to improve the army's proficiency. Some generals favored taking the offensive and making an attempt to liberate Philadelphia. The final option floated in discussions was changing the seat of the war and attacking the British in New York. Knox wrote a detailed opinion of the choices the Americans faced on Thursday, April 23. He thought that standing pat could be disastrous because not only would their army receive fresh troops, but so would the British.

Knox wrote to Washington that: "If theirs should be the greatest and earliest received, we shall the infinite mortification to have waited for nothing but disgrace. We shall be obliged to make a defensive war with an inferior force, to be perfectly attendant on the enemy's motions, move when they move, halt when they halt, retire when they advance or [risk] everything on the hazard of a general action where the probability of success will be apparently against us."

He kept in mind the need to maintain public support for the cause, believing that many would lose faith in American hopes if commanders declined to attempt a blow against the British. "Our friends, and those who wish to be our friends, will be dispirited, because we cannot protect them; neutrals will take an active part against us; the disaffected will be confirmed in their disaffection, and our army induced to desert. The enemy will be able to raise such numerous recruits from ourselves as when incorporated into their old troops, will enable them to garrison the conquered places without any sensible diminution of their principal force, which will be left free for new operations."[11]

Victory would cure many of the army's problems, he stressed. "Success in military matters procures applause, and covers every defect in planning or executing an enterprise."[12]

The chances of freeing Philadelphia through a prolonged siege did not seem promising, Knox explained to Washington. The army lacked the heavy battering cannons and military supplies needed for a protracted engagement, and given the British's ability to send reinforcements, such a plan would require 36,000 men. "I am afraid we should find great difficulty to obtain so large a number or subsist them." Instead, Knox favored leaving the enemy uncertain whether New York or Philadelphia would be their target.

He saw several advantages in attempting a siege of New York, believing that New Englanders would be more supportive of the army if the war were carried north.

"It is an enterprise of which the New England people are enthusiastically fond, and they would most cheerfully turn out as many men as to assist the Continental Army as would be required," he told Washington, estimating that the Continental force under the commander in chief could be boosted from 5,000 men to 25,500 merely by shifting the seat of the war. Knox believed that Massachusetts would provide 8,000 men, New Hampshire and New Jersey 2,000 each. New York could be counted on to supply 2,500 men and Connecticut another 4,500. About 2,500 Continental troops were already stationed in Albany along the Hudson River. He ticked off other advantages, such as better access to food and forage, navigable rivers to provide transport, and access to as many as fifteen large battering cannons from Boston, Providence, and forts along the Hudson. Knox laid out a detailed plan for recruiting and transporting troops as well as a blueprint for a two-pronged attack on Manhattan Island.

"New York, in my opinion, is of much greater consequence to the Britons in their design of subjugating America than Philadelphia or any other place whatever," he wrote.[13]

Washington's key advisors were divided on a plan of attack. Of the eleven generals who submitted their written opinions, only three joined Knox in recommending an assault of New York. Three, including Lafayette, wanted to stand pat and drill and train the army, while three wanted to pursue a siege of Philadelphia, and yet another general wanted to attack both cities.

When Congress had asked Washington to hold a war council to consider the summer campaign, Knox's name initially was omitted from the list of generals who should be consulted. The omission was corrected two days later. Washington suspected that Knox's reputation had suffered during the controversy surrounding Conway and Gates and reaffirmed his faith in Henry in a letter on Saturday, April 25, to New York congressman Gouverneur Morris, who had served on the committee that had visited Valley Forge. "Prejudices may be entertained by some against General Knox, there is no department in the army that has been conducted with greater propriety, or to more advantage, than the one in which he presides; and owing principally, if not wholly, to his management. Surely whatever plans may be come into, the artillery will have no small share in the execution."[14]

Three days later, a letter from Major General Conway was read in Congress. He complained that his talents were being wasted in the outpost in Albany, removed from the scene of action in the war, and offered his resignation. To his surprise, Congress accepted. Many delegates had begun to view Conway as a malcontent and malignancy in the army. Eight states voted to accept the resignation, and only Virginia voted against his departure. Conway immediately wrote to Congress that he had been misunderstood and that he had not intended to resign. But Congress took no action to reinstate him.[15] With the removal of Conway, the internal threat to the command of Washington and his key generals had passed.

As the spring temperatures warmed the air, news arrived at Valley Forge that France had agreed to an alliance with the United States and had signed a treaty on February 6. Congress immediately ratified the treaty in a unanimous vote on Monday afternoon, May 4. Knox and the rest of Washington's commanders knew that the nature of the war had completely changed and momentum had shifted. They were no longer battling the powerful British alone; now they were in partnership with the formidable French army and navy. Many of their problems in obtaining supplies and provisions could be overcome, while the British, now involved in a global conflict, could no longer commit as much of their resources to America.

Over the winter, Major General Frederick William August von Steuben, inspector general of the army, had drilled the soldiers in marching in formation and in using bayonets with remarkable success. He and Alexander Hamilton wrote the army's first military manual and imposed improved standards of hygiene. Knox watched as the soldiers marched with new precision. A cheer went up from everyone in the ranks: "Long live the King of France." Knox's men then fired another round of thirteen guns, which was answered by another general discharge of muskets and the cheer "Long live the friendly powers of Europe." Again Knox's men set off a thunderous explosion of thirteen cannons, and the soldiers responded with choreographed musket fire. The men cheered, "To the American States." With France changing the American prospects, Knox joined in the unanimous opinion of generals at a May 8 war council to decline attacking either Philadelphia or New York until the military situation could be reassessed. Washington believed the British could no longer provide much reinforcement for the troops already in America.

Signs appeared that the royal troops were preparing to evacuate Philadelphia. According to American intelligence reports, the British had moved their heavy cannons out of the city and were preparing wagons and teams of horses. Washington wrote Knox on May 17 that "this requires a state of readiness in us for marching at the shortest warning."[16] Knox responded the same day that the artillery was ready to move in a day or two but that he was waiting on horses from the quartermaster. He also said he was waiting on guns from New England and needed Greene to push through the shipping. Two thousand muskets were expected from Springfield and another 2,000 from Albany.[17]

Lucy arrived at Valley Forge accompanied by her escort, Major General Benedict Arnold, on Wednesday, May 20. Friends were struck by the tender nature of Henry and Lucy's relationship as well as the way their personalities seemed to complement each other. General Greene commented to his wife that he found Henry and Lucy to be "a perfect married couple." Arnold also received a warm welcome at Valley Forge, where his heroics at Saratoga had

been talked about throughout the winter. His limp—from a leg wound suffered in the battle—elicited sympathy mixed with admiration. As a result of
the wound, one of Arnold's legs was now an inch shorter, which precluded
him from assuming a field command. Washington gave Arnold an affectionate
embrace along with a finely adorned epaulette and sword knot that a friend in
France had presented to the commander in chief. Arnold's previous slight by
Congress had apparently been forgotten after the delegates restored his rank
and seniority.

Knox and the other military leaders around Washington daily expected
that the British would evacuate Philadelphia. They learned that the large cannons and the baggage of Howe's army had already been shipped down the
Delaware River or sent by transports to New Jersey. New York City was likely
the royal army's destination. The American army, however, still suffered from
the effects of the hard winter and smallpox. They were too weak to force a
battle. The anticipated English evacuation was delayed when the Frederick
Howard Carlisle peace commissioners arrived from England with promises to
repeal the Tea Act and to refrain from taxing the Americans in the future. The
English also sharply criticized the American alliance with France. Nathanael
Greene wrote to Knox, "Poor John Bull appears to be sick of his bargain and I
believe would gladly be off, could he do it with any kind of decency. Finding
he cannot subdue us by force, our enemy is trying to disunite us. They point
out the folly of a connection with a country [France] differing from us in language, customs and religion—all of which, however, will avail nothing. Arms
must decide the matter."[18] The American army was also delayed from action,
awaiting reorganization by Congress. By Wednesday, May 27, the final plan
was authorized and announced. Knox's artillery corps received a pay hike to
better retain qualified officers and gunners. The pay of an artillery captain, for
example, was boosted to $50 from just $20 a month, and the men in his regiment were generally paid 25 percent more than comparable soldiers in other
departments in the army due to the added expense of serving in the artillery
corps. His men had to buy their own supplies, which included items to maintain the cannons and horses. But Knox was given only three field commanders, which left him little room to promote men for heroism, initiative, or
outstanding service.

On Thursday, May 28, Washington appointed Major General Arnold to
command the American troops in Philadelphia when the British finally left. In
recent weeks, army soldiers had lined up to take an oath of allegiance to the
United States under an order by Congress. On Saturday, Knox administered

the oath to Arnold, who swore on his honor that "I, Benedict Arnold, do acknowledge The United States of America to be Free, Independent and Sovereign States and declare that the People thereof owe no Allegiance or Obedience to George the Third, King of Great Britain, and I renounce, refuse and abjure any Allegiance or Obedience to him."[19]

For the next two weeks, Knox kept his men ready to move. Washington could see no reason why the British had not already left Philadelphia; their baggage had been shipped out weeks earlier. He guessed that Howe and his replacement, General Henry Clinton, were waiting only for an American decision on a peace proposal they had offered Congress and for a separate offer from the Carlisle peace commissioners, sent by London.

The delegates flatly rejected the Howe-Clinton peace proposal on Saturday, June 6, and sent away the Carlisle peace commissioners on Wednesday, June 17, 1778, resolving that the body would not consider a treaty for peace with the British monarch unless given an "explicit acknowledgment of the independence of these states, or the withdrawing of his fleets and armies."[20]

That evening Knox attended a war council held by Washington to decide whether to attack the enemy. Washington explained that now, with the arrival of recent recruits, the Continental Army had 11,000 men fit for battle, and he estimated the British force amounted to 12,000 men. They discussed the option of shifting the seat of the war to New York. Washington wondered if they should wait for the enemy to quit Philadelphia and make a stand in New Jersey or march directly to New York. Knox wanted to harass and annoy the British as much as possible but was opposed to a major assault on fortified Philadelphia. This opinion was shared by four others in the sixteen-man council, which unanimously rejected an attack on Philadelphia but was divided on an alternative plan of action. Knox and the other generals put their opinions in writing the next morning: "It appeared to be the general sentiment that it would be the most criminal degree of madness to hazard a general action at this time,"[21] he wrote to Washington. Knox thought it ill-advised to attack the British, who could fire from behind entrenchments and batteries, and felt that attacking them in New Jersey was risky. For Knox, New York was the key position in America, linking the southern and northern states, especially New England. He wanted the army to wait until the British marched into New Jersey and then outrace them for the best position to battle for New York.

Shortly after 11 A.M. that day, news arrived that the British had slipped out of Philadelphia before sunrise and the enemy fleet was sailing down the

Delaware River and out to sea. Major John Andre, with whom Henry Knox had spent an engaging night discussing literature during his Ticonderoga mission, had made off with Benjamin Franklin's collection of books. The red-coats had crossed over the Delaware at Cooper's Ferry and Gloucester Point, about three miles from Camden, and into New Jersey. The royal army moved with 1,500 wagons in a procession that stretched twelve miles.

General Arnold led the American division of Colonel Jackson's Massa-chusetts regiment to take possession of the city the next day, Friday, June 19, with orders to prevent disorder or vandalism. The main body of the American army was ordered to move out to Coryell's Ferry and cross the Delaware into New Jersey. Knox's artillery held the rear of the procession. Rain began to fall and the air became muggy in the early summer heat, making the march ardu-ous and slow. Knox reached the Delaware by June 21 and spent the afternoon shipping the heavy artillery guns to the Jersey shore. He had an ample num-ber of boats on hand to facilitate the crossing, but the rain, heat, and soggy roads stalled the army's progress in New Jersey. A gill of spirits was issued to each man.

The British moved slowly as well, marching just forty miles in seven days. Washington sent troops and militia to harass the rear of their procession and further hinder their progress.

Washington desperately wanted to strike a crippling blow to Clinton's army. At a war council held about six miles north of Princeton on Wednesday, June 24, however, Knox sided with General Charles Lee and all but one of the advisors present in opposing a major battle and favoring instead to increase the troops annoying the British march. Lee argued that the French alliance assured an American victory in a war of attrition and that it would be foolish to risk the army in a major battle. Despite the strides made by the troops dur-ing the previous winter, Lee felt that they could not defeat the experienced and disciplined British soldiers. Knox agreed.

Henry wrote to his brother the following day: "Had we a sufficiency of numbers we should be able to force them to a similar treaty with [defeated British general] Burgoyne; but, at present, have not quite such sanguine hopes."[22]

Knox kept his artillery corps in motion as the army pressed through heavy rainstorms, humidity, and intense temperatures in a determined at-tempt to catch the British and prevent them from reaching New York. Several men fainted with fatigue, and some collapsed and even died of exhaustion. By Saturday, June 27, the two armies were five miles apart: the Americans at

Englishtown and the British at Monmouth Court House. Washington ordered an attack the next morning, fearing a delay would allow the British to reach an impregnable elevated position at Middletown Heights, twelve miles north. In the darkness, at 4 A.M., Clinton's red-clad soldiers began to move out. Intelligence reached Washington at 5 A.M., and General Lee was sent to lead an attack on the British rear while the rest of the Continental Army rushed to support the assault. The training and drilling Knox had put his men through in recent months would finally be tested under fire.

As Knox and Washington approached the battlefront, they were mortified to see the American vanguard troops in full retreat. The fleeing soldiers reported that General Lee had failed to give his officers coordinated orders, and instead of pushing for a strike against the 2,000-man British rearguard, had ordered the 5,000 troops under his command to wait to advance. Washington was furious. Riding up to Lee, he screamed that he expected his orders to be obeyed and unleashed a tongue-lashing replete with sharp profanities until, in Brigadier General Charles Scott's words, "the leaves shook on the trees." Lee answered that he thought an attack was unwise. Washington took command of the troops and rallied the men to form ranks. He rode from one end of the line to the other exhorting them to fight. Knox's booming voice called men to make a stand. He ordered his cannons to open fire to buoy the soldiers' resolve and push back the oncoming English.

Seeing the American flight, Clinton had turned his troops around and ordered a pursuit. At about 11 A.M., British cannons began to shell the Continental position. Knox worked furiously in what he believed was the hottest weather he had ever endured to move his gunners into position. "The enemy advanced with great spirit to the attack, and began a very brisk cannonade on us, who were formed to receive them," he recalled in a letter to Lucy.

The Americans took cover behind a hedgerow and woods, thanks to what Washington later described to Congress as "the brave and spirited conduct of the officers, and aided by some pieces of well served artillery, [which] checked the enemy's advance."[23]

As the American troops regained their composure, they reloaded to attempt another assault. Their newly acquired discipline surfaced, and the men sent coordinated volleys ripping through the British lines. A correspondent from the *New York Journal* reported that "the severest cannonade began that it is thought ever happened in America."[24] Knox's artillery belched explosive charges that scattered the enemy troops and were met with a furious response from the royal cannons. Knox later recalled of his men, "I was highly delighted with their coolness, bravery and good conduct."[25] Alexander Hamilton watched the firestorm and observed that the American "artillery acquitted themselves most charmingly."[26] The acrid smell of spent gunpowder filled the air and enveloped the battlefield as the armies fired almost blindly at each other. Men fell not only from enemy shots but from exhaustion and dehydration. The temperature topped ninety-two degrees, and the oppressive humidity, coupled with the heat emitted from cannons and muskets, drained fluids from the men dressed in heavy woolen uniforms. At the height of the battle, the wife of one of Knox's wounded artillerists, Mary Ludwig Hays, who would be celebrated as Molly Pitcher, heroically carted water to thirsty gunners trying to keep the Continental cannons blazing to match the British sallies. According to legend, she even manned a cannon after her husband fell. The duel dragged on throughout the afternoon. General Greene replaced Charles Lee and led his troops to circle around the enemy's left flank to Monmouth Road, emerging behind the courthouse and rear of the British line. The royal troops attempted to force Greene's men to retreat, but they made a spirited stand, and Knox's artillery gunners repulsed the charge with deadly precision. Exposed from behind by infantry and cannon fire, the redcoats fell back through a dense patch of woods and marsh. Washington ordered his troops to attack on both sides of the British line, and Knox's men sent galling cannon fire to the enemy front. The Americans gave chase but became bogged down in the terrain as twilight descended. They lay on their arms in the battlefield throughout the night, waiting for the morning light to renew the attack. Many were in critical need of water and were agonizing, some dying, from thirst. Washington found that the sandy ground in the area was "destitute of water." Knox did not rest but worked to get cannons in position to support the anticipated attack.

As the orange haze and the blue light of morning emerged, Knox could see that the British had slipped away in the night, leaving many of their wounded on the battlefield. The enemy had retreated so silently that even the American soldiers on outposts just a few yards away did not detect their movements. The redcoats left a trail of knapsacks, muskets, and personal belongings strewn for miles.

As Knox surveyed the battlefield, he thought it "a field of carnage and blood." Casualties on both sides were almost identical, each around 360. Henry felt his men and, indeed, the entire Continental Army under Washington had acquitted themselves. "Indeed, upon the whole, it is very splendid," he wrote in a letter to Lucy the following day. "The capital army of Britain defeated and obliged to retreat before the Americans whom they despised so much!"[27] To his brother William, Henry gloated, "The effects of the Battle of Monmouth will be great and lasting. It will convince the enemy and the world that nothing but a good constitution is wanting to render our army equal to any in the world."[28]

Henry realized the victory over the main British army was critical in establishing confidence in the Continental Army before French troops took to the field in the war.

Washington gave much of the credit to Knox and his artillery corps. A day after the battle, he issued a statement in the army's general orders, proclaiming "[i]t is with peculiar pleasure in addition to the above that the commander-in-chief can inform General Knox and the Officers of Artillery that the enemy have done them the justice to acknowledge that no artillery could be better served than ours."[29] And to Congress, he reported that "[a]ll the artillery both officers and men that were engaged, distinguished themselves in a remarkable manner."[30]

Charles Lee, however, would be court-martialed for failing to carry out Washington's orders; he was found guilty and suspended from the army for one year, thus ending his career in the service.

Knox had little time to recover from the battle. The army immediately resumed the march though New Jersey heading for New York. The British force reached Sandy Hook within a few days and waited for Admiral Howe's royal fleet to ferry the men to Manhattan. Congress, meanwhile, could finally return to Philadelphia after convening for ten months in Yorktown, Pennsylvania.

The French fleet arrived off the Capes of Delaware outside of Philadelphia on July 10 with eighteen ships, including transports carrying 10,000 soldiers and the news that France had formally declared war on Britain. Prepared to drive the British out of the city, instead the French were redirected to New York for an attempt to prevent the English from crossing New York Harbor. Clinton's force completed the naval evacuation, however, before the French gunships arrived.

Knox and the rest of the army crossed the Hudson River about fifty miles north of New York City and then marched south to White Plains. Washington wanted a coordinated land-sea, American-Franco attack to capture New York. But French admiral Comte d'Estaing was concerned that his ships might become grounded on the New York Harbor sandbar near Stanton Island. He was cautious about engaging the English fleet under Admiral Howe in unknown waters that demanded complicated navigation. Instead, he sailed for Newport, Rhode Island, for a joint attack with 10,000 American troops under General John Sullivan. The French ships, armed with 834 guns, sailed into Narragansett Bay by the end of July, and Howe's British fleet, with 914 guns, pushed off from New York City a week later to confront them.

Knox and the rest of the American army in New York awaited the outcome of the battle. Admiral d'Estaing, clearly more comfortable in fighting the British in the open sea, recalled his troops from land and headed back to ocean waters under a favorable wind. The two fleets spent days maneuvering for position when a violent sea storm intervened, scattering ships and damaging sails and riggings. When the tempest abated, many ships, including Admiral d'Estaing's flagship, the ninety-gun *Languedoc*, were crippled. Instead of a coordinated battle, ships engaged in skirmishes and attacks with enemy ships they happened to encounter. The French fleet reassembled off Newport, and the British returned to New York for refitting. The alliance already showed signs of strain as General Sullivan and Admiral d'Estaing insulted each other, and by late August, as hurricane season began, the fleet sailed to Boston for repairs. Many American soldiers and militia in Rhode Island became panic-stricken with the departure of French battleships and began to desert in hordes, leaving the troops under Sullivan in danger and forcing a retreat.

Knox became concerned when the British began reinforcing their garrisons in Rhode Island, and the American troops began leaving the state by August 30. He feared that Boston would become vulnerable to capture. He wrote to his brother, warning William to protect what little property they had left. But Henry also wondered if the British had tired of the war in America. "I believe [the enemy] are about to quit the continent, and perhaps only wait for their last orders to effect it." He thought that British confidence had been shaken at Monmouth. Lord Clinton's troops were deserting by the hundreds, cutting his strength by nearly a third. The Hessians were refusing to fight. Henry confided that he had lost much of his former admiration for the opposing commanders: "It is improper for a person in my station to speak thus, were it to be divulged; but I do not believe there ever was a set of men so perfectly disqualified by a total and profound ignorance of every thing that ought to constitute the characters of leaders of an army to conquest. I beg you not to imagine that by depreciation of their abilities I mean to exalt our own. God forbid! I shall say nothing about it but only this, that we never set ourselves up as great military men."[31]

But the British had little reason to evacuate America after Admiral d'Estaing decided to set sail for the West Indies, a move that ended any hopes of a major American offensive for the rest of the year. And perhaps, as Knox may have imagined, the British generals did not want to leave America as failures. The Continental Army, however, could do little to physically force the British out of New York City and back to England without a fleet to blockade the sea and hold off English warships and supply vessels. Washington had another problem that, unless solved, promised another winter of starvation, nakedness, and want for the troops. American credit was sinking and the currency of the fledgling country was nearly worthless, having plummeted 90 percent in value in recent months. To clothe his men, Washington had to plead for blankets, stockings, and shoes from the warehouses at Springfield, Massachusetts, and Hartford, Connecticut. Although he suspected that the British might abandon America, he knew that they could simply hold on and wait for the country's finances to collapse under heavy debt and high inflation. To Congressman Gouverneur Morris of New York, he wrote in early October that the question was not "simply whether G. Britain can carry on the War, but whose Finances (theirs or ours) is most likely to fail." Officers suffered along with the enlisted men because the equipment for their positions was becoming prohibitively expensive. Washington reported to Morris in exasperation: "A rat, in the shape of a horse, is not to be bought at this time for less than £200; a saddle under thirty or forty; boots twenty, and shoes and other articles in like proportion. How is it possible therefore for officers to stand this, without an increase of pay? And how is it possible to advance their pay when flour is selling (at different places) from five to fifteen pounds pr. ct., Hay from ten to thirty pounds pr. ton, and beef and other essentials, in this proportion."[32]

In the temporary stalemate, the British barricaded themselves in New York while the patriot army stationed troops in a forty-mile semicircle around the enemy. Knox moved with Washington in late November 1778 to Pluckemin, New Jersey. Lucy was again pregnant and spent the winter in Boston.

While the troops prepared winter quarters, Congress asked Knox and Greene to return to Philadelphia to help reorganize the ordnance department, which funneled supplies and weapons to men in the field. Washington also returned to the capital to meet with Congress over the war effort. The government was still learning as it went along and groping for ways to build a more efficient army to match the British. As Washington observed in a letter to one of his generals, "We are young in the business in which we are engaged."[33] Knox, who was just twenty-eight years old, oversaw the Continental ordnance. He laid out a detailed plan to organize America's war arsenal, streamline operations, and invigorate the flow of critical weapons and supplies. Around January 28, 1779, he paid a visit to delegate James Duane of New York, a member of the committee conferring with Washington, and unveiled his recommendations while offering guidance. Knox's knowledge left Duane feeling "not sufficiently master of the subject to decide,"[34] and he referred Knox's plan to the committee and Washington.

While in Philadelphia, Knox saw Benedict Arnold, who introduced him to the woman he planned to wed. Two years earlier Arnold had appealed for Lucy's help during fruitless efforts to court another young woman. Arnold's fiancée was the beautiful Margaret Shippen, daughter of a former chief justice of Pennsylvania, who attracted a bevy of suitors for her charm and vivacity as well as a keen gift for eliciting protective instincts in men, especially men in uniform. Although she was from one of the most prominent families in Philadelphia, she was socially ambitious. During the British occupation, she was a favorite among British officers, including Major John Andre. Arnold courted her with full ardor. Knox was impressed with Peggy and seemed willing to forgive her former attentions to British officers. To his brother William, he wrote: "The girls are the same everywhere—at least some of them: they love a red coat dearly. Arnold is going to be married to a beautiful and accomplished young lady—a Miss Shippen, of one of the best families in this place."[35]

Shortly thereafter, Benedict Arnold was charged by the state of Pennsylvania with war profiteering and with snubbing civilian officials by overstepping his authority and granting unwarranted passports while in command of Philadelphia. Knox refused to believe the accusations and held a steadfast belief in Arnold's character. The earlier criticisms against Knox, Washington, and several of the military brain trust had made Henry skeptical of attacks against Continental generals. To William, he wrote: "You will see in the papers some highly colored charges against General Arnold by the State of Pennsylvania. I shall be exceedingly mistaken if one of them can be proven. He has returned to Philadelphia, and will, I hope, be able to vindicate himself from the aspersions of enemies."

Knox left Philadelphia with Washington on Tuesday, February 2, as the members of Congress were preparing to host a lavish public celebration to commemorate the first anniversary of the French alliance. Knox returned to his artillery corps, which had set up winter quarters in Pluckemin. Huts had been constructed on the high ground of a hill in what one correspondent called "a very pretty manner as you approach," and said of the camp: "Its regularity, its appearance, and the ground on which it stands, throws over it a look of enchantment, although it is no more than the work of a few weeks."[36] Mobile field guns, howitzers, mortars, and cannons formed the front wall of the square-shaped park, which was marked off by smartly arranged barracks, military laboratories, and a military school. Ever since Knox had entered the army, he had tried to impress Congress and American leaders of the need for a military academy similar to those in Europe to train the Continental officer corps the principles of fighting a war. At Pluckemin, Knox ordered such a school to be built. It was the first military academy in America and a direct forerunner of what would later be the U.S. Military Academy at West Point, which would open in 1802. This military school was simply known as the academy. Knox took great care in the design and look of the building, as if, from its very conception and creation, to instill it with an aura of tradition. It stood several feet higher than any other building in camp and was adorned with a small cupola. The fifty-foot-by-thirty-foot lecture hall could hold several hundred students. At the end of the hall was an elevated enclosure, from which Knox and other speakers lectured.

For the most part, Knox was the school's sole professor. He wrote up a curriculum and demonstrated every kind of weapon in the American arsenal and the methods used in the laboratories for preparing munitions. He explained battle tactics and logistics, military principles, the considerations a commander had to make before engaging the enemy, the common errors and traps that officers fell into on the battlefield. Knox firmly believed that battles were won and lost in the planning and felt that the officers of Continental Army needed to be as knowledgeable as their counterparts in the British army and their comrades from France.

On February 18, Congress resolved to put the country's ordnance under the official control of Knox and granted him an additional $75 a month to be used expressly for his duties. He would be in charge of telling Congress the needs of the army and dispersing weapons and munitions throughout the continent. Congress was sensitive to the democratic ideal of civilian control of the country's stockpile of weapons. Arms and munitions could be removed from the permanent magazines only by express orders from the Board of War: a civilian, democratically elected body. But the delegates, acknowledging that the contingencies of war often demanded a quick response, gave Knox and Washington the exclusive power to pull weapons from the arsenals as needed.

In the reworked regulations for the ordnance department, Congress followed several of Knox's recommendations, including plans to improve the preservation of ammunition and arms. A colonel from his artillery corps would be assigned to regularly inspect weapons throughout the army, check procedures, and survey the arsenals. During lulls of activity in the war front, artillery officers would be sent to the military laboratories to learn more about munitions manufacturing and gain knowledge that might be helpful in the field. Knox also was ordered to make regular reports to Congress, to assess and project the army's needs.[37]

The scope of the responsibilities for which Congress placed their faith in Knox is remarkable for a young man not yet thirty years of age and who had been a professional soldier less than four years. He was responsible for the army's entire artillery corps, and had to maintain a full grasp of all the of battlefronts of the war to supply every regiment with arms.

By early 1779, Knox realized that the tiresome war would drag on for some time to come. The British shifted their focus to the southern states, invading Georgia and South Carolina. Knox's close friend, General Benjamin Lincoln, faced the enemy along the Savannah River near Augusta, Georgia. His men suffered a devastating defeat at Briar Creek on March 3, with many of the troops fleeing to the river and some drowning. The British were left in complete control of Georgia, and the Continental Army was helpless to send reinforcements as the English pushed farther toward Charleston, South Carolina.

As the spring weather brought rising temperatures, Knox expected the British to launch an offensive within weeks. Congress had let an opportunity to draft soldiers slip away, Knox believed, by resolving on March 15 to allow individual states to recruit artillery or cavalry regiments to fill their quotas but stopped short of giving the states the power to conscript men. As a result, the most educated and talented men either were pursuing business opportunities created by the war or were serving in posts to defend their states. Knox, like Washington, thought in national terms rather than provincial ones and was more concerned about the country's needs than state rivalries.

Knox's personal finances, however, took a brighter turn when the long-overdue reimbursement for his Ticonderoga mission three years earlier was finally paid on April 6, 1779. He received $2,500, out of which he had to pay himself, his brother, and a servant. He had earned $3 a day for their grueling efforts to preserve the American cause.

SEVEN

FORTITUDE

The American army stood better trained than ever. Grueling military drills by Baron von Steuben had transformed the enlisted ranks of soldiers, who could now perform complex, orchestrated battlefield maneuvers with discipline. And Knox's military academy had improved the Continental officers' understanding of tactics, strategy, and logistics. But the army was still too undermanned and short on provisions to launch an attack against the British fortifications in New York.

Both Henry and William Knox were concerned that the interruption of business during the war would leave them penniless. William sailed to Europe that spring with plans to visit France and the Netherlands in order to make business connections to import goods to Boston.

Henry's days were filled with a bewildering variety of responsibilities gearing up for the summer military campaign. He was filling requests for armament and munitions throughout the army, running an artillery corps consisting of forty-nine companies and 1,607 men. He also served on time-consuming court-martial boards, including the case against Benedict Arnold for accusations stemming from his command in Philadelphia. Citizens claimed Arnold ignored the civilian government and used his position to financially benefit himself. Arnold initially demanded a speedy trial but then delayed the hearings as he secretly withdrew his allegiance to the United States. Using the name of Gustavus, he sent a coded letter on Sunday, May 23, 1779, to Lord Clinton with detailed information about Washington's force and expressed his willingness to turn against the Continental army.

With Arnold's information in hand, Clinton sent 6,000 soldiers up the Hudson River aboard 70 sailing vessels and 150 flat-bottomed boats on May

30. Two days later, the redcoats captured Stony Point and Verplanck's Point and threatened the camp of the main American army at West Point.

Throughout the spring and early summer Lucy struggled with her second pregnancy, and gave birth to a daughter on July 2, 1779, in Pluckemin, New Jersey. The infant, whom Henry and Lucy named Julia, was not healthy, and died in infancy, leaving Lucy distraught and despondent. Henry was troubled that Lucy and his family struggled without him, and the realization of the enormous sacrifices that his family was making for the sake of the war became painfully apparent. Lucy decided that it was better if she returned to Boston, where she would be surrounded by friends. Henry wrote to her a few weeks later, alluding to his frustrations over his public duties and the war and expressing his deep desire to devote himself solely to his family: "I long with the utmost devotion for the arrival of that period when my Lucy and I shall be no more separated; when we shall sit down, free from the hurry, bustle and impertinence of the world, in some sequestered vale where the education of our children and the preparation on our part for a pure and more happy region, shall employ the principal part of our time in acts of love to men and worship to our Maker."[1]

Washington wrote a note of condolence to Lucy, and to Henry he inquired, "I wish you to make this an object of particular attention. I shall be glad to hear how Mrs. Knox is, to whom I beg my respectful compliments and best wishes for her health."[2]

Despite Knox's hope that the war would end soon, he continued to advise Washington to maintain a cautious defensive strategy while simultaneously making preparations for a joint campaign with the French fleet. Within weeks, however, these plans were disrupted. The French admiral did not want to navigate the difficult waters of New York Harbor and the Hudson, and instead sailed to Savannah to coordinate an attack with General Benjamin Lincoln against British forces occupying the city. Washington told Knox on November 12 to end any preparations for a joint campaign with the French fleet, and the army began to pack its bags to return to winter quarters in Morristown.

The trial of Benedict Arnold resumed at Morristown two days before Christmas, and Knox returned to his judicial seat. The court-martial was delayed again as Arnold asked for officers to testify on his behalf who could not leave their posts. Like everybody else in the army, Knox had no inkling of Arnold's duplicity and remained sympathetic, believing the accusations would prove baseless. After several days of testimony, Knox and the board acquitted Arnold of the charge that he ordered Philadelphia stores shuttered while he

made personal purchases and had slighted Pennsylvanians in appointing officers within the army, disregarding the authority of civilian leaders. But Knox
and the board found him guilty of allowing a ship from a British port to dock
in the United States and that Arnold used army wagons for personal business.
Washington issued him a mild, halfhearted rebuke, calling his actions "pecu-
liarly reprehensible." No other penalty was given.[3]

Despite the leniency, Arnold would later say that he was embittered by
the proceedings and the reprimand and thus felt fully justified to betray his
colleagues as he felt betrayed by them.

The winter of 1780 proved to be the most severe that anyone could remember, and was said to be the coldest of the eighteenth century. A three-day
blizzard in January buried the Morristown camp under snow that piled six feet
high. Henry's men had to dig the heavy iron guns out of the snow to prevent
ice from corrupting the barrels. As many as twenty-eight snowstorms blan-
keted the camp that season. The previous winter at Valley Forge had been
nearly unendurable, but this year proved to be even worse. Few supplies trick-
led in, and provisions became bogged down en route by impassable roads. A
forty-head herd of cattle was driven through the drifts to reach camp in early
January to save the men from starvation.

Needing a victory to inspire more support, Washington planned a surprise attack of Staten Island in New York. Knox allotted the number of cannons needed for the mission, in which troops were ordered to drive 500
sleighs through deep snow in an attempt to take the British by surprise.
Knox's provisions for the planned assault drew criticism from Lieutenant
Colonel Alexander Hamilton, who did not hesitate to question the estimates
of a superior. To Washington, Hamilton wrote on Friday, January 14, 1780:
"It appears to me the quantity of ammunition proposed by General Knox for
the artillery is inefficient. A larger consumption may be necessary—the stone
house in which the enemy may attempt to defend themselves may be obsti-
nate, and we should have it in our power by the severity and duration of our
fire, to bring them to reason."[4] Hamilton's reference to the "stone house" was
a clear allusion to the Chew House, where, in October 1777, Knox's artillery
guns had failed to dislodge 200 British soldiers, causing a costly delay in the
advance of Washington's army and contributing to the defeat at Germantown.
This would not be the last time Hamilton would question Knox's judgment.
Perhaps to be safe, Washington ordered Knox to send more artillery along
with the mission, which ended in failure. The British, well entrenched when
the Americans arrived and not surprised by troops, easily repulsed the attack.[5]

★ ★ ★ ★

American prospects for the war did not brighten with the spring of 1780. On May 12 in Charleston, South Carolina, British general Henry Clinton forced the surrender of General Lincoln, who turned over the American garrison and the city. It was the greatest defeat of the war, costing the United States 5,000 men, along with 400 guns and 6,000 muskets. The British were now unopposed in South Carolina. Knox sent a consoling letter to his friend Lincoln just as he had sent condolences to Nathanael Greene after his demoralizing defeat at Fort Washington in November 1776. Knox expressed his steadfast faith in Lincoln at a time when his military reputation lay in ruins: "The great defense made by you and your garrison in field fortifications will confer on you and them the esteem and admiration of every sensible military man. I hope and believe that Congress will most unequivocally bestow that applause which you have so richly merited. No event, except the capture of Sir H. Clinton and his army, would give me more pleasure than to see you."[6] Lincoln seemed deeply moved by Knox's abiding confidence. At a later period, he wrote to Henry in terms of overflowing affection: "The first moment I had the happiness of being acquainted with you I conceived a high degree of friendship, which uniformly has increased as I became more intimate, until the present period. I consider the confidential manner in which we have indulged as one of the happy circumstances of my life, and in all events of grief or joy there is no man from whose friendship I should more readily expect the most cordial balsam, or whose bosom would more cheerfully expand in a participation of my happiness."[7]

On Tuesday, May 23, 1780, Knox began to voice doubts over the prospect of success against the British in New York City. To lay siege to the town, he believed the Continental army needed 28,000 men to overtake the 14,000 redcoats nestled behind defensive fortifications. He provided Washington with a detailed if somewhat cautious plan for a coordinated Franco-American assault that expressed his concerns. Because the value of the American dollar had depreciated so much, many merchants and farmers were unwilling to sell goods to the army. Knox explained that any summer military campaign would be doomed if the army's quartermaster and commissary departments were not put on solid financial footing by Congress: "Those are the main springs of an army, and unless they are in perfect order, every movement depending on them must be wrong and will in the end, produce destruction."[8]

Many of the troops that Knox saw at Morristown were gaunt and emaci-
ated from months of malnourishment. Most went several days without meat,
and officers such as Knox subsisted on bread and water to set an example. Despite the strict diet, however, Henry remained a heavy man. But the troops
continued to die from disease or illness at an alarming rate, and Congress was
unable to raise money for the army to relieve the suffering.

During these lean times, Lucy was enduring another pregnancy. She gave
birth to a son, Henry Jackson Knox, on Wednesday May 24, 1780. He was
named after Henry's colleague and friend, Colonel Henry Jackson, commander of the Sixteenth Massachusetts infantry regiment.

The following day, Knox was forced to be at camp as several soldiers revolted over the dire conditions in the army. The troops had not been paid in
five months, and many feared that their depreciating wages would be worthless. Two Connecticut regiments paraded through the Morristown camp the
evening of Thursday, May 25, with their arms shouldered and carrying their
packs and accoutrements. A regiment of Pennsylvania soldiers appeared to
surround the protesters, who chose to return to their barracks.

Once again several members of Congress seemed to be losing faith in Washington and his circle of top advisors, including Knox and Greene. On June 13,
delegates unanimously appointed Horatio Gates to head the southern department of the Continental army, adding that he needed to answer only to Congress and not to Washington.[9]

Knox was frustrated with Congress's wavering faith in Washington and
believed that the army lacked provisions rather than leadership. The need for
flour to feed the starving soldiers was so great that Knox was sent to Trenton
on an emergency mission to speed up the arrival of rations. He left camp on
June 21 accompanied by twenty cavalry riders with a request for the head of
the Pennsylvania government to supply him with 250 wagons. Within a few
days, he had coordinated an express train of wagons carrying 2,213 barrels of
flour to troops posted in New Jersey at Morristown, Springfield, and along
the Hudson. The mission undoubtedly saved lives.

Knox also tried to address the army's critical needs for weapons, which
fell under his litany of responsibilities as the head of ordnance. He drafted an
estimate for Congress laying out the military stores needed for America to
join in a campaign with the French to liberate New York. The shortfalls were
staggering. Just as several states had failed to meet their recruitment quotas,

they had failed to send ordnance. According to Knox's estimates, the army could not join the French in a siege without another 8,649 barrels of powder, 21,182 ten-inch shells, 16,561 eighteen-inch shells, 54,151 eighteen-pound shots, and 59,679 twelve-pound shots.[10] Washington placed so much faith in Knox's assessments that he admonished Congress in a letter on Tuesday, July 4, that the army would have to decline the opportunity of French help unless the shortfalls were corrected: "If we aim at an important object, adequate means ought to be employed or it would be unreasonable to undertake it; if the means cannot be furnished we must desist from the undertaking."[11]

On July 14, news arrived in camp that 5,100 French infantry troops aboard ten ships of war had recently arrived at Newport, Rhode Island, led by Lieutenant General Jean-Baptiste Donatien Comte de Rochambeau.

Rochambeau disembarked and found, to his surprise, that the Newport streets were completely deserted and no delegation came to welcome him. Residents remained shuttered within their homes, uncertain if the impressive foreign fleet had come to conquer or to befriend them. The American general William Heath soon arrived to greet him.

News of the arrival of French troops sent expectations for an American victory soaring throughout the continent once again. The landing of troops from the famed French army, however, was not the salvation that the Americans had hoped for. Many of the men were sick or injured from a long and unusually difficult voyage and would need weeks to recover. And the British sent troops to prevent Rochambeau from marching to meet Washington.

When English ships of war appeared off the coast of New York City, state leaders became so alarmed that they demanded that Benedict Arnold be placed in the command of West Point. Arnold lobbied for the post as well, claiming that his leg wound from the Battle of Saratoga had left him unable again to take a field command.

Arnold's motive was to use the fort of West Point as a bargaining chip with the British to boost his value. He could not wait long to make the jump to the British; an audit of his command was beginning to uncover evidence of fraud. Knox continued have full faith in Arnold's character, however, believing him to be an exemplary soldier, and fully supported Arnold's appointment to take over the most important post in America.

As the summer wore on, it became more and more evident that not arms, nor powder, nor fresh recruits would arrive from the states in time to launch a siege of New York. Soon the French fleet would be forced to depart for warmer waters.

By August, British expectations for conquering America began to rise. Arnold took over the command at West Point on Thursday, August 3, and continued to provide General Henry Clinton detailed reports of Washington's movements. When the American army crossed the Hudson above New York to help defend the French force against a British attack, Arnold made certain that the patriots' maneuvers did not catch the British off guard. He promised to soon turn over West Point by leading its garrison of 3,000 men away from the fort.

British hopes also rose with the news of the Lord Charles Cornwallis's victory over Horatio Gates's troops at Camden, South Carolina. Gates surprised his supporters in Congress by abandoning his troops in the heat of the fighting, grabbing the fastest horse he could find, and fleeing at full gallop. By nightfall, he had reached Charlotte, North Carolina, a full 60 miles away, and was 120 miles away from the battle within three days. Gates would never again pose a threat to Washington's command or his circle of advisors.

Knox's place in the army was more secure than ever, however, not only because of Gates's actions but due to his own merits. He had become indispensable to the army and to Washington. He possessed a thorough and intricate knowledge of the army's bewildering inventory of weapons and armament along with the expertise to deal with contractors and find supply channels to get equipment into soldiers' hands. He had developed relationships with state leaders throughout the country. But what made Knox truly irreplaceable was that he combined this detailed knowledge with a strategic vision in which Washington placed a tremendous amount of faith.

After a war council of generals on Wednesday, September 6, Knox advised Washington to send help to the South and to forget about a siege of New York until spring. Henry proposed a joint American-French expedition to liberate Charleston. If the British were allowed to continue unopposed in Georgia and the Carolinas, the union might be irrevocably split, he wrote to Washington on September 9: "The full possession of those three states will confer immeasurable advantages on the enemy in the cause of the war and enable them to conquer the others. The principal inhabitants of spirit will be made prisoners, and the common people enjoying the sweets of ease, and commerce will be willing to remain under the British government even at the conclusion of peace, and will perhaps act of their own and refuse to return to the union."[12]

Knox broke with the majority of generals, who advised Washington against launching a southern expedition. They agreed, however, that any siege of New York should be postponed until the following year. Washington listened carefully, then passed on a summary of the war council opinions to Benedict Arnold, who continued to relay information to the British.

Quartermaster Nathanael Greene wrote to Arnold that same week: "We are starving here for want of provisions. Our troops don't get one day's meat in four. This can't hold long, what is to become of us?"[13] Through Arnold, the British had a full picture of the Continental army's shortcomings.

Knox was asked by Washington to attend the summit with General Rochambeau in Hartford, Connecticut, along with the Marquis de Lafayette to discuss strategy. Alexander Hamilton, Washington's aide, also made the trip. They set out from Bergen County on Sunday, September 17, and arrived that Wednesday.

Although aristocratic by birth, Rochambeau was well suited to work with commanders from a democratic society because of his congenial personality. He had been assigned to head the French army in America because of his military reputation rather than his impressive political connections. Knox was pleasantly surprised that Rochambeau brushed aside formalities and expressed a willingness to take orders from Washington.

Henry's self-taught fluency in French as well as his own gregarious nature helped foster an affectionate air between the officers as they made their introductions. Washington did not speak French, and relied on Knox and Lafayette to interpret. Knox listened diplomatically during the discussions, anxious not to reveal the Americans' limited ordnance supplies as plans for a joint campaign proceeded. Nothing of substance came from the meeting. Everyone agreed that until the second fleet of French navy arrived, they lacked the naval superiority to dislodge the British.

On the return trip from the meeting, Knox, Washington, and Hamilton detoured to confer with General Arnold, who had set up his headquarters at the home of a man named Robinson on the opposite side of the Hudson from West Point. As they neared the fort, they were surprised by signs of disrepair to the fortifications. Arnold was nowhere to be found, so Washington and the rest of the party proceeded on to the Robinson home. Along the way they had stopped to inspect a redoubt, during which time a letter arrived at the Arnold home from a nearby commander announcing the capture of a British spy. Arnold, who received the message while eating breakfast, was horrified, realizing his plot had been detected. He said a hasty good-bye to his wife and bolted, fleeing just minutes before Washington, Knox, and their party arrived. The men immediately realized that something was profoundly wrong. Mrs.

Arnold, whom Knox had met in Philadelphia, was weeping inconsolably and seemed to be in shock. Holding her infant in her arms while swaying through extremes of emotion—one minute melting into tears while lamenting her state of abandonment and in the next screaming wide-eyed that the American generals had come to kill her baby—she seemed insane.

Washington and Knox examined the letter that had tipped off Arnold that his conspiracy had unraveled. It had been sent by Lieutenant Colonel John Jameson, commander of the American outpost at Lower Salem, New York. The suspect had been traveling under the name of John Anderson and wearing civilian attire, yet he claimed to be no spy at all. A note was attached to Jameson's message identifying Anderson as none other than John Andre, the top aide of the British commander in chief, Lord Henry Clinton. Andre had been captured by three militiamen who had searched him and uncovered several military documents concealed in his boots. All were in the handwriting of Benedict Arnold, and included notes from Washington's most recent war council, which Knox had attended, along with estimates of the number of soldiers posted at West Point and the surrounding posts and layouts of the fortifications, artillery orders, and a flag-of-truce pass written by Arnold that authorized "John Anderson" to pass the guards at White Plains without question.

Although Jameson recognized Arnold's handwriting, he did not suspect that the general had plotted with Andre. Instead he complied with an order from Arnold to notify him if anyone answering the name of "John Anderson" appeared along the American lines.

As the American generals tried to piece together what had happened, Knox remembered that he had spent an entertaining evening with prisoner-of-war Andre at Fort George in 1775 during his Ticonderoga mission. At the time, Andre was on his way to take part in a prisoner exchange. Knox had been immediately impressed with the British officer. As Knox and Washington discussed Andre's capture, it soon became apparent that Arnold had had a hand in the plot. Mrs. Arnold cried that she had been deserted by her cad of a husband despite her unwavering love for him. She did not deserve this fate, she sobbed, rocking back and forth and pressing her child to her breast. To Knox, Washington, and Hamilton, she appeared to be plunging toward a breakdown.

The scene of the abandoned mother tearfully clinging to her baby tugged at the empathetic instincts in Knox and the other generals. They believed that Mrs. Arnold had been completely unaware of her husband's duplicitous plot and that both she and the nation had been betrayed in the same treasonous act. The officers tried to comfort her with soft words, assuring her that they meant no harm to her child but instead extended their deepest sympathies for her plight.

Her manner would have "pierced insensibility itself," wrote Alexander Hamilton, who was present. In describing Mrs. Arnold in a letter written that same day to his future wife, Elizabeth Schuyler, Hamilton explained: "All the sweetness of beauty, all the loveliness of innocence, all the tenderness of a wife, and all the fondness of a mother showed themselves in her appearance and conduct. We have every reason to believe that she was entirely unacquainted with the plan, and that the first knowledge of it was when Arnold went to tell her he must banish himself from his country and from her forever."[14]

Peggy Arnold was not, however, an innocent bystander. She had supported her husband's overtures to the British from the beginning and pushed him to betray his command to satisfy her social ambitions. As she cried and moaned before Washington, Knox, Hamilton, and Lafayette, she was giving the manipulative performance of her life—as she would later admit with glowing pride.

Knox was stunned by Arnold, a man whom he had continued to trust even after presiding over his court-martial. Uncertain how extensive the plot with the British was or whether the enemy was on the verge of attacking, Knox sent off a dispatch to Major Sebastian Baumann, who was stationed at West Point, for the troops to stand ready to fight, expressing dismay over Arnold's betrayal: "The strangest thing in the world has happened. Arnold has gone to the enemy. . . . It is incumbent on us to be on our guard." Washington, no less surprised and disheartened by Arnold's defection, turned to Knox and Lafayette and asked, "Whom can we trust now?"[15]

Hamilton was sent to King's Ferry in pursuit of Arnold, who had managed to escape by climbing aboard a barge and sailing south down the Hudson to reach the British sloop *The Vulture*. Safely aboard, he sent a message under a flag of truce to Washington, asking that his wife be protected from acts of vengeance and justifying his actions: "I have ever acted from a principle of love to my country since the commencement of the present unhappy contest between Great Britain and the Colonies, the same principle of love to my country actuates my present conduct, however it may appear inconsistent to the world; who very seldom judge right of any man's actions."[16]

Realizing that Arnold was now providing the British with detailed intelligence about West Point, including its layout, the position of its artillery, and the location of its most vulnerable points, Knox had to rearrange its guns to offset the redcoats' precise intelligence.

He was also given the unenviable task of sitting on the fourteen-man board of general officers appointed to try Major Andre as a spy. At his hearing, Andre pleaded that he was innocent of this charge and that he had left *The Vulture* dressed in his regimental uniform rather than civilian clothes. He explained that he had rendezvoused with Arnold the night of Thursday, September 21, for a meeting in neutral territory at a secluded clearing along the banks of the Hudson. The meeting continued longer than planned as they discussed the details for the British to attack and capture West Point and for Lord Clinton to ostensibly take Arnold prisoner. Dawn broke with elements of the conspiracy yet to be settled. Rather than return to the river and risk detection, Andre claimed that he followed Arnold on horseback to a safe hiding place and that Arnold and one of the general's associates had betrayed him by leading him to a house behind American lines. Arnold may have done this in order to sacrifice Andre if they were discovered. Andre said he had no choice at this point but to change out of his regimental uniform and into civilian clothes. In a written statement, he explained: "I [was] betrayed into the vile condition of an enemy in disguise within your posts."[17]

Whatever fondness Knox had for Andre, whatever sympathies he felt for the plight of a British officer who had been unwittingly betrayed by Arnold, Henry sided with the rest of the board of generals that Andre should be hanged as a spy. Knox signed the board's verdict, which was handed down on September 29, and reported its findings: "Major André, Adjutant General to the British Army, ought to be considered as a spy from the Enemy and that agreeable to the Law and usage of nations it is their opinion he ought to suffer Death."[18]

Andre impressed Knox and nearly everyone else with the dignity in which he faced his fate. On the eve of his hanging, he sketched a self-portrait that showed himself in relaxed repose, his hair pulled back to reveal the delicate features of his boyish face with his eyes wistfully transfixed in distant thought. He asked for the honor of being shot like a soldier rather than hanged as a spy. Washington turned down this request. Knox watched as Andre was ordered at noon to mount a wagon beneath the gallows on Monday, October 2, 1780, at the army camp at Tappan. The condemned man drew admiration for his grace and composure in his final moments. Wearing a new suit of his regimental colors and with a sword by his side, he opened his shirt, placed a tied handkerchief over his own eyes, and uttered his last earthly words: "I have said all I had to say before, and have only to request the gentlemen present to bear testimony that I met death as a brave man."[19]

With that, the cart was pushed forward and Knox watched Andre hang. A journalist from the *Pennsylvania Packet* wrote of Andre's death: "Perhaps no person (on like occasion) ever suffered the ignominious death that was more regretted by officers and soldiers of every rank in our army; or did I ever see any person meet his fate with more fortitude and equal conduct."[20]

Nathanael Greene, who had recently resigned from the post of quartermaster after serving two years in that capacity, had returned to field duty. He believed that Henry Knox should be given the command of the Continental army's southern department and succeed the discredited Horatio Gates. After two successive American generals, Lincoln and Gates, had both suffered demoralizing defeats at the hands of the British in the morass of the southern states, the task of reviving American hopes in the region seemed monumental. Nevertheless, Greene told Washington that Henry had demonstrated time and time again an ability to achieve the near impossible with ingenuity and perseverance: "Knox is the man for this difficult undertaking. All obstacles vanish before him; his resources are infinite."

"True," Washington replied to Greene, "And therefore I cannot part with him."[21]

This was no idle compliment to Knox or a polite way to dismiss Greene's recommendation. By now Knox had become more critical to Washington's own success as commander in chief than even a talented strategist and battlefield leader such as Greene. Washington was fully capable of leading troops into battle himself and could live without one of his top field generals. But Henry's specialized knowledge and skills in artillery as well as his understanding, expertise, and management of the entire U.S. arsenal of weapons could not be easily replaced. It was clear to Washington that Knox's importance had far transcended his title as brigadier general or even his position as the head of the corps of artillery. His experience in erecting the military machinery and channeling supplies and ordnance from various states, his diplomacy with congressional delegates and various governors and French allied commanders, along with his talent as a strategist and battlefield technician, meant that he influenced nearly every move the army made. No other man possessed the wide array of skills that Knox had developed in the course of the war or could step in as his replacement without crippling the Continental military. Washington could not plan any campaign without Knox at his side.

Washington therefore informed Greene on Saturday, October 14, that he, not Knox, had been appointed to lead the Continental Army's southern department.

Writing the news of Greene's promotion to South Carolina congressman John Mathews on October 23, Washington expressed his faith in Nathanael while alluding to the difficulties the southern commander would face: "I think I am giving you a general; but what can a general do, without men, without arms, without clothing, without stores, without provisions?"[22]

Washington spelled out to Congress just how vital Knox had become to the army after news arrived that delegates promoted William Smallwood of Maryland to the position of major general. Washington viewed the promotion as a purely political move based upon "the principle of a state proportion" of top generals. Building an officer corps based on geography rather than merit threatened the most outstanding generals in the army, foremost among them Knox. Washington wrote to New Hampshire congressman James Sullivan on Saturday, November 25, warning that if Knox were passed over for promotion due to political appointments, "he will undoubtedly quit the service; and you know his usefulness too well not to be convinced this would be an injury difficult to be repaired."[23]

A month later, Washington wrote New York congressman James Duane that the army could not lose Knox or pass over his promotion and risk his resignation: "I am well persuaded that the want of him at the head of the artillery would be irreparable."[24]

Lucy had left Boston with the couple's two children and accompanied Henry as the army moved into winter quarters at New Windsor, New Jersey, near Morristown. They took up lodging in a small, quaint farmhouse in a secluded wooded area a short distance from the artillery park. Washington and Lafayette brought Francois-Jean de Beauvoir, Chevalier de Chastellux, a major general under the command of Rochambeau and one of only forty members of the French Academy, to visit Knox's home. Knox received them, standing at the head of his artillery, which had been formed in a manner that mirrored artillery formations of the best European armies. Knox wanted to demonstrate that the American artillery corps, which he had built and trained virtually from scratch, met the standards of the leading armies in the world. The monumental nature of this achievement was not lost on Chastellux, who nodded in wonder that Knox had been able to develop into a first-class officer and produce a professional artillery corps without attending a renowned military academy or without experience in the military prior to the war. Chastellux later wrote of Knox: "From the very first campaign, he was entrusted with the command of the artillery, and it has turned out that it could not have been placed in better hands." Chastellux believed that Du Coudray, the career French artillery general who had tried to replace Knox earlier in the war, was far inferior to Henry as an officer.

Knox was at his likable best with Chastellux. With a wink, Knox explained that he would have been happy to greet the esteemed Frenchman with a full military salute of booming cannon fire, except that British soldiers were posted on the opposite side of the river, and he did not want rouse them for battle. Knox rode with Washington and the French general down the wooded trail that led to his rural lodging. Chastellux was touched by the sight of Henry's family following him to war. "We found [Lucy] settled in," Chastellux later recalled, "at a little farm where she had passed part of the campaign, for she never quits her husband. A child of six months and a little girl of three years old formed a real family for the general." He described Knox as "very fat, but very active and of a gay and amiable character."[25]

As winter weather set in, Henry dreaded the thought of another miserable season in which the army was ill-fed, ill-clothed, and again neglected by Congress and the states. Many men wanted to return home rather than face another year of deprivation in the Continental army. Henry wrote to his brother on Saturday, December 2 that the soldiers were fighting for people who had failed to support them: "We depend upon the great Author of Nature to provide subsistence and clothing for us during a long and severe winter; for the people, whose business, according to the common course of things is to provide the materials necessary, have either been unable or neglected to do it."

To William, Knox poured out his feelings of concern over the plight of the enlisted men and expressed his admiration at their resolve: "The soldier, ragged almost to nakedness, has to sit down at this period, and with an axe—perhaps his only tool, and probably that a bad one—to make his habitation for winter. However, this, and being punished with hunger in the bargain, the soldiers and officers have borne with a fortitude almost superhuman." Knox told himself that each of these men would someday return home to a hero's welcome and bask in the gratitude of his wartime achievements. He tried not to entertain the thought that the soldiers who had borne such suffering would be greeted with apathy by their countrymen. He told William: "The country must be grateful to these brave fellows. It is impossible to admit the idea of an alternative.[26] Yet he and other officers were concerned that the resentment running through the ranks was a powder keg ready to explode.

By the end of the year, some soldiers had reached their breaking point and decided they could no longer take the missing paychecks, the starvation, and neglect by the national and state governments who had sent them to war. At 9 P.M. on Monday, January 1, 1781, several noncommissioned officers and privates from Pennsylvania stormed from the barracks at Morristown, carrying their muskets and swords, and shouted for others to join them in a march to Congress to demand their back pay. They carted off mobile artillery and raided ammunition to fire on any troops that stood in their way. Commissioned officers ordered the mutineers to stop and placed themselves in the path of the angry men. In the confusion and shouting, shooting erupted, with both officers and enlisted men killed. Nevertheless, the dissidents were not dissuaded, but marched down the road to Philadelphia in full gear.

Knox received an urgent message from Washington, who was uncertain if the unrest would spread through other regiments in the army, that Henry must travel immediately to Connecticut, Rhode Island, Massachusetts, and New Hampshire to make a direct appeal for supplies to help keep the army together. In a circular to New England leaders, Washington said he was sending Brigadier General Knox to solicit help "that you may have every information that an officer of rank and abilities can give of the true situation of our affairs." For the army to make it through the winter, Knox needed to bring back money, flour, and clothing, especially shirts, vests, breeches, stockings, and coats.[27]

The mutineers marched to Princeton, New Jersey, where they stopped and settled in at the campus of the university. There the renegades set up a board to issue their demands to Congress. After a tense few days and the intercession of General Anthony Wayne, the mutineers agreed to terms with congressional delegates. The entire Pennsylvania regiment was allowed to take a furlough until March, and the mutiny ended, although some of the instigators were later hanged.

Knox returned to Boston with news of the mutiny and to plead the case of the neglected Continental soldiers before the Massachusetts general court and governor John Hancock. On Tuesday, January 16, he detailed their grievances: "The non-commissioned officers and soldiers of Massachusetts, in common with the troops of the other states, labor under a total want of pay for a year past." Soldiers who had joined regiments in Massachusetts were especially bitter that their enlistment bounties had been deducted from their pay, a practice not done in other states. "Until this measure shall be repealed, no peace or contentment can be expected in the Massachusetts line." Henry explained that the recent mutiny was symptomatic of the perpetual suffering throughout the army and that this latest revolt could trigger even more unrest and cost America the war. "The revolt of the Pennsylvania line may possibly infuse new ideas and induce them to extend their expectations further. From the critical situation of the revolted troops it is probable that part of those terms will be a new bounty," he stressed.[28]

Knox's warnings proved prophetic. Four days after his address to Massachusetts leaders, a group of New Jersey soldiers ignored their officers and marched out of camp at Pompton. Washington responded by sending General Robert Howe and 500 troops to put down the mutiny. The dissidents then reentered the Pompton camp and barricaded themselves in. A loyal force of soldiers surrounded them and restored military order. Two of the mutiny's ringleaders were sentenced on the spot and shot.

Knox meanwhile proceeded to the other New England states and made similar appeals. By mid-February, he reported to Washington that the "Eastern States are awakened by the late tremendous crisis to greater exertions than have hitherto been made."[29]

The mission had demanded diplomacy and judgment to deal with sensitive state governments. Knox had to gently convey to the representatives the frustrations of the soldier, subtly chiding them for neglecting their own fighting men and tugging at their sense of embarrassment or shame for the condition of their home-state troops. Yet at the same time, Knox could not alienate the leaders who could offer help. Washington praised the success of Knox's mission in a letter to him on Wednesday, February 7, adding that his tactful approaches to the various state leaders all had "my entire approbation and merit my warmest acknowledgments for the zeal and judgment so conspicuous in them. The result of your applications, I hope, will be as satisfactory as it will be beneficial to the troops."[30]

But Knox had a litany of reasons for not placing his trust in the promises of state leaders, regardless of how genuinely concerned and committed they seemed to be over the plight of the suffering soldiers. Past applications for help had been received with enthusiastic offers to send food, clothing, and money and prayers. Yet time and time again, those supplies and wages never materialized. Upon his return to New Windsor, this fact played on

Knox's mind as he sat down to estimate ordnance needs for the 1781 summer campaign with the French. The report had become a yearly ritual of frustration for Henry. As he calculated the number of shells, the amount of shot, gunpowder, cannons, and other equipment needed for a possible siege of New York, the inventory seemed like a wish list. He wondered where these materials would come from. Unfortunately for him, he was in charge of obtaining them. He felt compelled to express his anxiety over the prospect of meeting the army's equipment needs to Washington in a letter written Tuesday, February 13: "Your Excellency well knows our present supplies of ordnance & stores are totally inadequate to the demands of an arduous operation—I have strained every nerve public and private to obtain an ample supply of shot & shells."[31]

Knox's counterparts elsewhere did not have to deal with the problems that besieged him in trying to run his various departments. Unlike the more established military institutions of other nations, America did not have well-grooved channels in which to route supplies and no long-established arms manufacturers. Other countries were not split into thirteen state governments, each with its own bureaucracy contributing to the national army. Ordnance and artillery officers of other nations did not have to solicit for critical supplies from national and state legislators and deal directly with civilian contractors.

Knox wondered if he had been given an impossible task that no amount of heroic effort or ingenuity could overcome. Upon his shoulders rested all the hopes of the American army—and even those of the county itself. He worried that, despite his best efforts, the supplies would not come and that the failure would leave him in dishonor and disgrace.

EIGHT

YORKTOWN AND SURRENDER

Henry Knox had little reason to believe that the military campaign of 1781 would put an end to the war. Another year of failed promises and unrealistic expectations appeared to lay ahead.

He did not entertain high hopes as he saddled up and rode with Washington along the winding roads through Connecticut farmland to Wethersfield for a meeting with the top French generals, Rochambeau and Chastellux. On Monday, May 21, the generals decided to again attempt to lay siege to New York, even though similar plans had been aborted the previous two summers because the Americans lacked virtually everything required for such an ambitious undertaking. And no siege could be successful without help from the French navy.

But Knox and the other generals believed they had no other option. Part of their dilemma lay in the fact that the enemy British fleet could transport troops up and down the American seacoast whenever needed. Unless the French fleet arrived to cut off the British sea-lanes, Washington and Knox thought it pointless to march the army south to help Greene when the redcoats could simply send fresh reinforcements to outnumber their troops. The only other option was again to plan an assault of New York City.

Knox meanwhile closely read reports of Greene's struggles against Lord Cornwallis's army in the Carolinas. Greene continued to lead the British on hopeless chases that were beginning to wear out British supplies and patience. Green was demonstrating his own exceptional strategic and tactical abilities. He even split his force to leave the British searching for him, then attacking and retreating before the enemy could capture his army. Greene explained to the French ambassador in America, the Chevalier de La Luzerne: "We fight, get beaten, and fight again."[1] Knox was amazed at Greene's resilience, writing to a friend: "[Without] an army, without means, without anything, [Greene] has performed wonders."[2]

Knox was given the order to put the nation's ordnance and artillery in motion for an all-out siege of New York on Monday, May 28. In issuing the command, Washington acknowledged the limitations that Knox faced as well as his own personal doubts about the probable success of the siege: "Put the whole business for the operation (so far as is within your reach) in the best train of execution, which our embarrassed circumstances will possibly admit."[3]

Henry tried to offset the shortfalls in the army's supplies by pressing the governors of Massachusetts and Connecticut for loans of gunpowder from state magazines. Much of his time was spent supervising the military laboratories and overseeing the preparation of munitions, and drilling his artillery corps. As if these responsibilities were not exhausting, he even found time to come up with an improved baking plan to feed the army.

Lucy, in the third month of another pregnancy, accompanied Henry along most of the trip as the army moved to Peekskill, where the French and American armies were ordered to rendezvous. She parted with her husband to travel farther north along the Hudson with Mrs. John Cochran, the wife of the director general of the military hospitals of the United States. The two women proceeded toward Albany to find lodging. The separation was difficult for both of Henry and Lucy. They both had fears over her health and that of the unborn child. Her resentment over the war was growing, leading her to plunge into bouts of self-pity, especially over being deprived the company of her husband while facing the significant risks of pregnancy. She continued to lament the loss of her father, mother, sister and brother, yet thought that even the loss of her childhood family would be bearable if Henry was not absent for so much of the time. The separation left Henry feeling lonely as well. His family had become a lifeline that helped sustain him in the midst of war. Lucy was critical to his own stability, he believed, and his brother William, had returned to Boston after his trip to Europe.

Yet Henry's duties took priority over his personal wishes. As the army geared up for the summer military campaign, he had a myriad of errands to attend to each day. Rochambeau's 4,000-man French force arrived at Dobbs Ferry the first week of July, and both armies made final preparations to attack New York City while awaiting the arrival of the French fleet. As Knox watched the 9,000-man force of American and French soldiers intermingle, he was pleasantly surprised at the lack of friction between the men and the air of camaraderie that pervaded. The French sympathized with the under-manned Continentals and viewed their struggle for independence and liberty through a romantic prism.

He was clearly weary with the war, however. He wrote to William on Friday, July 20, that he longed for an end of the conflict, for the return of civilian life, and to be able to build a permanent family estate for the comfort of his family: "Although we are not bad in accommodating ourselves to our circumstances, yet I sensibly feel the inconveniences we labor under, to accumulate in proportion to the increase of our family. I sincerely pray God that the war may be ended this campaign, that public and private society may be restored."[4]

To his brother, he expressed his frustration over the weak national government and state rivalries under the Articles of Confederation, which he already viewed as inadequate and as a severe handicap to their effort: "The vile water-gruel governments which have taken place in most of the states are totally disproportioned to the exigencies of the war, and are productive of sentiments unworthy an energetic republic."

He passed his thirty-first birthday on Wednesday, July 25, longing for his family. Lucy's twenty-fifth birthday, a week later, proved painfully lonely. Writing to her from Dobbs Ferry on August 3, Henry lamented: "Yesterday was your birthday. I cannot attempt to show you how much I was affected by it. I remembered it, and humbly petitioned Heaven to grant us the happiness of continuing our union until we should have the felicity of seeing our children flourishing around us, and ourselves crowned with virtue, peace, and years and that we both might take our flight together, secure of a happy immortality."

As he wrote, his mind fluctuated from heights of optimism to pangs of doubt over the upcoming military campaign. In one sentence he observed, "All is harmony and good fellowship between the two armies. I have no doubt, when opportunity offers, that the zeal of the French and the patriotism of the Americans will go hand in hand to glory." Yet in the very next line, he admitted that much of the army's plans were still unsettled and that it was entirely uncertain when the French fleet might arrive—if at all. The prospect of victory seemed to be founded on sanguine dreams rather than solid expectations. "You know what we wish, but we hope more at present than we believe."[5]

Lucy wrote back expressing her bitterness over the war and the tribulations she endured: "Oh, horrid war, how hast thou blasted the fairest prospects of happiness. Robbed me of parents, sisters and brother, thou are depriving me of the society of my husband, who alone can repair the loss."[6]

All of the plans for the siege of New York were canceled when Washington received a dispatch on Tuesday, August 14, telling him that Admiral Francois Joseph Paul Comte de Grasse, commander of the French fleet, declined to sail to New York because he did not want to risk his ships navigating the difficult waters of the harbor and the Hudson. De Grasse proposed instead to sail up the Chesapeake with twenty-nine ships; his fleet would be available for a joint campaign of just a few weeks. Washington and Knox were crestfallen. All their hopes of ending the war by liberating New York had failed to materialize once again as the war dragged on into its sixth year.

Trying to salvage the situation, Washington then made the pivotal decision of the war by ordering his army to immediately march 450 miles south to hook up with the French fleet in an attempt to trap Cornwallis's army, which was now entrenching in Yorktown, Virginia, trying to regroup after vainly chasing Nathanael Greene.

This change of plans meant that Knox had to devise ways to transport artillery from New York to Virginia and to find siege guns that could be shipped to the battlefront. The task must have reminded him of his Ticonderoga mission. It demanded the utmost celerity, since the Continental and French armies were engaging in a foot race to reach Yorktown before the British could reinforce Cornwallis or rescue him by sea. Despite the pressures on Knox, he made plans for the pregnant Lucy and their children to accompany him on the trip to Virginia. Clearly he could no longer live without them nearby.

The vanguard of the American army crossed the Hudson at King's Ferry at 10 A.M. Monday, August 20, and Knox had the artillery over the following day. He then rode ahead of the marching troops with Washington and Rochambeau, playing interpreter as well as general. His brother realized that Henry's study of French was proving invaluable once again. Writing from Boston on August 22, William observed: "I suppose, from necessity, you are obliged to speak much French, which, you having long since learnt the theoretic part, I should imagine from a little practice, would come easy to you. I recollect, the Compte Rochambeau doesn't speak a word of English."[7]

The army paused a few days near the New York Harbor to help foster the illusion that it was merely circling around New Jersey to reach Sandy Hook as part of a plan to begin the siege of New York. But on Thursday, August 30, the troops were ordered to face south and to march as quickly as possible

more than 200 miles to the Head of Elk at the northern tip of the Chesapeake. The race was on. Within a day or two, the British would realize that
Cornwallis was in grave danger.

Knox arrived with Washington in Philadelphia on Friday. At 3 P.M., they
paid their respects to Congress and met with delegates to discuss the war. Afterward, they dined with congressional president Thomas McKean and finance superintendent Robert Morris. Knox enjoyed a pleasant evening as he
watched marine vessels fire salutes into the night sky, and countless toasts
were hoisted to the officers and the army. As night fell, the city was illumi-
nated with every kind of light, and Washington and Knox were greeted as heroes in the streets.

The next morning, Knox continued to scramble to equip the army. Once
the bombardment and attack began against the British at Yorktown, he believed that the stream of firepower could not slacken even momentarily to
allow the enemy to escape or strike a counterblow. In Philadelphia, he drafted
an appeal to the congressional Board of War asking that all the arms that
could be spared be shipped to the Chesapeake. He asked for three-pound, six-
pound, and twelve-pound guns, hundreds of rounds of ammunition, 300,000
musket cartridges, 20,000 flints, priming wires, musket balls, 1,000 powder
horns, and a supply of cartridge papers.

Knox continued south. Lucy had accepted an invitation to stay with
Martha Washington at the Mount Vernon estate for the duration of her pregnancy and the siege of Yorktown. She planned to enroll their daughter, Lucy,
in a boarding school in Philadelphia, and to then proceed with their son,
Henry Jackson Knox, to the Washington home in mid-September.

Knox had little time to pause. As he was traveling through Chester,
Pennsylvania, on Wednesday, September 5, an express rider galloped up
with an urgent dispatch for Washington. The message reported the news
that de Grasse's fleet had already landed at Jamestown, at the mouth of the
Chesapeake. Knox and Washington had been concerned that the French
fleet would fail to arrive—or that it would sail to the wrong location. Suddenly that groaning weight was lifted from their shoulders. For the first
time in the war, they had the advantage over the British. The fleet, it was reported, included twenty-five large battleships or ships of the line, each with
two decks of cannon, ranging from sixty-four to eighty guns. The fleet also
included six smaller frigates along with 3,000 French infantry soldiers to reinforce Lafayette, whose force was holding Cornwallis at Yorktown. An
overjoyed Washington and Knox turned back on the dusty road to look for

Rochambeau, who was traveling down the Delaware River. As Rochambeau's boat approached a wharf to dock, the Frenchman was surprised to see the normally taciturn Washington frantically waving his hat and screaming that the fleet had arrived.

That same day, the masts of nineteen battleships and seven frigates sailing under the Union Jack were spotted. The English fleet decided to attack the French ships. A three-day sea battle ensued in which the French emerged victorious, forcing the British ships to sail back to New York for repairs. Knox realized that Cornwallis would have no relief from the sea, and was now pinned in.

His optimism over the prospect of victory soared, and he sent a letter to William, inviting him to travel to Virginia to witness the triumph he anticipated. Writing on Saturday, September 8, from Head of Elk, he laid out his expectations: "I rob my business of one moment to inform you that our army is here, and will, with all its stores, proceed down the Chesapeake in three days. Our prospects are good; and I shall hope to inform you, in fifteen days, that we have had Cornwallis completely invested. The Count de Grasse's squadron is a noble one, and will prevent the enemy's escape by water. I hope we shall do it by land."[8]

Knox beamed as the allied forces marched into place at Williamsburg, Virginia, on Saturday, September 15, for a grand military review. Washington and Rochambeau stood at the head of the columns. The force, which had swelled to 16,000 troops, amply outnumbered Cornwallis's 7,000-man army. At Cape Henry on Monday, Knox accompanied Washington and Rochambeau as they boarded the cutter *Queen Charlotte* and sailed to the French fleet for a meeting with de Grasse aboard his towering, 110-gun *Ville de Paris*. The aristocratic de Grasse, who was born into one of France's oldest families, was cordial and cooperative, if condescending. He kissed Washington on both checks, referring to the American commander in chief as "my dear little general." After an awkward silence, Knox laughed to defuse any tension.

The American and French officers agreed on most of the strategic issues for carrying out the siege and naval blockade. They would encircle Cornwallis's fortifications with a series of trenches and then bombard the British with cannons and heavy siege guns landed from the French fleet and from Knox's artillery. But de Grasse was clear that he could not continue the blockade around Yorktown beyond November 1 because of the advent of the hurricane season. For Knox, this added even more pressure to come up with all the necessary ordnance and artillery for the siege to succeed. To complicate matters, on the return trip aboard the *Queen Charlotte*, contrary winds prevented Knox and Washington from stepping back on land until Saturday, September 22.

Knox learned that the British fortifications at Yorktown were more extensive than previously believed. He drafted an augmented list for the congressional War Board, which Washington passed on with Knox's advice, writing: "General Knox has for these reasons thought it prudent to increase his requisition for shot and shells. His letter accompanies this and I must entreat the board to use every exertion to forward the articles required, and as expeditiously as possible, for should we be under the necessity of slackening our fire on account of the consumption of our stock, the loss to us would be perhaps irretrievable."[9]

Knox's artillery regiment sailed down the Chesapeake and reached Williamsburg by Friday, September 28, where a shortage of horses and wagons hindered their efforts to disembark the cannon. The rest of the army, meanwhile, marched to the outskirts of Yorktown and enveloped Cornwallis's force.

Newspapers across the continent reported the march of the American and French army and a major campaign in Virginia, raising patriot expectations for victory. Nathanael Greene wrote Knox on September 29 with hopes that Henry was engaged in the Yorktown campaign. "My Dear Friend, Where you are I know not, but if you are where I wish you, it is with the General [Washington] in Virginia; the prospect is so bright and the glory so great, that I want you to be there to share in them."[10]

Yorktown was a small village of about sixty houses, many of which were strikingly elegant. The town sat on a sandy plain on the south side of the York River, which flowed into the Chesapeake. The American and French armies set up below the town, pinning Cornwallis against the river. The strategy of the siege was to dig protective trenches closer and closer to the British post and then to bombard the position into submission. To his surprise, Knox found, that Cornwallis conceded his farthest line of fortifications at Pigeon Quarter and three other redoubts, evacuating them without a fight under the belief that his only escape could come by sea. To Lucy, Henry wrote on Monday, October 1, "[T]his gives us a considerable advantage in point of time. Our prospects are good, and we shall soon hope to impress our haughty foe with a respect for the continental arms."[11]

For Knox, a respect for Continental arms was a paramount concern. He wanted to impress not only the British, but also the French, that the corps of gunners which he had built up from an ill-equipped unit of amateurs could stand professionally alongside the best artillery regiments in the world.

Working in secret through an unusually dark night and into the morning hours of Sunday, October 7, approximately 1,500 men moved tons of dirt to dig out the first parallel of American and French trenches. Knox's friend Major General Benjamin Lincoln, who had been exchanged as a prisoner after his capture at Charleston, led the force. Knox sent wagons carrying cannons and ordnance and bags swelling with sand to arm and fortify the trench. The work proceeded in near silence, undetected by the redcoats, who woke that morning to peer through the early dawn light to find their opponents burrowed in a mere 600 yards away.

Cornwallis sent infantrymen to clear this trench, but they were repulsed with heavy musket fire. Knox directed his regiment as the soldiers worked tirelessly to drag the heavy guns through the trench and then nestled the cannon barrels between small openings in the earthen fortifications. Knox proudly stepped aside on Tuesday, October 9, to allow Washington the honor of igniting the bore hole of a heavy siege gun and ceremoniously discharging the first shot from the American battery at Yorktown. The shell was clearly visible as it streaked across the sky and landed with precision within the British compound, setting off cheers throughout the American ranks.

The Continental artillery corps then continued an uninterrupted stream of fire that produced a relentless, unnerving, and deafening roar. Cornwallis would later recall: "The fire continued incessant from heavy cannon, and from mortars and howitzers throwing shells from 8 to 16 inches, until all our guns on the left were silenced, our work much damaged, and our loss of men considerable."[12] The soldiers could see the red-hot shells racing overhead. During the day, they appeared as black balls streaking across the horizon while giving off a high-pitched whistling sound. The shells spun wildly as they hit the earth, excavating craters and then bursting to throw shots flying in all directions. Cannonballs that plunged into the York River sent up streams of cascading water. British boats went up in flames under the bombardment, their rigging and sails creating small infernos. At night, the blazing shells curved across the star-filled heavens and fell like streaking meteors, each followed by a tail of fire.

Knox took personal command of the artillery guns. The French general Chastellux would later write of Knox's performance at Yorktown: "We cannot sufficiently admire the intelligence and activity with which he collected from different places and transported to the batteries more than thirty pieces of cannon and mortars of large caliber for the siege. . . . The artillery was always very well served, the general incessantly directing it and often himself pointing the mortars: seldom did he leave the batteries."[13]

While working in a redoubt, Knox and his former artillery officer, Alexander Hamilton, who was now an infantry colonel, argued over whether it was unmanly to yell at the sight of an oncoming shell before jumping for cover behind the wooden blinds set up to shield the men from explosive shrapnel. Washington had issued orders approving warning cries to save lives. Hamilton, however, maintained that being a soldier meant braving danger without flinching. As he and Knox argued, the cry went up that a shell was headed their way. Knox moved toward the blind, and Hamilton grabbed Henry as a shield. They battled each other to reach protection just seconds before the shell exploded. Knox told Hamilton not to use him as a breastwork ever again.

It was not uncommon during the day for Knox and Washington to walk above the trenches to view the damage done by the artillery. Once a nervous aide pleaded with them not to endanger themselves in the open. Washington responded with bravado. If the aide felt unsafe, he should retire to the protection of the trenches. Knox could see not only the destruction to the British earthworks, but the human toll of the battle. The exploding shells and cannonballs often sent limbs and other body parts flying through the air. It was a repeat of the ghastly vision that had haunted him earlier in the war.

The British tried to return fire as American and French soldiers burrowed through the sandy earth, moving closer and closer to their earthworks. The allied soldiers covered the excavation with planks that provided shelter from musket fire and shells. The work was dangerous, however, and skirmishes erupted daily, causing casualties on both sides. By Thursday, October 11, Knox noticed that the combined American and French artillery barrage had silenced nearly every British gun. He no longer attracted enemy fire when he emerged from the trenches. A second line of parallel trenches was begun that same day, this time only 300 yards from Cornwallis's main works. By nightfall, the trench extended more than half a mile as the excavation pushed in both directions toward the York River on each side of the town. To reach the water, however, the allies needed to capture two remaining British batteries that protected the enemy flanks. During the night of Sunday, October 14, Alexander Hamilton led a furious bayonet charge to capture one of these redoubts. This daring act of heroism would give Hamilton the battlefield glory and military fame he had so long coveted and would enable him to launch his political career.

The French captured the other redoubt that night; soon the British would be completely walled in by trenches. More cannons were moved into place at the captured redoubts, giving the allied armies more than 100 guns firing without interruption and making the entire peninsula shake beneath the soldiers' feet.

Cornwallis's men pleaded with their commander to allow them to attempt a desperate escape through the allied line. He relented, and 350 British soldiers charged the nearest allied trench at four in the morning on Tuesday, October 16. The redcoats were able to spike four French cannons and two of Knox's guns before being sent back in a cloud of musket fire. In the ensuing firefight, Knox received a minor wound in the ear.

At ten the next morning, a curious figure appeared on the British parapet as the American and French cannons continued their bombardment. A moment later, a British officer emerged on the top of the fortification, waving a white handkerchief high above his head. Slowly the cannon fire slackened, and Knox and the other soldiers could hear the drummer's plaintive cadence beating out a parley. All eyes watched as the officer and drummer began to walk toward the allied line. An American officer ran to meet them. The drummer returned to his line, and the British officer was blindfolded with a handkerchief. He was then led to Washington and the other allied generals. Washington demanded that Cornwallis surrender unconditionally, terms that, by the end of the day, the British general knew he had no choice but to accept.

Knox and his brother William watched more than 7,000 dejected British troops march out to surrender their arms on October 19. Many, bitter over the defeat, threw their muskets violently against the ground to render them useless. Knox rounded up 7,320 muskets from the defeated soldiers.

Henry had been sensitive to what he viewed as a haughty attitude displayed by the British during the war and a lack of respect for the American army. He took a personal satisfaction that the captured English soldiers were forced to accept similar terms to those once offered Major General Lincoln upon his capitulation of Charleston, which included a denial of American independence by refusing to allow his force to display the Stars and Stripes or to play a patriotic song as they laid down their arms. The redcoats now were required to march with their colors cased rather than unfurled and without patriotic music. The English officers looked only at their French opponents and drew Knox's indignation by failing to make eye contact with the Americans. Cornwallis begged off attending the surrender by complaining of an illness.

General Lincoln was given the honor of accepting the sword of the British general Charles O'Hara as a token of the English defeat. Knox dashed off a letter at eight o'clock that evening for William to carry to Lucy at Mount Vernon. "I have detained William until this moment that I might be the first to *communicate good news* to the charmer of my soul. A glorious moment for America! This day Lord Cornwallis and his army march out and pile their arms in the face of our victorious army. The day before yesterday he desired commissioners might be named to treat the surrender of his troops, the ships, and everything they possess."[14]

While the British were reluctant to give the American army credit for their defeat, they did not fail to express their awe over the destructive efficiency of Knox's artillery corps. In his memoirs, the French general Chastellux wrote: "The English marveled no less at the extraordinary progress of the American artillery, and at the capacity and instruction of the officers. As to General Knox, but one-half has been said in commending his military genius. He is a man of talent, well instructed of a buoyant disposition, ingenuous and true: it is impossible to know him without esteeming and loving him."[15]

After the victory, Knox collected a considerable amount of artillery; the British had not lacked firepower at Yorktown. The American and French artillery had outdueled a potent British gun corps, armed with 74 brass cannon and 140 iron cannon.

Knox's performance in the victory drew high praise from Washington, who lauded him in his dispatch to Congress announcing the victory. Washington reiterated this praise of Knox and his artillery counterpart in the French army in orders to the troops on Saturday, October 20, expressing gratitude to "General Knox and Colonel [François Marie, Comte d'Aboville] for their great care and attention and fatigue in bringing forward the artillery and stores and for their judicious and spirited management of them in the parallels [trenches]."[16]

The triumph at Yorktown did not immediately end the American Revolution, but Knox realized that the British war effort was critically wounded. The English had been driven from the interior of the continent and now clung to two harbors. In a letter written on October 21 to John Jay, the American minister to Spain, Knox explained his view of the significance of Cornwallis's defeat: "The consequences will be extensively beneficial. The enemy will immediately be confined to Charleston and New York and reduced to a defensive war of these two posts, for which they have not more troops in America than to form adequate garrisons.[17]

For Knox's performance at Yorktown, Washington recommended to Congress that he be promoted to the rank of major general. Writing on Wednesday, October 31, he stated that "the resources of his genius have supplied, on this and many other interesting occasions, the defect of means: his distinguished talents, and services equally important and indefatigable entitle him to the same marks of approbation from Congress."[18]

Knox went to Philadelphia with Washington as most of the Continental Army filled in the trenches around Yorktown before heading back to the fortifications along the Hudson River in November. With no major campaign to plan, Henry could turn his mind to private life and spend more time with Lucy. She gave birth to another son, whom they named Marcus Camillus, after a Roman soldier and statesman whom Knox admired, on December 10. The couple spent several anxious days after the birth, plagued by the memory of Julia's death just eleven months earlier. The boy appeared to be healthy as Lucy nursed him to strength. George Washington was named the child's godfather. His brother William was unable to restore the bookstore in Boston to profitability. William chose to embark on a second business trip to Europe. He set sail in 1781 with plans to visit the Netherlands and France in an attempt to further establish business connections.

The end of the war seemed to be in sight, and Knox could bask in the glory of Yorktown. From South Carolina, Nathanael Greene wrote Knox on the same day as the birth of Henry's son: "Your success in Virginia is brilliant, glorious, great and important. The Commander-in-chief's head is all covered with laurels, and yours so shaded with them that one can hardly get sight of it."

Greene and Knox were both enjoying the kind of military fame that they had so coveted as youths. Now, however, they wished only for an end to military life. Greene wrote to Knox that "I hope at some future day, when the cannon shall cease to roar, and the olive-branch appears, we shall experience a happy meeting. Your great success in Virginia gives me the most flattering hopes that this winter will terminate the war."[19]

Knox's duties took a diplomatic turn. An agreement needed to be reached with the English to exchange thousands of prisoners of war, which included not only soldiers but civilians who had been rounded up by both sides. Washington appointed Knox and Gouverneur Morris to negotiate the prisoner exchange. Morris was a cock-eyed former New York congressman who now lived in Philadelphia and served as assistant to the secretary of finance. Morris, whose artful pen would later help write most of the U.S. Constitution, continued to be a prominent figure in Philadelphia despite the handicap of having had a leg amputated after falling from his carriage in 1780.

The task of exchanging American and British prisoners was complicated, not only because the costs of housing them had to be negotiated equitably but because the British commissioners still refused to concede American independence. They had every reason to stall the talks while the British government decided whether to renew the war.

Knox and Morris set out on Tuesday, March 12, 1782, for Elizabethtown, New Jersey, to meet with the British commissioners, William Dalrymple and Andrew Elliot. Knox was familiar with Dalrymple, who had commanded the two British regiments that occupied Boston from 1768 to 1770.

While Knox was in Elizabethtown, Congress finally acted on Washington's recommendation that Henry be promoted to the rank of major general. A year earlier, Congress had resolved that promotions to major general should be based on age rather than battlefield performance. This mandate left Knox, who was not yet thirty-two, ineligible for promotion for several years. Washington sent several letters to congressional leaders lauding Knox's performance and supporting his promotion. A month after the victory at Yorktown, Rhode Island delegate James Varnum rose in Congress to declare the seniority system "stupid," particularly in Knox's case. After deferring the question for several months, delegates granted Knox the appointment of major general on Friday, March 22, "on account of his special merit and particularly for his good conduct at the siege of Yorktown."[20] Knox became the youngest major general in the America army.

Negotiations with the British over prisoner exchanges began on Sunday, March 31, and were immediately bogged down with postponements and heated debates. Knox soon realized that no agreement could be reached and that the British commissioners had no authority to grant the American demands. He and Morris rejected several of the British proposals, including an offer to exchange American citizens taken prisoner directly for British soldiers. Knox thought this policy would quickly augment the number of British troops in America without adding any more soldiers to the American army. The British meanwhile refused to agree to several of Knox and Morris's demands, including a requirement that all Americans held anywhere in the world by English authorities be set free. At the time, Henry Laurens, the former president of Congress and father of Washington's aide John Laurens, was being held in the Tower of London.

Negotiations grew much tenser when Knox and Morris learned that an American officer had been murdered while being transported from New York to Elizabethtown to be exchanged. The victim, Captain Joshua Huddy, was hanged on Friday, April 12, by the British captain Richard Lippincott in retaliation for the earlier murder of a loyalist named Phillip White. A sign pinned to Huddy's hanging body served as a warning to anyone who did harm to loyalists: "Up goes Huddy for Phillip White."

Knox and Morris sent Washington a report of the murder on Tuesday, April 16. Washington immediately polled twenty-five of his officers as to what action to take, and twenty-two said that a demand should be made for Lord Clinton to turn over Huddy's murderer to the Americans.

Washington demanded that Lord Clinton hand over Lippincott or else a British captain would be randomly chosen by lots from the ranks of prisoners and be put to death in retaliation and to discourage further mistreatment of U.S. prisoners. The British responded that Lippincott had been tried by the British and exonerated after claiming that he was merely following orders, although Clinton denied sanctioning Huddy's murder.

Unable to resolve the issue, Knox and Morris decided to wrap up the prisoner-exchange negotiations without reaching accord on any of the key issues. Feeling slighted and disrespected by the English commissioners, Knox wrote to Washington on Sunday, April 21, explaining why he believed the negotiations had been fruitless: "Every circumstance we observed convinced us, that we never shall obtain justice or equal treatment from the enemy, but what were in a position to demand."[21]

In the same letter, Knox thanked Washington for his hand in Congress's decision to promote him. "I cannot express how deeply I am impressed with a sense of your kindness, and the favorable point of view in which you have regarded my feeble attempts to promote the service of my country. I shall ever retain, my dear General, a lively sense of your goodness and friendship, and shall be happy indeed if my future conduct shall meet with your approbation."[22]

Knox and Morris reported the circumstances surrounding the failed negotiations to Congress, where delegates approved their decisions "for refusing to admit the other propositions insisted on by [the British]."[23]

Knox and Lucy then packed their bags and, with their three children, left Philadelphia in mid-May and headed to Newburgh, New York, along the Hudson, where Washington had set up his headquarters and the American army was encamped to keep watch over the British in New York City.

Washington's hard-line policy seeking retaliation for Joshua Huddy's murder, meanwhile, became highly controversial and stirred emotions across the country. Many believed that the tactic of threatening to execute an innocent British soldier as a way to discourage acts of violence against American prisoners was misguided and unjust. Charles Asgill, a nineteen-year-old captain from a well-connected British family, was chosen as the potential victim of the policy, and sympathy for him welled. Among those who questioned the practice was Alexander Hamilton, who suspected that Knox might feel equally uncomfortable with it. Writing from Albany on Friday, June 7, Hamilton reminded Knox of his role on the board that decided to execute Major John Andre: "If we wreak our resentment on an innocent person, it will be suspected that we are too fond of executions." Hamilton recognized that Washington placed a great deal of faith in Knox's judgment. He conveyed his opinion through Knox, in part because his relationship with Washington had become strained in the previous year. To Knox, Hamilton appealed: "I address myself to you upon this occasion, because I know your liberality and your influence with the General."[24]

Knox, however, responded that as draconian as the measure appeared, he knew of no other way to prevent the murder of American prisoners by loyalists. He told Hamilton that Washington was not fond of executions and did not take the drastic policy of hanging innocent soldiers lightly. Asgill's life was spared, and he was set free by Washington later that year after mounting pressure from the French.

Knox set up his headquarters at West Point, where he placed the artillery park and stored much of the army's ordnance. Ever fond of entertaining, he orchestrated a celebration of the birth of the French Dauphin, the son of Louis XVI. A huge shelter was erected, and thousands of soldiers attended the daylong festivities. The highlight of the event was the evening ball. Lucy was in high spirits and enjoyed herself dancing. A newspaper reported that "His Excellency General Washington was unusually cheerful. He attended the ball in the evening and with a dignified and graceful air, having Mrs. Knox for his partner, carried down a dance of twenty couple in the arbor on the green grass."[25]

After Knox had a chance to thoroughly inspect West Point and its tributary posts, he was alarmed at their vulnerability. Due to the army's depleted finances, he had been unable to transport shells and ordnance to the fort. Knox did not think it could withstand more than ten days under siege and estimated that as much as 1,000 tons of ammunition were needed to secure its safety. In July, he urged Washington to place more emphasis on such a vital link in the country's defenses, whatever the costs.

Washington decided to appoint Knox as the commander of West Point. In notifying Knox of the assignment on Thursday, August 29, Washington wrote: "I have so thorough a confidence in you and so well am I acquainted with your ability and activity that I think it needless to point out to you the great outlines of your duty."[26]

With Knox in charge at West Point, the location attracted prominent visitors, especially French officers and Henry's colleagues in the army. He had a reputation for hospitality and was popular in the army, and had forged many sincere relationships. Washington later commented on Knox's character and the attraction he represented to visitors in a letter to Benjamin Lincoln, saying that Henry possessed "great politeness, hospitality and liberality."[27]

As Knox went about strengthening the defenses at West Point, his family was again struck with personal tragedy. Their nine-month-old son, Marcus Camillus, died on Sunday, September 8. The usually buoyant Knox was thrown into a deep despondency. The loss of the child, coupled with his concern for Lucy and the emotional toll of the war, all left him grasping to cope with his pain. In a letter written to Washington just two days after his son's death, he tried to make sense of the loss: "I have the unhappiness my dear General to inform you of the departure of my precious infant, your Godson. In the deep mystery in which all human events is involved the Supreme Being has been pleased to prevent his expanding innocence, ripening to such perfection as to be a blessing to his parents and connections, when by their advanced years they may find every comfort necessary to sweeten life rendered bitter by a thousand stings."

In the same letter, Henry expressed his concern over whether Lucy could endure the anguish of losing another child. "Mrs. Knox by leaning upon the great principles of reason and religion will be enabled I hope to support this repeated shock to her tender affections."[28]

Washington expressed his sympathies in a letter written on Thursday, September 12: "In determining to submit patiently to the decrees of the all-wise disposer of human events, you will find the only true, and substantial comfort under the greatest of calamities. In addition to this, the lenient hand of time will no doubt be necessary to soothe the keener feelings of a fond and tender mother."[29]

Henry found it difficult to shake off his depression. He became more solitary than at any time in his life. Letters from even close friends languished without reply. Benjamin Lincoln, who had been named secretary at war under the Confederation government, became concerned.

Lincoln persisted with the correspondence, however, and in one letter raised the issue of pay for the soldiers, suggesting that the men might accept a lump sum for their pension because many state leaders opposed the plan to grant half pay for life. Knox responded apologetically for staying out of touch but expressed his willingness to help lobby Congress and state leaders on behalf of the Continental soldiers.

Knox felt unsettled by fears that another revolt would erupt if the soldiers continued to be denied the emoluments promised prior to enlistment. If the troops decided to march to Philadelphia to coerce Congress at musket point to pay them, the unrest would lead to the ruin and disgrace of the army, Knox believed, and the suffering and sacrifices endured by the troops throughout the Revolution would have been in vain. To Knox, the unblemished honor of the Continental force after eight years of hardship needed to be preserved, even at a high cost.

But there was even a larger issue at stake. If a battle over pay erupted between the army and civil authorities, America's attempt at republican government might be sacrificed in the struggle and the goal of the revolution might be lost to intemperate passions.

Yet Knox also had to consider his own financial situation. Since the beginning of the war, he had longed to provide Lucy with a stable home and give her the style of life she had been accustomed to during her youth. She had been the daughter of privilege and the wife of misfortune. His wife and children had been deprived of countless comforts during the conflict, and Knox felt an acute anxiety over whether he would receive his considerable back pay. How could he tell Lucy that their trials and tribulations would not be rewarded by peacetime prosperity?

To Secretary at War Lincoln, he penned on December 20, 1782: "The expectations of the army, from the drummer to the highest officers are so keen for some pay, that I shudder at the idea of their not receiving it."[30]

The concern that ran through the ranks was that once the threat of the war had passed, the soldiers would be completely forgotten and their promised wages and benefits would not be paid. The British evacuated Charleston in December, raising hopes that the fighting was all but over but also reducing the need for the army, and therefore lessening the urgency to pay the soldiers.

The issue of how to compensate the soldiers was hopelessly complicated. Congress had made the promise of half pay for life to many of the soldiers before the Articles of Confederation were approved. Under the Articles, Congress had no constitutional power to fulfill its promises because it had no authority to levy taxes and could only "recommend" to the states that money be raised to compensate the troops. The Articles also required that nine of the thirteen states agree on any proposal.

Knox realized that getting nine of the thirteen states to agree on a pension was unlikely, especially since leaders and residents in nearly every state believed they had already contributed more than their fair share to the war effort. Added to these complications, the prospect of peace led to poor attendance in Congress. Georgia declined to send any delegates to Philadelphia, and many delegates did not show up for sessions.

While his home-state Massachusetts legislature debated whether to grant its soldiers half pay for life, Congressman Samuel Osgood complained to Knox in a December letter that the costs would be "excessive" because the plan rewarded soldiers who served a short stint equally with those who served for the entire war. Osgood objected that Massachusetts would create problems in poorer states by agreeing on half pay for life, and therefore he could not support it.[31]

Knox felt that with the fighting over, it was a little late for delegates and state leaders to find reasons not to fulfill promises made to soldiers. His high standing in the army and his popularity among the troops made him a point man on the issue. He received a constant stream of letters from Philadelphia keeping him abreast of congressional deliberations over the matter from delegates as well as correspondences from fellow officers such as Baron von Steuben and well-connected friends such as Gouverneur Morris in the finance department.

Several Continental officers came together in December to plan a strategy to plead with Congress to address the army's pay grievances. Knox was chosen as chairman of the committee and drafted a petition offering a solution. As the promise of receiving their due pension of half pay for life appeared more and more unattainable, he offered Lincoln's compromise of a lump-sum pension payment. He also stated that the men's back pay, which he calculated to be between $5 million and $6 million, should be paid immediately to prevent unrest or mutiny.

Major General Alexander McDougal, Colonel Matthias Ogden, and Lieutenant Colonel John Brooks were deputed to travel to Philadelphia and present the Knox-authored memorial to Congress.

The men arrived in Philadelphia on Sunday, December 29. James Madison, a thirty-one-year-old Virginia delegate, commented in a letter that the feeling around Congress was that the proposals offered in Knox's memorial "breathe a proper spirit and are full of good sense."[32]

McDougal, Ogden, and Brooks had nearly depleted their funds for the trip waiting to meet with a congressional committee. McDougal, suffering from painful bouts of rheumatism, was initially too ill to attend sessions, and asked if committee members could meet at his lodging at the Indian Queen Tavern to discuss the collective grievances of thousands of soldiers. But delegates balked that this would be beneath "the respect due to themselves, especially as the mission from the army was not within the ordinary course of duty," Madison recorded in his notes of the debate.[33]

McDougal, Ogden, and Brooks addressed Congress on Monday, January 30, detailing the suffering of the soldiers and their need for some kind of immediate payment while offering to compromise on the pension. They expressed the deep bitterness and anger among the soldiers that Congress had found ways to pay civilian salaries but had failed to come up with funds for men who risked their lives on the battlefield. Madison recorded in his notes: "General McDougal said that the army [was] verging to that state which we are told will make a wise man mad," and "They mentioned in particular that the members of the legislatures would never agree to an adjournment with[out] paying themselves fully for their services."[34]

Horatio Gates, meanwhile, had returned to the army after his disgrace at the Battle of Camden, South Carolina. His aides began to circulate rumors in Philadelphia that the army was ripe for revolt and would not lay down their arms and return to civilian life until being fully compensated for their service. Alexander Hamilton, who had been elected to Congress the previous July, was uncertain how much weight to ascribe to the whispers. It was said that many soldiers in the army grumbled that Washington was too delicate in dealing with civilian leaders to adequately pressure or threaten politicians on behalf of the men. Hamilton reestablished his relationship with Washington, writing him on Thursday, February 13, 1783, that he should use his influence with elected officials. Hamilton also advised Washington to confide in discreet officers within the army to manage the building torrent of anger within the ranks in order to avoid the risk of appearing to interfere with civil authority. Hamilton suggested: "General Knox has the confidence of the army & is a man of sense. I think he may be safely made use of."[35]

As weeks dragged on, Congress failed to act decisively on the pay issue. Knox was crestfallen when he received news from McDougal that Congress was content to leave the soldiers' compensation in doubt. He replied on Friday, February 21, from his headquarters at West Point, pouring out his exasperation and writing for the eyes of congressmen: "The complex system of government operates most powerfully in the present instance against the army; who certainly deserve every thing in the power of a grateful people to give. We are in an unhappy predicament indeed, not to know who are responsible to us for a settlement of accounts."

Knox pointed out that the soldiers had placed their faith in the integrity of national and state legislatures in enlisting and fighting. "Posterity will hardly believe that an army contended incessantly for eight years under a constant pressure of misery to establish the liberties of their country without knowing who were to compensate them or whether they were ever to receive any reward for their services."

In the same letter, Knox gently warned political leaders: "My sentiments are exactly these. I consider the reputation of the American army as one of the most immaculate things on earth, and that we should even suffer wrongs and injuries to the utmost verge of toleration rather than sully it in the least degree. But there is a point beyond which there is no sufferance. I pray we will sincerely not pass it."[36]

In the political morass surrounding the issue, Knox pinpointed the source of the complications: America's framework of government under the Articles of Confederation. As early as the opening months of 1783, he began writing to influential leaders with the extraordinary suggestion that a constitutional convention be called together to replace the existing form of government with a compact that created a stronger union and gave the national legislature the authority to tax.

On the divide between supporters of a strong union and supporters of strong states, Knox clearly fell on the side supporting a vigorous national government. As a member of the Continental army, Knox's allegiance to Massachusetts had yielded to his love of country, which for him was "the United States of America." Many American political leaders—including Virginia's Thomas Jefferson, Patrick Henry, and Richard Henry Lee and Massachusetts'

John Hancock and Samuel Adams—viewed the states as more important than the national government, which was seen as little more than a skeletal framework that loosely held the alliance of states together. Many state leaders feared a strong national government as much as they had detested British oversight. The national army only brought fears of a growing national government and bureaucracy.

Knox was convinced that the army was the victim of provincial thinking. As a member of a Continental army, he had mixed with soldiers from all regions of the country. Within the ranks of American army, state allegiances blurred and disappeared as soldiers forged close, lasting relationships with men who hailed from towns throughout America. The troops looked to Congress as their government and "the United States" as a single country rather than a wartime alliance of thirteen individual provinces.

Knox was closer to the Virginian Washington and Rhode Island's Nathanael Greene than he was to any of the political leaders from Massachusetts. Henry explained his perspective within the army in a letter to Gouverneur Morris, written the same day that he had written McDougal with his frustrations: "The army generally have always reprobated the idea of being thirteen armies. Their ardent desires have been to be one continental body looking up to one sovereign. . . . It is a favorite toast in the army, 'A hoop to the barrel' or 'Cement to the Union.'"

Knox believed that Congress needed to be empowered with the authority to levy taxes to raise general funds for the army. The absence of taxing authority in the national government had plagued the army during the war.

In his letter to Morris, Knox then made a remarkably prescient recommendation: "As the present Constitution is so defective, why do not you great men call the people together and tell them so; that is, to have a convention of the States to form a better Constitution?"[37]

He made this recommendation four years before the U.S. Constitutional Convention would be held in Philadelphia. And Gouverneur Morris, to whom he made this suggestion, would one day draft much of the language for the U.S. Constitution.

Knox observed that the slight regard with which the states viewed Congress was a telltale sign of the poor design of the Articles of Confederation and was manifestly demonstrated by the delegates' poor attendance. To McDougal, he wrote on Monday, March 3: "It is enough to sicken one to observe how light a matter many states make of their not being represented in Congress—a good proof of the badness of the present constitution."[38]

In Philadelphia, wild rumors of unrest within the army continued to circulate, including the claim that soldiers had vowed not to disband and return to civilian life until all their claims had been settled. Delegates began to fear that the army might seize control of the government and launch a counterrevolution. Both the army and the Congress seemed suspicious of the other. In a letter written to Washington on Thursday, February 27, Virginia congressman Joseph Jones openly wondered if the country was bordering on a civil war: "When once all confidence between the civil and military authority is lost, by intemperate conduct or an assumption of improper power, especially by the military body, the Rubicon is passed and to retreat will be very difficult."[39]

While Knox vociferously stated the soldiers' case for compensation, he was careful not to inflame an already volatile situation. Knox's letters to friends in Philadelphia painted a more moderate view of the army's discontent, as James Madison noted in a letter to Edmund Randolph on Tuesday, March 4, 1783: "A letter from General Knox is in town which I understand places the temper and affairs of the army in a less alarming view than some preceding accounts."[40]

At Washington's main camp at Newburgh, New York, about ten miles from West Point, agitators played on the anger of the men and stoked feelings of resentment toward Congress. On Monday, March 10, an artfully written anonymous letter was circulated among the officers. Referred to as the Newburgh Address, it sharply criticized Congress for failing to live up to its promises and recommended that Congress's authority be disregarded and that the soldiers take the law into their own hands if not given what had been promised. The letter also advised soldiers to refuse to fight any longer for the country but to leave the populace defenseless and open to foreign attack, telling the men to "retire to some yet unsettled country, smile in your turn and mock when their fear cometh on."[41] The address called for the soldiers to gather for a meeting the next day to take up their cause.

It was not commonly known at the time, but the address was written by Major John Anderson, an aide of Horatio Gates.

Washington and Knox moved quickly to, at the very least, redirect the movement. They believed that General Gates had been behind the rumors buffeting Philadelphia as well as the Newburg Address. Washington issued general orders on Tuesday expressing his disapproval of the irregular meeting proposed in the address, yet acknowledging that the men had reason for complaint. He recommended that the soldiers instead wait four days, until a

Saturday meeting, to decide a course of action and allow passions to subside. Washington tied Gates's hands by appointing him to chair the meeting. The commander in chief also realized that the trust and respect that the men had for Knox could help defuse the situation. In preparing for the meeting, Knox wrote up a series of moderate resolutions that he hoped would preserve the honor of the army, and he sent off letters to influential leaders pleading for help.

He wrote a letter the following day to McDougal in Philadelphia, imploring delegates to act: "Endeavor, my dear friend, once more to convince the obdurate of the awful evils which may arise from postponing a decision on the subjects of our address."

He prayed that the situation would not end in the disgrace of the army and believed that those who played on the injured pride and desperation of the soldiers acted criminally: "I sincerely hope we shall not be influenced to actions which may be contrary to our uniform course of services for eight years. The men who, by their illiberality and injustice drive the army to the very brink of destruction, ought to be punished with severity."[42]

That same day, he wrote Secretary at War Lincoln in Philadelphia explaining that a Saturday meeting had been called by Washington in response to the Newburgh Address: "What will be the result, God only knows. Congress ought not to lose a moment in bringing the affairs of the army to a decision. Push the matter instantly, my dear sir, with all your might and main."[43]

On Saturday, March 15, Knox and hundreds of soldiers gathered at noon at a newly built, 40-foot by 70-foot building at Newburgh. The room was silent as all eyes rested on Washington. A second letter had been circulated around the camp that warned: "Suspect the man who should advise to more moderation and longer forbearance."[44]

Washington, however, rose and walked slowly to the pulpit, as if the first signs of age and infirmity were beginning to creep into his unusually hardy constitution. He pulled a piece of paper from his coat and unfolded it in an unhurried manner as if for dramatic effect. He squinted slightly as he strained to read his own writing. Apologizing, he reached into his waistcoat and pulled out spectacles that had been given to him by the astronomer David Rittenhouse. None of the men had ever seen him wear eyeglasses before. In a hushed, barely audible tone, he said, "Gentlemen, you will permit me to put on my spectacles, for I have not only grown gray, but almost blind, in the service of my country."[45]

Many of the most battle-hardened veterans were visibly moved. Washington reminded the men that he had shared their every hardship since the beginning of the war, that he had never left them even during the most difficult times. He observed that the anonymous writer of the incendiary documents could not be a friend to the country but rather was an insidious foe; quite possibly he had even been sent by the British or loyalists in New York to destroy the harmony between the army and the American government in an effort to prove that republic government could not survive. Washington told his men: "The secret mover of this scheme (whoever he may be) intended to take advantage of the passions, while they were warmed by the recollection of past distresses, without giving time for cool, deliberative thinking."

Knox was deeply touched by Washington's words. He thought the performance "masterful" and that the moment displayed not only Washington's gift as a natural leader but an index of the noble tenor of his heart.

Knox was fully aware that history contained only a few examples of military leaders who declined to take control of the country's government when given the opportunity and blessed with an army behind them that was willing to follow. At that moment, Washington demonstrated his commitment to republican government and that his service during the war had not been born of blind personal ambition. Rather than seizing the opportunity at Newburgh, Washington chose to reaffirm his subordination to Congress and remind the army of its obligation to subvert its will to civil authority.

At the conclusion of Washington's words, Knox moved his series of resolutions thanking Washington for his patriotism and a statement of the men's unwavering attachment to the commander in chief as well as their "unshaken confidence in the justice of Congress." A resolution was also offered to make an unequivocal statement that "the officers of the American army view with abhorrence and reject with disdain the infamous proposals contained in a late anonymous address to them."

Horatio Gates realized that as chair of the meeting, he had little choice but to put the resolutions up for a vote. They passed unanimously.

Knox was overjoyed. In his eyes, the soldiers had acted with a sense of honor and patriotism that deserved the esteem of their countrymen. To Benjamin Lincoln, he wrote on Sunday describing the meeting: "The occasion, though intended for the opposite purposes, has been one of the happiest circumstances of the war, and will set the military character of America in a high point of view. If the people have the most latent spark of gratitude, this generous proceeding of the army must call it forth."[46]

On Saturday, March 22, Alexander Hamilton brought the issue of the officers' pay before Congress. Delegates voted to grant the officers five years' pay plus 6 percent interest in lieu of half pay for life. When told about the congressional vote four days later, Washington wondered if the news was too good to be true, but sent Knox a note overflowing with gratitude for his role in supporting the issue: "My dear Knox: Such as I have, I give unto *thee*. God grant the news may be true. But whether it is, or not, the late conduct of the Army will redound to the immortal honor of it."[47]

NINE

CONFEDERATION SECRETARY

C ongress declared an end to hostilities with Great Britain on April 11, 1783, bringing the American Revolution to a close after eight arduous years of fighting. Even before the soldiers laid down their muskets, Henry Knox was already envisioning the future of the U.S. Army in a peacetime America. In the coming months, thousands of troops would return home, and many political leaders wanted to dismantle the army completely, believing that a strong but idle military posed a threat to republican government and democracy.

After watching the Continental army struggle to train officers and soldiers during the Revolution, Knox felt that it would be foolish to tear apart the force and all that the soldiers had built only to resurrect it when inevitable war clouds threatened. Just six days after Congress declared peace, he submitted a detailed blueprint for a standing peacetime army, including the recommendation for a United States Military Academy at West Point.

Calling the West Point fort "the key to America," Knox wrote to George Washington on Thursday, April 17, stressing that the post was vital to keep open even during peace. To save money, he recommended the dual purpose of locating a forty-student military school on the grounds and devising a curriculum that embraced "the whole theory of the art of war as practiced by the most enlightened nations."[1] He also laid out a complete plan to raise state militias that might be used as building blocks for a national army in time of war.

Washington wholeheartedly supported Knox's plan and sent it with his endorsement to Congress. Although delegates did not immediately act on Knox's proposals, most of his recommendations were eventually enacted.

Knox wanted to maintain the wartime relationships in the American and French armies. In April 1783, he drafted a plan for an organization he called "The Society of Cincinnati," named after a Roman soldier who gave up military power. The first meeting of the Society of Cincinnati was chaired by Alexander Hamilton and held at Fishkill, New York on the evening of Tuesday, May 13. Knox was elected secretary of the society, and Washington was named president in his absence.

The society was opposed by many civilian leaders such as Thomas Jefferson, Elbridge Gerry, and John and Samuel Adams, who believed the group represented the beginnings of a noble class of soldiers.

The pace of life in a peacetime army gave Knox more time to spend with his family. He was thankful that after missing the births of several children during the war, he was with his family on Wednesday, July 6, when Lucy gave birth again. She bore a son whom they christened Marcus Camillus, the same name as that of the infant who had died the previous year. Knox was thrilled to write to friends that both Lucy and the children were in a perfect state of health.

Washington placed Knox in charge of the army in August while he visited Congress to pave the way for his return to Mount Vernon. In weighing his return to civilian life, Knox was apprehensive about his own prospects. Unlike Washington, he had no profitable estate to which to return. Henry could not imagine himself returning to the humble life of a store owner.

Knox decided to attempt to create a position for himself in the government as "master general of ordnance." Writing to Washington on Wednesday, September 17, 1783, he stressed the need to maintain the country's military stores and offered himself as a candidate for the job: "Although my expectations and wishes are for private life, yet if any office similar to the above, should be formed upon the broad scale of national policy, I might if thought worthy, find it convenient to give it my zealous assistance."[2]

He also sought a more prestigious national office. Benjamin Lincoln, the secretary at war under the confederation government, wanted to resign and recommended Knox as his successor. Washington wrote Henry on Thursday, October 23, pledging to lobby Congress to secure his appointment.

On Sunday, November 2, Knox commanded that Washington's farewell orders to the army be read to the troops at West Point. Upon hearing the orders, which discharged the men and allowed them to return home to their families, the soldiers shouted with joy and embraced. Knox was moved to pen a reply to Washington from the army that expressed the wish that "when you quit the stage of human life, you may receive from the unerring judge the rewards of valor exerted to save the oppressed, of patriotism and disinterested virtue."[3]

The following day, thousands of troops packed their bags and headed home. As the commander of the forts around New York City, Knox notified the British commander, General Guy Carleton, on Sunday, November 9 that the time had come for the British to leave America. Carleton responded that his troops would begin moving out from the outlying skirts around New York on Thursday, November 20.

Knox took possession of the city on Tuesday, November 25, 1783, riding at the head of a long procession. He greeted residents, riding in a row of eight officers, in a triumphant parade into the city that had been occupied for seven years. Once again he saw his former headquarters at the foot of Broadway, and could remember that frantic morning when he and Lucy had spotted the British fleet from the window of their home. The officers were followed by a row of political leaders who waved to residents shouting in celebration. The speaker of the state assembly appeared, and then Washington and New York governor George Clinton arrived.

Knox and Washington enjoyed a tranquil week of celebrations. The governor hosted a lavish dinner for the officers, and tavern owner Samuel Fraunces, an ardent patriot, hosted a victory banquet at his establishment at the corner of 54 Pearl Street and Broadway. The tavern had been a favorite meeting place for the New York Sons of Liberty before the British occupation.

On Thursday, December 4, Washington called together Knox and fellow officers for a farewell meeting at noon at the elegant Long Room at Fraunces Tavern. Washington planned to leave New York that day and head to Annapolis, where Congress was temporarily sitting, and then to resign his commission. In an order issued to Henry that same day, Knox was named as Washington's successor as the commander of the American army: "Finding it essential to the public interest that you should superintend the posts and military affairs in this department until some further arrangement, or until the pleasure of Congress shall be known; I have therefore to request that you will remain in service."[4]

Knox was in an emotional mood as he considered his own relationship with Washington; with the exception of his wife, undoubtedly it was the most significant relationship of his life. Knox had shared all of Washington's military successes during the Revolution, from the liberation of Boston in 1776 to the victory at Yorktown five years later. For his part, Washington had warmly supported Knox and his career at every step, from the beginning of his career as a citizen volunteer to his entrance into the Continental army at the rank of colonel and through his rise to major general. But their relationship was not merely professional. Washington, who had no children of his own, had played a paternal role in Henry's life. Lucy had stayed at Mount Vernon during one of her pregnancies. Knox had developed a sincere admiration for Washington.

After the officers waited for several moments in the Long Room, Washington finally appeared. He did not act like the austere commander that they were accustomed to seeing even during the most trying times. Washington was visibly emotional, willing to let loose the grip on his feelings within the circle of comrades. He filled his glass with wine, turned his attention to the downcast faces around him, and tenderly said: "With a heart full of love and gratitude, I now take leave of you. I most devoutly wish that your latter days may be as prosperous and happy as your former ones have been glorious and honorable."

Washington drank to the toast and then told the men, "I cannot come to each of you to take my leave, but shall be obliged to you, if each of you will come and take me by the hand."[5]

Washington then turned and immediately grabbed Knox's hand. Choked with emotion, Washington appeared unable to utter a word. He wept openly as he wrapped his arms around Henry and embraced him, kissing him on the cheek.

One by one, all of the officers made their way to Washington at the head of the room. They shook his hand and accepted his embrace, but no one spoke. A dignified silence pervaded the room, as if any words would be inadequate to convey the feelings between men who had experienced so much anguish and triumph together. Hardened veterans brushed back tears, and Knox fought to maintain his composure.

Washington then walked slowly from the room and exited the tavern, passing a corps of light infantry posted outside. He proceeded to the wharf at Whitehall, where he planned to embark on a barge that would ferry him across the Hudson River to Paulus Hook in New Jersey. Knox and the other officers looked forlorn as they followed Washington in procession, perhaps never to parade behind the general again. As the barge pulled away, Washington removed his hat and waved it slowly, bidding a silent adieu to Knox and the other officers.

★ ★ ★ ★

Knox's mission in the final months of his command of the army was to dismantle the American force for peacetime. The size of U.S. military dropped to a mere 700 men by late 1783, a skeletal garrison spread thinly over several locations, including the arsenal at Springfield, Massachusetts, and Pittsburgh and the forts in New York. With his duties winding down, he sent Lucy and their three children, Lucy, Henry, and Marcus, home to Boston in December. Henry relinquished the command of West Point in January and headed for home on a chilly Monday, February 9.

He had little choice but to await Congress's decision on appointing a secretary at war or a master of ordnance. Back in Massachusetts, he and his family made a home in Dorchester, not far from the spot where his guns had pounded the British in 1776. The house was a comfortable, picturesque structure owned by an international banker and located on the road to Milton near the Second Congregational Church. One day it would be the summer home of Daniel Webster.

His state legislature tapped Knox for diplomatically sensitive assignments. In the summer of 1784, he was named as a member of a three-man commission to negotiate a treaty with the Penobscot Indians, whose presence along the Penobscot River was alarming white settlers in the district of Maine. Knox and the commission convinced the Penobscot to move farther west. He was also asked by Massachusetts to help settle a border dispute between the people of the British-owned Nova Scotia and the American residents in Maine. The border, according to the peace treaty, was the river St. Croix, which proved to be a confusing line of demarcation because of its many tributaries and winding stretches. The problems were too complicated for a quick resolution, and despite Knox's efforts, the issue would remain unresolved for years.

Knox welcomed the work because he was having trouble finding a way to make a living. After spending nine years in the military, he had trouble adapting to civilian life, and found himself ill suited to return to the life of a merchant. Henry's certificates for his service in the army were not yet redeemable for their full value because of the state of American finances. Meanwhile, his family expenses were growing as Lucy gave birth to daughter in November, whom the couple named Julia, the same name as the daughter who died in infancy in 1779.

While awaiting word of Congress's decision to fill the secretary at war post, Knox received a letter from Washington written Wednesday, January 5,

1785, continuing their ongoing complaint with the anemic national government under the Articles of Confederation. Washington was exasperated by what he viewed as myopic thinking and provincial jealousies in Congress and among the state leaders, which seemed to work to oppose any positive step for the country as a whole. "Would to God our own countrymen, who are entrusted with the management of the political machine, could view things by that large and extensive scale upon which it is measured by foreigners, and by the statesmen of Europe, who see what we might be, and predict what we shall come to," he complained to Knox.

"In fact, our federal Government is a name without substance: No state is longer bound by its edicts than it suits *present* purposes, without looking to the consequences. How then can we fail in a little time, becoming the sport of European politics, and the victims of our own folly?"[6]

Knox thought that the national problems stemmed not solely from the politicians but from inherent flaws in the design of the Articles of Confederation that created a federal government with little power over the thirteen states. He responded on Saturday, January 13, 1785, conceding that the federal government could not act decisively on any measure, including funding the army or even clothing the small peacetime garrisons of soldiers. Knox believed a completely new constitution needed to be written: "We are entirely destitute of those traits which should stamp us one nation—and the Constitution of Congress does not promise any capital alteration for the better."[7]

Even filling a national office such as the job as secretary at war seemed to be a difficult task for Congress. After leaving a post so critical to the nation's defense vacant for sixteen months, delegates finally elected Knox on Tuesday, March 8, 1785. He was nominated by the Virginian James Monroe, a fellow member of the Society of Cincinnati. Unfortunately for Knox, the cash-strapped Congress approved a modest annual salary of only $2,450 for the post, a sum that was $1,000 less than he had expected.

Some congressional delegates were embarrassed by the meager compensation for such a prominent national office and urged Knox to take the job with the realistic expectation that the salary would soon be increased. Congressman George Partridge of Massachusetts wrote to Knox the same day as his nomination that "[i]t is rather doubtful with some of your friends whither you will accept on account of the deficiency of salary . . . but I have no doubt but there will be an addition."[8]

Delegate Rufus King of Massachusetts was also apologetic, writing Knox on Monday, March 14, asking him to be patient concerning compensation:

"This sum is too small, but in the existing situation of affairs it was not practicable to obtain a larger sum. The office is certainly a very honorable one; and the U.S. will not suffer the head of so very respectable a department to remain unsupported."[9]

King pressed Knox's sense of duty and admitted that the country's humble military structure had fallen into such a delinquent state that only Knox could revive it: "If the wishes of your particular friends, and the entire satisfaction of the states would be an inducement to your acceptance, you cannot refuse. I could not excuse myself, did I not make these observations to you; the present wasting condition of the department requires the hand of a master; if you decline, I fear we shall be driven into an election, that will neither aid the dignity, nor preserve the interest, of the union."

Knox suppressed whatever disappointment he felt over the salary and expressed only a sense of honor for the appointment. Nine of the eleven states represented in the poorly attended Congress had elected him. The position provided him with a respectable office in keeping with his status as a major general and prevented him from the humiliating embarrassment of stepping into a humbling job in private life. Writing to the secretary of Congress, Charles Thomson, on Wednesday, March 17, Knox thanked the delegates for their faith in him: "I have the most grateful sentiments to Congress for this distinguishing mark of their confidence."[10]

Knox realized that the task of setting up the nation's defense would be mired in complications because of the deadlocked Congress. He believed the main flaw of the Articles of Confederation was its provision that a three-quarters majority approval was required to pass any legislation, including military funding. As a result, just three states could block any proposal. Instead of majority rule, the Articles set up a scenario where the minority held sway. In Knox's eyes, this arrangement was undemocratic. In a letter of Tuesday, March 29, to the Connecticut general Samuel Parsons, he explained: "A democracy so constituted that a small minority shall operate to check the great majority cannot be upon durable principles."[11]

Knox made plans to travel to the seat of the national government in New York by mid-April and for his family to join him in June. Before he left his home state, he and Lucy laid claim to tens of thousands of acres of land that had legally fallen to her as the last remaining Flucker in America. She was the maternal granddaughter of General Samuel Waldo, who had led a militia regiment that successfully captured the French fort at Louisburg in 1745. Waldo garrisoned the post out of his own expenses until a regiment of British regular soldiers arrived. To compensate him, the governor of Massachusetts granted him a patent for a tract of virgin land in Maine. Waldo died before laying hold of the land, and the patent fell to the Fluckers. Henry and Lucy's claim, which if resolved would solve their money troubles, was still unsettled when he headed off to New York.

Upon arriving at the capital and taking an oath of office, Knox began assessing the army's needs. When he took over the war office, its total staff consisted of just two people, a secretary and a clerk. No "War Department" yet existed, and therefore his title was "Secretary at War." The entire U.S. military, modest though it was, fell under his control along with the responsibility for the government's relations with American Indian tribes. He was required to take stock of all U.S. troops, military stores, ordnance, supplies, and clothing and report to Congress and to travel to each of the military posts annually, in keeping with his recommendation that the nation's western frontiers be garrisoned with U.S. soldiers.

The Knox family moved into a home on Bowery Lane in the city. Henry enjoyed a rare season of domestic tranquility, surrounded by his four children. His daughter Lucy had reached ten years of age and his youngest child, Julia, was a year and a half old. Lucy was again pregnant.

A note arrived from Lafayette, who had returned to Paris bearing news of Knox's errant brother, William, who had remained in Europe throughout the previous four years to nurse his mental health, and during that time had lost touch with his family as he traveled on business and personal matters. At Henry's urging, the marquis located William but was dismayed to find that he had become a recluse. Lafayette tried to ease Henry's concern, promising in the letter written Wednesday, May 15, 1785, that he would take William into his own home and oversee his care. This provided some relief for Henry, who feared that his brother was going insane. In letters to friends, he expressed his willingness to spend everything he had to find a cure for him. A letter soon arrived from a family friend, however, stating that William had already set sail for Boston.[12]

Knox meanwhile found that his concerns over running the War Office proved well founded. Even with the army under his control, he was unable to engineer improvements due to ongoing fears of a standing army and a formidable central government and budget concerns. His dream of establishing a military academy at West Point met with opposition because of costs and objections that such a school would foster a military class that would dominate society.

Knox realized that in order to fulfill his obligation to manage the nation's defenses, he needed to change minds concerning men in uniform. As he saw it, the problem with traditional military arrangements had arisen because armies had been controlled by kings and nobles for their personal welfare, not the general welfare. The relationship between the military and civilian authorities in most countries had not been planned but had evolved uneasily through wars and political turmoil. He believed, however, that America's army could be planned in the tranquility of peace, using wisdom, experience, and reason.

He thought that if America represented an experiment in republican government, then a blueprint for an army could be designed in the same innovative spirit. If armies had traditionally threatened liberty, then a new kind of army could be created that actually supported democratic ideals.

Throughout the early months of 1786, Henry worked to flesh out his vision for a workable, democratically driven American army. Recognizing that many political leaders would never consent to a formidable national army, he set down a plan designed to make use of the state militias. He estimated that by raising militias in each state and rotating three years of service, the nation could have an impressive fighting force of 325,000 men.

It was an ambitious plan. After reading a preliminary version, South Carolina congressman David Ramsay conceded its usefulness but wrote to Knox on Sunday, March 12, that he was expecting too much from his countrymen: "I think it is excellent in theory but I fear the supineness of our citizens would make its execution impracticable."[13]

Knox, undeterred, officially unveiled his "Plan for the General Arrangement of the Militia," which filled thirty-four folio pages, on Saturday, March 18, 1786. He opened his proposal with an attempt to change people's perceptions about the military, arguing that soldiers did not have to necessarily represent a distinct class from the rest of the populace; instead, a citizen army could be raised that reflected society's values and could even instill in recruits America's most cherished values. "It is the intention of the present attempt to suggest the most efficient system of defense which may be compatible with the interests of a free people," he wrote.

At the time that Knox was writing, America had not yet established state-run school systems or federal educational programs. There was no cohesive system to foster a national identity or inculcate the principles that the patriots had fought for during the Revolution. He believed that the militias could play a vital role in promoting civic education through military training. "Youth will imbibe a love of their country—reverence and obedience to its laws—courage and elevation of mind—openness and liberality of character—accompanied by a just spirit of honor. In addition to which their bodies will acquire a robustness—greatly conducive to their personal happiness as well as the defense of their country."

Although his plan was well ahead of its time, it became the basis for training programs for decades to come and was included in National Selective Service manuals well into the twentieth century. It even served as the basis in 1920 for the formation of the Citizens Military Training Camps, which ran from 1921 to 1940.

Knox's plan also provided something of an index of his mind. He did not view himself exclusively as a military leader but as builder of the republic, willing to play the role of architect in creating institutional pillars of American society. He was not content to borrow foreign patterns in formulating the design for the U.S. military; rather he looked at the problem from the vantage point of a statesman and political theorist. For Knox, the American military needed to embody distinctly American ideals.

A congressional committee later in 1786 recommended that Knox's plan be sent to each state and that it could "not only put their militia upon a very respectable but formidable footing."[14]

Knox continued to maintain his correspondence with friends who had served in the army during the war. He was delighted that Congress ordered that two cannons be presented to Nathanael Greene to commemorate his heroic service, and he supervised the engraving of inscriptions in his honor. But life had soured for Greene, who felt little joy in the public honors that he had once so desired. Like many soldiers, he had returned home deeply in debt. Greene still owed money for rations purchased for his men. North and South Carolina and Georgia had voted to grant Greene large plots of lands taken from loyalists. He sold the land to help pay his wartime expenses, but the proceeds did not completely satisfy creditors.

Greene moved his family to a Georgia estate called Mulburry Grove, fourteen miles north of Savannah, and hoped for a season of prosperity, only to endure crop failures and other setbacks. Knox was among those who lobbied Congress to provide relief for Greene's debts. Henry received a letter from Greene dated Sunday, March 12, 1786, thanking him for the inscriptions on the cannons but confessing: "I have been so embarrassed and perplexed in my private affairs for a long time past, which originated in the progress of the war, that I have but little spirit or pleasure on such subjects."

Greene's letter conveyed a pervading sense of hopelessness: "My family is in distress, and I am overwhelmed with difficulties; and God knows when and where they will end. I work hard and live poor, but I fear all this will not extricate me." He asked for Knox's advice on an offer from Lafayette to oversee and finance his son's education in Paris.[15] "Let your answer be as candid as I trust your friendship is sincere," Greene implored. Shortly after receiving this letter, Henry was notified that Nathanael Greene had died. He was forty-four, and died surrounded by his wife and friends.

Upon hearing the news, Knox pulled out Greene's most recent letter and read over the words as if to hear his friend's voice one more time. He could recall their first meeting in Boston during the British occupation in 1774 and remember their discussions of military strategy, their shared hopes for military glory. Henry became emotional as he read the letter expressing Nathanael's distress, writing across the margin of the page, "This is the last letter I ever received from my truly beloved friend, General Greene."

Knox was haunted by fears that he might also face poverty in private life. His current position lacked security and did not allow him to save for the future. The nation's economy was mired in depression because of high taxes and inflation. He and Lucy continued to pin their hopes on the Waldo patent, which would provide them with enough land to satisfy their financial needs. He also had to worry about the future of his brother, William, who was now living in Boston and was in need of employment. Henry found a solution to this problem when Samuel Shaw, who served as a clerk in the War office, resigned. Henry quickly hired William as a clerk.

His fears that conditions under the Articles of Confederation would lead to civil unrest were realized when crowds of debt-ridden farmers in Massachusetts began storming country courts on Thursday, August 31, to prevent their land from being taken by foreclosures. Many of the insurgents complained that they had been impoverished by the economic conditions and taxes. Congress immediately sent Knox to his home state to oversee the situation and advise state leaders.

Back in Boston, he found that the issues stirring up the insurgents had grown well beyond tax complaints. Many of the rebels, in fact, had never paid taxes, but were stoked with dreams of creating a society in which all property was publicly owned and private debt was abolished. They proposed paying off any public debts with unfunded paper money. Landowners became frantic that they would be attacked or driven off their land by the insurgents. Everyone looked to the state government, wondering if it was strong enough to repel an attack from the rebels or if the situation would explode.

On September 26, 1786, approximately 500 renegades under Daniel Shays, a former captain during the Revolution and a veteran of Bunker Hill, stormed the state supreme court and demanded that it close its doors.

Knox was embarrassed that the national army could not provide help in reining in the unrest—or even to fully protect its own armory at Springfield. Rumors spread that Shays planned to seize the arsenal of weapons. The Massachusetts governor called up 4,000 state militiamen, who were placed under the command of General Lincoln. The state was bankrupt; donations for the effort had to be coughed up by local businessmen and affluent citizens. The troops were hastily sent to Springfield, where the armory housed 1,300 barrels of powder, 7,000 muskets, and 200 tons of shot and shell. Knox reported from Hartford to Congress on Sunday, October 1, that the number of renegades had quickly swelled to 1,200, and were armed with bayonets, muskets, and even sticks.[16]

The rebels marched to Springfield, where they intimidated the state supreme court from sitting. Knox wrote an urgent note to Congress on October 3, reporting that the national armory was in danger and that the insurgents had formed ranks: "They were embodied in a military manner, and exceedingly eager to be led to action, but the prudence of their leader prevented an attack on the government troops."[17]

It seemed to Knox as if the fabric of society was unraveling. According to intelligence, Shays was gaining sympathetic support in the neighboring states of Rhode Island, Connecticut, and New Hampshire. Many people welcomed the possibility of annihilating all debts. Throughout the crisis, Knox sent regular reports to Mount Vernon to keep Washington abreast of the situation. Writing on October 23, he stated that the country could no longer wait and that a stronger constitution had become absolutely necessary to prevent lawlessness from spinning out of control. If Americans thought that liberty and reason would elevate them above the shortcomings of human nature, they had been sadly mistaken: "Our government must be braced, changed or altered to secure our lives and property. We imagined that the mildness of our government and the wishes of the people were so correspondent that we were not as other nations, requiring brutal force to support the laws."

Congressional delegates led by Alexander Hamilton decided to use an economic conference slated for May 1787 to overhaul the Articles of Confederation. Knox pressed Washington's sense of duty and patriotism in admonishing him to support the convention and changes to the Articles: "Every friend to the liberty of his country is bound to reflect, and step forward to prevent the dreadful consequences which shall result from a government of events."[18]

Washington became alarmed as he read Henry's words. He quoted extensively from Knox's letter in a November 5 note to Virginia congressman James Madison, lamenting that the British had apparently been correct in scoffing: "Leave them [Americans] to themselves, and their government will soon dissolve."[19]

Knox, characteristically, took it upon himself to come up with a solution, and created a blueprint for a new constitution, which he sent to Washington in a letter written Sunday, January 14, 1787, offering it for consideration at the Philadelphia convention: "Where I to presume to give my own judgment, it would be in favor of the convention, and I sincerely hope it may be generally attended."

Knox's "Plan for a General Government" resembled to a remarkable degree the eventual outline of the U.S. Constitution. Knox seemed almost prescient in his ability to anticipate the country's next step and offer sound suggestions that would closely reflect the eventual remedy. He already believed that the Articles of Confederation could not merely be altered to solve the nation's problems; the present form of government needed to be swept away and a completely new plan formulated. He told Washington that it was not premature to begin thinking of a new constitution even before the Philadelphia convention convened: "It would be prudent to form the plan of a new house before we pull down the old one."

In laying out his solution, Knox acknowledged that an ideal American constitution should establish a democratic republican government but that the federal government needed the power to oversee the state governments and set the course for the entire country.

His proposed a federal government that would consist of three branches: an executive, a legislative, and a judiciary. The legislature would be bicameral, with House members serving one- to three-year terms and senators serving five- to seven-year terms. The executive would be chosen to a seven-year term by the House and the Senate, and could be impeached by House members and tried in the Senate. The judiciary would be chosen by the executive and serve for life during good behavior.

Knox thought that the sovereignty of the United States should reside with the federal government: "The laws passed by the general government to be obeyed by the local [state] governments."

He realized that his proposal for a powerful central government was a drastic step, but he believed the time for half-measures had long passed. To Washington, he stated: "To attempt to establish less will be to hazard the existence of republicanism, and to subject us either to a division of the European powers, or to a despotism arising from high-handed commotions."[20]

Knox was aware of Washington's desire to remain out of politics and continue a life of tranquil seclusion as a Mount Vernon planter. But Henry believed that the crisis caused by the weak national government had become too serious to ignore. "There may indeed arise some solemn occasions in which you may conceive it to be your duty again to exert your utmost talents to promote the happiness of your country," he admonished Washington.

Shays's men closed in on the Springfield armory on Thursday, January 25. Shays appeared outside, shouting his demand for military stores and provisions for his men. The troops inside the armory threatened to fire, and Shays ordered his men to seize the arsenal. When the rebels came within 300 yards, a shot was fired over their heads. When they stepped within 100 yards of the arsenal, the soldiers lowered the sight of a cannon and fired a blast of grapeshot directly into the throng.

Three men were killed and another lay wounded. The insurgents fled, retreating to Pelham.

Knox returned to New York to await intelligence reports. He threw himself into the cause of promoting a new constitution and rounding up support for the Philadelphia convention, writing to prominent leaders urging the necessity of changes and exploring legal means for replacing the Articles of Confederation. To Massachusetts congressman Stephen Higginson, he wrote on Sunday, January 28, that the "poor, poor federal government is sick almost unto death." Some politicians questioned the legality of the upcoming convention and pointed out that it had no authority to change the Articles of Confederation. Only Congress had a public mandate from voters.

Knox suggested to Higginson that the convention and new constitution could be established legally by following the steps that both Congress and the Articles had to become the law of the land: The state legislatures could elect delegates to the convention and a new constitution could be sent to the states for ratification. Knox asked the rhetorical question: "Would not this, to all intents and purposes, be a government derived from the people and assented to by them as much as they assented to the confederation?"[21]

In Massachusetts, Shays and his insurgents retreated to Worcester County and stopped at Petersham on Saturday, February 4. General Lincoln's militia caught up with them by 8 P.M. In a surprise attack, the next morning 150 rebels were taken prisoner as the renegades dispersed in all directions. Shays escaped.

In Knox's updates to Washington, he reported the encouraging news. But he continued to pin his hopes for a long-term solution to the national troubles on the Philadelphia convention. Washington was uncertain, however, whether to attend and was concerned that the event might tarnish his reputation if it failed. He was among those who questioned the legality of the convention. Yet like Knox, Washington had little faith that the delegates were capable of fostering the kind of fundamental changes needed to steady the national government. He did offer his opinion on Knox's plan for a federal government; he thought it certainly represented a more effective constitution than Articles of Confederation but that Knox was perhaps overly optimistic and far reaching. Washington believed that state leaders would never give up any of their power and submit to the authority of a central government. To Knox, he wrote in early February: "The System on which you seem disposed to build a national government is certainly more energetic, and I dare say, in every point of view more desirable than the present one."

After Shays fled to Vermont, the insurgency was soon broken. Many of the rebels returned to their homes, and Lincoln's militia restored order. Knox informed Congress on Monday, February 12, that "the rebellion in Massachusetts is in a fair train of being speedily and effectually suppressed."[22]

Two days later, he sent a letter to Benjamin Lincoln congratulating him on his handling of the Shays crisis and urging his friend to support the Philadelphia convention and a new constitution. "The convention will be at liberty to consider more diffusively the defects of the present system than Congress can, who are the executors of a certain system."[23]

On February 21, Congress sanctioned the Philadelphia convention to be held beginning on May 14, and recommended that state legislatures choose delegates to attend for the purpose of revising or amending the Articles of Confederation and that the changes would be sent back to the states for approval. This was the plan that Knox had supported.

As the date for the convention approached, Washington felt mounting pressure to attend. Uncertain where his duty lay, he turned to Knox and a close circle of advisors. In a letter to Knox written Thursday, March 8, he asked: "Inform me confidentially what the public expectation is on this head, that is, whether I will, or ought to be there? You are much in the way of obtaining this knowledge, and I can depend upon your friendship, candor, and judgment in the communication of it, as far as it shall appear to you."[24]

Knox realized that Washington would be compelled to sit as the convention's president and, therefore, the success or failure of the proceedings would be attributed to him. But Knox told Washington in a letter of Monday, March 19, that without his approbation, the convention would lack credibility in the eyes of the public. "Your attendance will be grateful, and your non-attendance chagrining; that your presence would confer on the assembly a national complexion, and that it would more than any other circumstance induce a compliance to the propositions of the convention."[25]

By attending the convention and risking failure in Philadelphia, Washington was putting at stake the honor and fame that he had sacrificed so much to achieve during the war. Realizing this, Henry carefully crafted his appeal by prodding Washington with an almost irresistible temptation: "It would be circumstance highly honorable to your fame, in the judgment of the present and future ages, and doubly entitle you to the glorious epithet— Father of Your Country."

This is believed to be the first time that anyone of significance referred to George Washington as the "father of his country." It is likely that Knox was drawing parallels between Washington and other historical figures who had been given paternal homage, such as Cicero in 64 B.C. and Peter the Great in 1721.[26]

To Knox's satisfaction, Washington informed him in a letter dated Friday, April 27, that he would attend the convention. Knox was genuinely concerned for the fate of his country, but his own personal fortunes were also completely tied up in the success of the nation and its government. He was deeply in debt, in part because he and Lucy loved to entertain and were unable to curtail their spending. As one of the handful of individuals who held a national office, he needed the federal government to become effective for his own prosperity. The waning state of the confederation troubled him on a visceral level; an American collapse threatened all that he had worked for during the agonizing hardships of the war, the sacrifice he made in giving up his most energetic youthful years to public duty as well as the promise of a future basking in the honors due a leader of a new nation.

Without a stable government, his army pension was in jeopardy. American dollars would remain nearly worthless unless a federal government could back the currency and stabilize the economy. Knox seemed to internalize the national troubles. In April he wrote to Winthrop Sargent, his former artillery captain and fellow Cincinnati member, that he felt like "the most wretched man on earth . . . the poverty of the public is so great that all national operation might soon cease."[27]

Knox received regular updates from Constitutional Convention delegates working in the sequestered sessions of the secretive deliberations, including notes from George Washington, Elbridge Gerry, and Rufus King. On May 27, King notified Henry that Washington had been named president of the convention, as he had predicted.[28]

In July, he received a letter from an exasperated King: "I wish it was in my power to inform you that we had progressed a single step since you left us."[29]

Henry and Lucy's life then took another downward spiral in August when their one-year-old daughter, Caroline, died from an infection. From Philadelphia, Washington wrote an August 19 letter of condolence: "[I] am sure, however severe the trial, each of you have fortitude enough to meet it. Nature, no doubt, must feel severely before calm resignation will over come it."

In the same letter, he confessed that the deliberations at the Constitutional Convention were proving tedious: "By slow, I wish I could add and sure, movements, the business of the Convention progresses; but to say when it will end, or what will be the result, is more than I can venture to do."[30]

The slow process came to a successful conclusion by Monday, September 17, when delegates adjourned with a draft of a completely new Constitution.

Knox received the news with joy. The proposed system for a federal government was not dissimilar to the plan that he had outlined in his letter to Washington earlier in the year. Although he did not believe the new Constitution was perfect, he believed that it would create a more vigorous government and cement the union. Much of the language of the draft had been composed by Pennsylvania's Gouverneur Morris, whom he had written four years earlier with the strong suggestion that just such a convention be held.

Although Knox had not been a delegate to the constitutional convention, he had played a major role in rounding up support for the proceedings and sounding the alarm against the weak national government. Even before the peace treaty that had ended the American Revolution was signed, he had pressed prominent civil leaders with the need for a more vigorous central government. And perhaps most of important of all, he helped convince George Washington to take the risky step of attending the convention and supporting the move toward a new Constitution.

In his private life, Knox believed that a remedy for his family's financial problems was near. He and Lucy cleared their claim on the Waldo patent, which provided them with thousands of acres of uncultivated land. His former army colleague Henry Jackson sent him news that this land contained many settlers, some of whom were willing to pay for their property and some who denied his right. Knox wrote a land agent who was about to embark to Europe with an offer that he was willing to sell well-timbered land, suitable for farming, on the St. George's River and Penobscot Bay at $2 an acre. He told the agent he could deliver perfect titles and to sell any amount, from a single acre up to 80,000 acres.

On Tuesday, November 27, Lucy gave birth to a boy, whom Knox described as a "fine black-haired, black-eyed boy." He named his son after George Washington, and notified the child's namesake in a letter: "As an evidence of our respect and affection for you, which we hope will survive ourselves, we have done him the honor of giving him your name."[31]

Five states had ratified the Constitution—Delaware, Pennsylvania, New Jersey, Georgia, and Connecticut—by the time the ratifying convention in Knox's home state of Massachusetts opened on Wednesday, January 9, 1788. Massachusetts emerged as the critical swing state, upon which the success or failure of the constitution rested. The size and influence of the state would likely sway delegates in ratifying conventions in New York, Rhode Island, and New Hampshire.

Knox wrote a stream of letters to influential leaders lobbying support for the constitution. He explained that landowners, or "Federalists," wanted a strong government to ensure stability to protect their homes and businesses, but that many former Shays men sat at the convention as "anti-Federalists" and opposed any viable government. Knox was exasperated by those who favored state rights over federal sovereignty. To Washington, he wrote: "Mr. Samuel Adams has declared that he will oppose it to the very great disgust of the people of Boston, his constituents. It is said Boston was about to take some spirited measures to prevent the effect of his opposition."

Knox overstated Samuel Adams's opposition, however. As the debate progressed, Adams became persuaded of the imperative need for greater federal power and finally threw his support behind the Constitution. After delegates scrutinized and argued over the document line by line, paragraph by paragraph, for nearly a month, Massachusetts became the sixth state to ratify the compact by a narrow margin of just 18 votes: 187 to 168. Church bells rang and cannons fired in celebration in Boston.

An overjoyed Knox wrote to Washington on Thursday, February 14: "It may with great truth be asserted that no subject was ever more candidly debated."[32]

Knox continued to lobby support for the Constitution through his connections around the country, which provided him with greater knowledge of Federalist efforts than almost any other leader at the time. Even Washington was forced to ask Knox about the identity of the writers behind the *Federalist Papers:* "Pray, if it is not a secret, who is the author, or authors of Publius?"[33]

Knox replied that the essays were the work of his former aide, Alexander Hamilton, along with James Madison and John Jay. Knox's passions were caught up in the prospective fate of the proposed Constitution. Rhode Island invoked his ire when he received news that the state had rejected ratification in a referendum on Monday, March 24, by the wide margin of 2,945 to 237. To Lafayette, he wrote on Saturday, April 26: "As to Rhode Island, no little State of Greece ever exhibited greater turpitude than she does. Paper money and tender law engross her attention entirely: this is, in other words, plundering the orphan and widow by virtue of laws."[34]

When New Hampshire ratified the Constitution on June 21, it was formally adopted as the government of the United States. Major Doughty at Fort Pitt wrote Knox with congratulations and credited the predominately Federalist-party Society of Cincinnati with the achieving its ratification. He pointed out that the former soldiers in the society were the group who "more generally advocates for good government than perhaps any other class of individuals."[35]

TEN

ILLUSIVE BUBBLES

Henry Knox had become one of the most prominent figures in national politics. His name consistently popped up as a possible candidate for the vice presidency of the United States.

Under the new Constitution, the candidate with the most electoral votes was elected president while the runner-up became vice president. Everyone agreed that Washington would be chosen as nation's first chief executive, but the field of vice presidential candidates was wide open. The most astute political observer in the city, Virginia congressman James Madison, thought the vice president should hail from New England to balance the Washington administration.

In gauging the prevailing political sentiment, Madison pared the possibilities down to John Adams, John Hancock, John Jay, or Knox. Writing to Thomas Jefferson on Wednesday, October 8, 1788, Madison said he preferred Jay or Knox but thought that neither would accept the job, since it was a largely impotent post. The following day, Alexander Hamilton sounded out Massachusetts congressman Theodore Sedgwick in a letter discussing the vice presidency: "What think you of Lincoln or Knox?" he asked.[1]

Sedgwick responded on Thursday, October 16, opining that: "Lincoln & Knox I love, their characters too, I respect. But it is now too late to push in this state the interest of either. The minds of all men here seem to be fixed either on Adams or Hancock."[2]

Hamilton realized that Knox faced financial struggles and doubted whether he could afford to take the vice presidency, which lacked the financial perks and expense account that came with running and staffing the war office. Writing to Madison on Sunday, November 23, he observed: "As to Knox, I cannot persuade myself that he will incline to the appointment. He must sacrifice emolument by it, which must be of necessity a primary object with him."[3] Knox, in fact, did not want to leave the war office, and wrote to Washington on Sunday, December 21: "Mr. John Adams will probably have the plurality of views for vice President."[4]

Henry had cause to reflect on the path his life had taken after receiving a letter from a childhood friend, David McClure, who had risen to become a clergyman in Hartford, Connecticut. McClure reminded Knox of their adolescent games, of sliding down a ship's oar from atop a building owned by Henry's father. "Have you forgotten that diversion?" McClure asked. "I have often rejoiced with gratitude that the Supreme Disposer of all events has preserved you through the dangers you have encountered, and made you so great a blessing to your country, for whose happiness and glory your labors have been directed."[5]

Knox remarked on the divergent roads that their lives had taken in a letter of Sunday, January 25, 1789: "You have been deeply exploring the natural and moral world, in order to impress on the minds of your fellow-mortals their relative connection with the great scale of intelligent being; leading them by all the powers of persuasion to happiness and humble adoration of the Supreme Head of the universe; while I have been but too much entangled with the little things of a little globe. But, as it is part of my belief that we are responsible only for the light we possess."[6]

★ ★ ★ ★

Washington was elected as the nation's first president on Monday, April 6, 1789, by a unanimous vote of sixty-nine electors, and John Adams won the vice presidency with thirty-four votes. Secretary of Congress Thomson arrived at Mount Vernon to notify the president-elect on Tuesday, April 14. Washington answered with muted appreciation: "Silence can best explain my gratitude."[7]

Thousands of spectators gathered outside Federal Hall in New York City, where Washington emerged on a small, half-enclosed portico overlooking Broadway and Wall Street. Congress had deemed that the swearing-in should be as public as possible. Knox stood behind Washington as he placed his hand on the Bible and took the oath from the chancellor of New York, Robert R. Livingston. Washington leaned over and kissed the Bible, and afterward returned to the House chamber to deliver his inaugural address. That evening, Knox hosted the president at his home, where they enjoyed fireworks. A week later, on May 7, a dinner honoring Washington was held at the Assembly

Room on the east side of Broadway, near Wall Street. As one of the city's leading socialites, Lucy Knox helped planned the ceremonials.

Knox had little time to enjoy a season of high society. Their son, George
Washington Knox, was stricken with dysentery and grew weak to the point of
death by early July. Henry and Lucy pushed aside everything to take him on a
sea cruise in hopes of reviving his strength. The child's condition weighed on
Knox as they returned and Henry was forced back into duty by the pressing
need to gear up for the new government.

Congress was in the midst of creating the federal departments set forth in
the U.S. Constitution, one of which gave Knox the mandate he needed to create a permanent, standing army. During the Confederation government,
Knox had served merely as secretary at war, a title that denoted a temporary
position that was expected to be terminated in peacetime. Congress created
the Department of War on August 7, 1789, and Knox's title changed to secretary of war. (The U.S. Department of War would be merged into the U.S.
Department of Defense in 1947.)

Some members of Congress in the new government under the U.S. Constitution, such as the anti-Federalist William Maclay, thought that the country had no urgent need for a war secretary.

The uneasy relationship between the branches of the government immediately became evident. Secretary Knox appeared with Washington at the
Senate Chamber on August 22 to discuss problems arising from tensions between white settlers in North and South Carolina and Georgia and American
Indian tribes. Knox thought that it was important to develop a good relationship with the Indian chiefs not only to preserve harmony and avoid war but as
a buffer against encroaching European powers, such as Britain and Spain.

Washington and Knox thought it would be proper to ask the Senate for
its advice and consent on the attempt to treat with the Indians, since the Constitution gave the Senate authority over treaties. As they appeared at the Senate door, Washington handed Vice President Adams a lengthy explanation of
the problems and history of recent treaties with the hostile tribes, written by
Knox. As Adams read the statement in the Senate chambers, several senators
became irritated. The noise from carriages outside made it difficult to hear,
and several congressmen felt the issues were new and complicated and needed
to be sent to committee for further study. Washington, angry, said: "This defeats every purpose of my coming here."

Knox had appointed Benjamin Lincoln as an agent to deal with the
problems between the state of Georgia and tribes along its border. One of

the senators asked Knox directly when Lincoln would arrive, and Henry responded "not till Saturday next."[8]

This is still the only time in American history that a member of the president's cabinet was openly questioned before the full Senate. Washington had seen enough. To avoid getting entangled in tedious Senate discussions, he decided to address Congress in writing rather than appearing in person. Senators did, however, allocate $20,000 for an attempt to treat with the Indians as Knox had asked.

As Henry sat before the senators, his mind must have been elsewhere. The following day, he wrote to Henry Jackson that his son George Washington Knox had died. Once again, the Knoxes were plunged into anguish. The frequent deaths of their children had not made them numb to the pain of losing another child.

Henry Knox officially became the first United States secretary of war on September 12, and Congress established a standing 1,000-man army on September 29. John Marshall, the future chief justice of the U.S. Supreme Court, wrote in praise of Knox's appointment, noting two virtues that were often used in reference to Henry: honesty and judgment. Marshall observed: "To his past services and an unquestioned integrity, he was admitted to unite a sound understanding; and the public judgment as well as that of the chief magistrate pronounced him in all respects competent to the station he filled."[9]

In putting together his cabinet, Washington tapped Knox along with Alexander Hamilton to head the Treasury Department, Thomas Jefferson, who would soon return from Paris, as his secretary of state, Edmund Randolph of Virginia as attorney general, and Samuel Osgood as postmaster general. Knox, the only carry-over from the Confederation government, was therefore the senior official in the nation's first cabinet.

His primary goal was to place the army on firm footing. He arranged the army into a legionary formation, which became the basis of the regular army for the United States, and once again he tried to get approval for a military draft for the state militias. Washington sent the plan to Congress on January 11, 1790, with his approval. But Congress, in no mood to enact an unpopular draft, dropped the idea.

America's failure to raise a formidable army caused its own set of problems. In dealing with hostile Indian tribes, Knox found that chiefs had little respect for the fighting force of the United States and had little reason to sign peace treaties. Knox thought that many of the tribes' complaints were completely justified and that they had been victimized by white settlers. But without an army, he was powerless to prevent violence. He wrote Washington on January 12 that troops were needed to maintain harmony along the nation's borders: "The lawless whites, as well as Indians, will be deterred from the commission of murders when they shall be convinced that punishment will ultimately follow detection."[10]

He drew up provisions to raise a 5,040-man army at a cost of $1,152,000 annually to put pressure on the Creek nation along the country's southwestern frontiers. Washington gave his approval for the plan on January 21, 1790, and Knox personally presented it to Congress on January 22. Senator Maclay, who sharply disagreed with any proposal to augment the size of the federal government, thought that Knox would eventually entangle the country in war if given an army. When Knox appeared before the Senate, Maclay noted in his journal: "In now came General Knox with a bundle of communications. I thought the act was a mad one, when a Secretary of War was appointed in time of peace. I can not blame him. The man wants to labor in his vocation."[11]

Meanwhile, that spring the hostilities along the frontier grew more deadly. Brigadier General Josiah Harmar wrote to Knox on March 24 that settlers going up the Ohio River were being murdered or taken captive. Knox authorized Harmar to lead an expedition from Fort Washington (present-day Cincinnati) consisting of 1,700 militia and 400 federal troops at a cost of $156,000 to punish the Wabash and discourage further attacks. He wrote Harmar on June 7: "No other remedy remains, but to extirpate, utterly, if possible, the said banditti."[12]

Yet Knox also used his personality as a tool to forge alliances. To entreat the hostile tribes of the Creek nation, he invited twenty-four leading chiefs to New York to meet with him and tour the capital. Tensions between white settlers and the Native Americans continued to rise as settlements further encroached on hunting grounds that were vital to the tribe's survival. The chiefs who arrived in New York commanded a powerful fighting force of 14,000 warriors. Henry thought that the Americans should emulate the British, who strengthened their bond with the chiefs by offering gifts and titles of distinction. Knox hosted the chiefs and, in not-so-subtle message, orchestrated a military parade of American soldiers for their entertainment. The top Indian leader was Alexander McGillivray, the son of a Scottish trader and a Native American mother. Knox told the chiefs that he felt their complaints were justified and promised that white settlers who committed crimes against them would be punished.

At a meeting with the chiefs in Federal Hall, Knox negotiated a historic treaty on August 7 that ended hostilities along the nation's southwest frontier and established boundaries between the state of Georgia and the territories of the Creek nation. The treaty demonstrated Knox's commitment to fairness in his dealing with the rights of American tribes and that he held their legal rights to be equal with whites. The agreement acknowledged that the Indians needed vast areas of land on which to hunt and stipulated that "[i]f any citizen of the United States, or other person, not being an Indian, shall attempt to settle on any of the Creeks' lands, such person shall forfeit the protection of the United States, and the Creeks may punish him or not, as they please."[13] The treaty also made provisions to supply the Creek with tools to develop agriculture so that they could survive on less land by tilling the soil. To further cement the bond, Knox designated McGillivray a brigadier general.

As Knox ended hostilities between settlers and American Indians in the South, more trouble erupted along the frontier borders in the Northwest. Knox ordered General Harmar's expedition to use coercion to deal with the belligerent Miami and Shawnee Indians in the Ohio Territory who were killing whites and refusing to treat with the U.S. government.

More than 1,450 men marched from Fort Washington on September 30, 1790, on a mission to bring order to the region. As they progressed, the Indians abandoned their camps and disappeared into the forest. The Miami and Shawnee sent runners to tribes throughout the region with messages to send warriors. As Harmar's men reached the site of present-day Fort Wayne on October 18, the tribes launched an attack and killed 183 soldiers, while 120 Indians were killed.

Because news was slow to travel from the wilderness, weeks passed without any word from the expedition. In New York, Knox waited anxiously and was embarrassed that he could not update the president on the fate of men.

Washington, impatient, finally wrote Knox on November 2, "I am a little surprised that we have not heard . . . of the issue, the progress, or the commencement of the expedition."[14]

When the disastrous news arrived in New York, Knox thought that the country faced a long, drawn-out war with the Miami and Shawnee. Other tribes, he believed, would be emboldened to attack the settlements that were his sworn duty to protect. Harmar's expedition had been the first major military mission under his watch as secretary of war. He had placed his faith in the general, despite rumors that he had a drinking problem.

Washington openly second-guessed Knox's confidence in Harmar in a pointed message of November 19: "I expected *little* from the moment I heard he was a *drunkard*."[15]

With this defeat weighing on Knox's mind, he and Lucy closed their home in New York and headed for Philadelphia, which was to serve as the temporary capital for the United States while builders and architects readied the permanent government seat at the District of Columbia along the Potomac River in Virginia. Vice President John Adams offered to rent them a home on the outskirts of the city on a piece of elevated ground, called "Bush Hill." The house was an elaborate mansion designed by Andrew Hamilton, the architect who had created Independence Hall, where the Continental Congress had convened.

Henry had little time to settle into the home, however. He moved into the War Department office on Chestnut and Fifth, diagonally across from the State House and Congress Hall. In an attempt to avoid war with the Indians, he invited friendly tribes such as the Senecas and Chickasaws to the city in December to discuss complaints and to induce them to make peace overtures to the belligerent tribes. Knox assured them that he would seek the prosecution of any white person who committed crimes against them, and explained that the federal government alone had the power to treat with them rather than the individual states. The failure of the Harmar expedition became a national embarrassment, and much of the criticism was leveled at Knox. Washington tried to assure frontier settlers that the federal government could still protect them. In a December 11 message to the House of Representatives, he pledged that his government "will make the aggressors sensible that it is their interest to merit by a peaceable behavior the friendship and humanity which the United States are always ready to extend to them."[16]

Knox spent weeks planning another expedition in which a line of forts would be built in the northwest Ohio Territory to protect the settlers. In his orders to General Arthur St. Clair on March 28, 1791, he emphasized the need to restore confidence in the army: "You are well informed of the unfavorable impressions which the issue of the last expedition has made on the public mind."

The tensions within Washington's cabinet were beginning to split the administration. Knox and Hamilton were in an ideological and political battle with Thomas Jefferson as each man struggled to win the favor of the president. Knox often found himself aligned with Hamilton, although Henry continued to view the treasury secretary as "Colonel Hamilton," and his inferior in rank. But he found little in common with Jefferson, and the sage of Monticello had a natural aversion to Knox.

Knox had risen from New England, where inhabitants disdained distinctions of class. Jefferson, like Washington, was an affluent planter who sat among the elite of patriarchal Virginia. Henry's experiences during the war as well and his services as war secretary had led him to favor a strong federal government. He had been part of a national army in which state allegiances held little meaning, and the weakness of the central government had continually hindered his ambitions as an artillery commander and as an architect of the nation's military. Jefferson's political orientation was completely opposite. Educated as a lawyer, Jefferson had served as the representative of his state in the Continental Congress and also as Virginia's governor during the Revolution, which led him to think in terms of his state rather than from the perspective of the national government. He saw himself as a protector of state's rights, fighting against the encroachment of national power. He abhorred businessmen, bankers, and land jobbers, discounted the merit of military service, and put little stock in the heroics of men such as Knox and Washington.

Hamilton and Jefferson were also at odds. Hamilton emerged as the dominant figure among the Federalists, who favored strong national defense and the encouragement of business. Jefferson became the leader of the anti-Federalists, who favored a strict interpretation of the Constitution and fought the growth of the War and Treasury departments.

As the divide in his cabinet widened, Washington left for a tour of the southern states and for a visit to Mount Vernon in the spring of 1791. Jefferson and James Madison began a tour of New England states and New York to garner anti-Federalist support.

Lucy gave birth to a daughter in July, whom they named Caroline. But no sooner had they added one child then they lost another. Marcus Camillus, their eight-year-old son, died in September 1791, at his school in Princeton. On September 8, Washington wrote in condolence to Henry and Lucy: "Parental feelings are too much alive in the moment of these misfortunes to admit the consolations of religion or philosophy; but I am persuaded reason will call one or both of them to your aid as soon as the keenness of your anguish is abated."[17]

No words could console Knox, who responded to Washington that "[i]n this moment, neither philosophy nor reason have their proper office." He wrote a letter to the headmaster of the Princeton school thanking him for sending the remains of his son home. Knox's friend and wartime colleague, Henry Jackson, sent a letter expressing his sense of loss over the death: "That so lovely, promising and amiable a boy should be taken from his parents and friends who love and adore him, while the lives of thousands are spared who are a burden to themselves and society."[18]

Lucy and the children had returned to Boston for the summer, and their son, Henry Jackson Knox, had been placed in a boarding school. With the frontier troubles unresolved, Henry stayed in Philadelphia. Life in the capital became dull in Knox's estimation. He wrote to Lucy that she was not missing out on any tempting social events, only two teas had been held that summer. On Sunday, July 15, he wrote her "[m]y evenings cannot possible be any cause of jealousy. They are stupid indeed. I drive out pretty often, come home, read the evening paper, then got to a solitary and painful bed—painful from the reflection that the companion of my soul is at a distance and that I am deprived of the blessed solace of her arms."

In a letter to his daughter Lucy, he confessed that his passion for public accolades had waned. "All my life I have been pursing illusive bubbles which burst on being grasped, and 'tis high time I should quit public life and attend to the solid interests of my family."[19]

By early 1793, the world plunged into a global war. Knox was concerned about the country's ability to defend itself, but he was handcuffed in his efforts to prepare the nation's defenses because of budget concerns and the huge federal debt amassed during the Revolution. The War Department not only had to deal with the domestic troubles regarding the Indians but with the prospect of an invasion by a foreign European power. France was in the throes of a revolution. The French king, Louis XVI, who had been so helpful to the American's during its revolution, was guillotined with Marie Antoinette before a jeering mob on January 21, 1793. The new French government declared war on Great Britain, Spain, and the Netherlands on February 1, 1793.

The Girondist regime of the French republic sent an ambassador to America by the name of Edmond Charles "Citizen" Genêt, who arrived in Charleston on April 9, 1793. Genêt was welcomed with great fanfare, as many Americans hailed the French Revolution as an extension of their own struggle for liberty against monarchy. While in Charleston, he commissioned privateers and armed ships to prey upon British merchant ships even before presenting himself for recognition before Washington's administration. Genêt never questioned the Franco-American alliance and the treaty between the two nations that had been signed during the American Revolution with the now-deposed royal French government. Many political leaders in America also viewed the treaty as perfectly valid, despite the change in French governments. The governor of South Carolina applauded Genêt's efforts, and the Frenchman was enthusiastically greeted all along his trip to Philadelphia. Washington, who took the oath of office for a second term on March 4, was apprehensive that Genêt's actions would drag America into a war with Britain and sent a list of questions to his cabinet asking if the French treaty was still valid and whether Genêt should be received.

The issue split the administration along party lines. Secretary of State Jefferson loved France, where he had served as an American minister. He welcomed Genêt as a friend and believed that the United States was bound by treaty to align itself with France. Knox and Hamilton disagreed, and believed America should avoid insulting Britain and risking another war.

Jefferson again felt the odd man. In an April cabinet meeting called to discuss the Genêt issue and the validity of the French treaty, Hamilton, followed by Knox, voiced their opposition to Genêt. Jefferson had little patience with either man and wrote derisively of Henry in his journal: "Knox subscribed at once to Hamilton's opinion that we ought to declare the treaty void, acknowledging, at the same time, like a fool as he is, that he knew nothing about it. It was clear it remained valid."[20]

Washington sided with Hamilton and Knox. He requested that Genêt be recalled and the French obliged. The president also issued a "Neutrality Proclamation" on April 22 that warned American citizens not to aid any nation in its war effort.

Meetings within the administration grew increasingly contentious as the split between the Federalist and Republicans widened. Jefferson's relationship with Washington and his influence within the administration were irreparably harmed by the Genêt affair. Realizing that he had lost the political rivalry with Hamilton, Jefferson turned in a letter of resignation on July 31 and agreed to serve out the remainder of the year as the secretary of state.

Both France and England were unhappy with the U.S. policy of neutrality. Each nation sent warships to prey on vulnerable American merchant vessels under the pretense of stopping any shipments of supplies destined for their enemy's docks. Shipping lanes on the high seas across the globe suddenly became a lawless haven for piracy. American merchant ships sailing across the Atlantic and through the Mediterranean were especially targeted because the United States did not possess a navy to protect its vessels or exact retribution on those who attacked its ships. On October 8, 1793, the American minister to Portugal, David Humphreys, sent a letter to U.S. authorities with the warning that Barbary pirates from Algiers were also capturing American vessels. Panic spread among captains shipping cargo in the Mediterranean under the Stars and Stripes. Every American vessel bound for Lisbon, Cadiz, or the Straits of Gibraltar was in danger of being attacked and its crew thrown into slavery.

In mid-December, American newspapers reported that ten American ships, including the *Hope of New York*, had been captured along with 110 sailors who were brought to Algiers, where they were stripped, shackled, and sold into slavery. The Algiers pirates used brutal tactics. Fast-sailing corsair ships preyed on slow, unarmed American business vessels, with pirates throwing long lateen yards across their prey's rails and then hopping aboard, armed with cutlasses and pistols. Any merchant seamen who resisted were killed, and the rest were sent below decks in chains.

A public clamor rose for the War Department to defend Americans on the high seas and for the formation of a navy. Knox had argued the need for a naval force as far back as the Confederation government. By the end of the Revolution, all but two of the Continental Navy's thirteen ships had been captured or destroyed, and the navy was disbanded.

Any project to establish a navy would fall under the authority of the War Department. A separate naval department would not be created until 1798. On January 2, 1794, a closely divided House resolved by a vote of 46 to 44 "[t]hat a Naval force, adequate to the protection of the commerce of the United States against the Algerine corsairs, ought to be provided."[21] The issue was sent to a committee to estimate the cost of building the naval force.

Although Knox was the son of a shipwright and grew up along the Boston docks, he knew little about building ships or what kind of vessels would suit America's needs. He walked the numerous shipyards of Philadelphia, talking to master shipwrights, captains, and sailors. At the time, the city was the largest shipbuilding center in the United States. More than 8,000 tons of shipping were constructed there, twice the tonnage of any other port in America. More than a quarter of the nation's $7 million in total exports sailed from its docks.[22]

Knox was swayed by a proposal given to him the previous year, dated January 6, 1793, from the city's leading shipwright, forty-two-year-old Joshua Humphreys, who observed that: "As our Navy must for a considerable time be inferior in numbers, we are to consider what sized ships will be most formidable and be an overmatch for those of an enemy."[23]

Knox faced a variety of complicated decisions in choosing a design for the ships. Congress wanted ships to deal with the Barbary pirates, who used light, quick corsairs. America could not afford the large, expensive battleships used by England and France. Yet Knox believed that sooner or later U.S. Navy vessels needed to be equipped with enough firepower to compete with the warships of Europe.

Humphreys proposed an intermediate ship, a super-size frigate that would weigh more than 1,000 tons with a deck length of 175 feet and a keel as deep as 150 feet. He reasoned that because America could not compete with the massive scale of large European battleships, its navy should use better technology to produce a more compact yet sturdy, efficient fighter that would be both quick and powerful, with enough guns and speed to subdue corsairs and frigates and elude large battleships, also called ships of the line.

Battleships generally carried seventy-four guns on two decks with cannons that could discharge twenty-four- or thirty-two-pound shells. Frigates typically were smaller ships sent out as the eyes of the fleet to scout the waters ahead. They were ideal for poking into harbors and up rivers, and usually possessed a single deck of no more than thirty-eight guns, modest eighteen-pounders. Most frigates would be outgunned against a battleship.

The design was highly controversial, however. Other ship designers charged that Humphreys's idea would not work, that the frigate was much too large and that the hull would crack under the enormous strain of bearing 1,000 tons of wood, copper, and iron scantlings. They believed that the massive frame and exaggerated keel would cause structural weakness that would force the hull to distort under the weight of the heavy guns and extra deck. Some pointed to a common drawback inherent in the design of frigates: The guns sat high above the water to increase the distance of the firing range. This elevated the ship's center of gravity, making it unstable. Adding bigger and more numerous guns to a frigate would increase that instability, and several of Knox's advisors maintained that Humphreys's design should be made lighter and reduced in size to avoid disaster.

Although Knox harbored reservations about Humphrey's design, he was inclined to favor innovative technology. Humphreys believed that his frigates could be strong enough if built from live oak and red cedar, materials that were difficult to obtain in Europe but available in the southern U.S. states.

Aside from establishing a navy, Knox believed that America needed to build a line of coastal defenses to prevent enemy warships from venturing into its harbors unopposed. On February 28, 1794, he submitted to Congress a detailed plan for federal installations along the eastern seaboard in sixteen port towns, including Boston, New York, Philadelphia, Baltimore, Norfolk, Charleston, and Savannah. He estimated the cost of building the forts at $76,000 and pegged the expense of 200 cannons for the project at $97,000, for a sum total of $173,000. Another $90,000 would be needed to pay the soldiers to garrison the posts.

To many in Congress, his plans seemed overly ambitious. The bill to fund the navy was finding heavy opposition in the House, where James Madison argued that the country could not afford a navy until it paid off its war debts. He suggested that the United States hire the Portuguese navy to fight its battles. Many anti-Federalist Republicans claimed that the navy would be a tool for Federalists like Knox who could use it to expand the federal government. A navy would also be a source of influence and patronage.

Jefferson had long argued that "a Navy will be [a] ruinously expensive, aristocratic institution, subversive of Democratic ideals, whose glory-hungry officers will drag the country into unwarranted adventures overseas."[24]

Nevertheless, heeding the clamor to protect American shipping, the U.S. House finally gave its approval in a 50 to 39 vote on March 10, 1794 for "An act to provide a naval armament."[25] The Senate quickly approved, and Washington signed the measure into law on March 27. The appropriation that launched the United States Navy was a mere $688,888.

On April 15, Knox sent Washington his recommendation in favor of the Humphreys design, writing that the ships would "combine such qualities of strength, durability, swiftness of sailing and force, as to render them equal, if not superior, to any frigate belonging to any of the European powers."[26] Washington gave his approbation to begin work.

Knox established the first U.S. Navy yards. Each frigate would be built in a separate city. He initially leased shipyards and then transformed them into federal installations. Throughout the spring and summer, Knox held meetings at the War Department on Chestnut and Fifth in Philadelphia. He laid out detailed instructions for master builders, ship captains, and shipyard agents and going over plans and budgets with Humphreys that included every piece of wood, copper, or iron used in constructing the frigates. Teams of men were sent to the islands off Georgia to cut the live oak necessary for construction to begin. It has been estimated that each of the six frigates required as many as 460 live oak trees.[27]

The controversial decision Knox made in choosing to build super frigates rather than more conventional warships demonstrated his far-reaching vision of the nation's future. In planning the frigate project, he considered not only the immediate need of dealing with the Barbary Pirates, as many in Congress myopically had, but he also looked to the long-term future of the navy and indeed the country. Just as Humphreys had promised, the oversize frigates, with their wider and longer hulls, extra guns, and reinforced live-oak frames, put the United States Navy on the cutting edge of the science of building and designing warships. This was the beginning of a long tradition of world-class innovation and leadership that would continue for centuries.

The six frigates that Knox helped plan—the *Constitution, United States, President, Congress, Chesapeake,* and *Constellation*—went on to perform legendary service. In the War of 1812, *Constitution* captured three British frigates, *Guerriere, Java,* and *Cyane,* along with the sloop *Levant* as well as many smaller vessels. She was nicknamed "Old Ironsides" after broadsides from *Guerriere* bounced off her twenty-two-inch-thick, live-oak-framed hull. Casualties aboard the original six frigates were much less than on comparable enemy ships.

Chesapeake also became part of sea lore. She was commanded by Captain James Lawrence in the War of 1812. After suffering a mortal wound during a battle with the British cruiser *Shannon,* Lawrence cried out with his last few breaths the immortal words: "Don't give up the ship."

Both Thomas Jefferson and James Madison, who each had opposed a navy, would come to be thankful that Knox had championed the cause of a naval armament. Jefferson wrote to John Adams in 1822 that the six frigates "[c]ertainly raised our rank and character among nations."[28]

Despite the launch of the navy, Knox became more and more dissatisfied with his role in the administration. Yet he felt he could not yet step down with much of the business of his department unfinished, including building a new corps of artillery, the frigates projects, and erecting the nation's fortifications. He also worked to oversee General Anthony Wayne's expedition against the Indians in the Ohio Territory to quell hostilities against settlers. "I cannot leave my situation in this critical state of affairs," he wrote his friend Henry Jackson, who managed his estate, in a letter of May 10, 1794.[29]

He felt his influence with Washington waning as Hamilton's rose. Knox became embroiled in a struggle with the Treasury secretary over the power to buy supplies for War Department, a powerful source of political patronage. Hamilton thought that the Treasury Department should handle all contracts concerning the federal government. Unlike Hamilton, Knox harbored no political aspirations and did not need political patrons, but nevertheless felt that the secretary of the Treasury was trying to enlarge the influence of his department. This was the same charge that Jefferson had leveled against Hamilton so often in letters to Washington.

Knox's personal finances and interests needed urgent attention. Taxes were due on the Waldo patent, and work on his home in Thomaston, Maine, needed direction or contractors would have to suspend the project, and therefore increase its cost. He decided to ask Washington for a six-week leave of absence to return to Massachusetts and his Maine land to put his life in order. Washington agreed. But just as Knox began to pack for the trip home, the fledgling federal government again faced a critical test that demanded the use of the military. In 1791, Hamilton successfully spearheaded a federal excise tax on distilled spirits, which were used as a kind of currency in the far frontier regions of the country. The funds generated by the tax were the second most lucrative source of revenue for the federal government and helped pay for the War Department's expeditions against the Indians.

On the western side of the Alleghany Mountains in the Pennsylvania frontier, the Scotch-Irish pioneers found that because of the expense of transporting wheat and corn over the mountains, the only way to turn a profit on their grain was to convert it into whiskey. Several distillers claimed that the tax was an excessively heavy burden and tried to elude or intimidate federal revenue officers, which led to several instances of minor violence. "Revenuers" were tarred, feathered, beaten, and whipped. On August 1, 1794, however, the situation erupted into an open rebellion. Law officers tried to round up sixty tax evaders to bring them to trial in Philadelphia. A riot ensued as 6,000 settlers from around the region banded together at Braddock's field, muskets in hand, threatening any federal officer who ventured into Washington and Alleghany counties.

Many of the rebel settlers believed that the federal government had become as oppressive as the British before the Revolution and urged similar tactics to defeat the tax measure. The chief tax collector's home was set ablaze in an act of vandalism reminiscent of a colonial protest during the 1765 Stamp Act controversy. A U.S. soldier was killed in Pennsylvania, and the rebels pledged to form their own government and secede from the union.

Washington thought that the U.S. government could not tolerate its laws to be trampled on and called out 12,900 militia troops from Pennsylvania, New Jersey, Maryland, and Virginia on August 7. He warned the insurgents to disband and return to their homes by September 1 or the militia would force them to do so. In a proclamation issuing the order, he told the country of his "most solemn conviction that the essential interests of the Union demand it; that the very existence of Government, and the fundamental principles of social order, are materially involved in the issue."[30]

For nearly two decades, Knox had heeded every call to duty that his country had demanded. He had rushed to Washington's side at every summons, regardless of the costs to his family or private interests. But with his estate in need of urgent attention, Knox turned his focus away from his government duties and looked to his future. Despite Hamilton's grasping ambition, Knox went so far as to arrange for the Treasury secretary to take control of the War Department in his absence. Henry seemed to be anticipating leaving office and accepted even the risk of completely losing control of the department to Hamilton.

Washington gave Knox permission to begin his furlough, writing him on August 8 at 8 P.M.: "I consent to your pursuing your plan, and wish you a good journey and a safe and speedy return."[31]

Knox reached Boston a little more than a week later. His son Henry arrived to discuss his ongoing problems at school. As father and son came together, both became overcome with emotion. Recalling the moment, Knox wrote to Lucy, who had remained in Philadelphia, on August 17: "I had one of the most affecting moments of my life. I intended to talk to him seriously about his errors, but my soul was too full for utterance and we wept in each other's arms for a long space. He saw my agony and I hope he will be more regular in the future."[32]

Knox stayed in Boston only a few days before venturing into the frontier wilderness to the site of his rising home in Thomaston. Along the way, he met with squatters who had taken up residence on his land. While he paid them for their work in clearing and cultivating the soil, he told them that they must vacate his property within the next year, when he planned to begin development.

When he arrived at his future home along the St. George River, he was pleased to see that the builders had laid out the outlines of the foundation and frame for the structure. He seemed to picture himself in repose with Lucy and envisioned lavish dinners surrounded by friends and distinguished guests. He met with the builder, Ebenezer Dunton, and detailed plans for dozens of guest rooms in the mansion that he was to call Montpelier. The ceilings in the parlors would be thirteen feet high, and eleven in the chambers. Guests would enter the home into an ornate oval room, enveloped on both sides by staircases. Knox ordered twenty-four fireplaces to be built in the home, and directed that trees be planted near the house and scenic landscaping planted.

As Knox lingered in the tranquility of his wilderness refuge, the whiskey crisis in the country was growing. A dispatch arrived from John Stagg, the chief clerk of the War Department, that reported that the Pennsylvania insurgent force had not dissipated at the threat of force, as Knox had hoped. The rioters had refused to return to their homes as the militia from various states gathered to deal with the unrest. Unlike so many crises in his past, Henry did not rush to the scene. For some reason, he remained at the Thomaston property even after his six-week furlough ended. He seemed to be emotionally or spiritually worn out from years of exhausting duty and personal sacrifice. His public ambition no longer drove him; instead he yearned for private solace in the distance wilds, far from exasperating political life.

The Whiskey Rebellion, as it came to be known, still was not resolved. The rebels failed to desist by Washington's September 1 deadline. As Knox remained out of touch in Maine, on September 9, the president ordered the militia to march to western Pennsylvania and quash the insurrection. Virginia governor Henry Lee led the 12,900-man force with the aid of Alexander Hamilton, who seldom refused an opportunity to exercise power. Hamilton also dealt with all the logistical responsibilities that Knox should have handled.

On September 25, Washington issued a final proclamation to the insurgents, threatening military coercion to force them to disband and reminding them that unlike British tyranny, the federal laws had been enacted by elected officials rather than a king: "[The] people of the United States have been permitted, under the Divine favor, in perfect freedom, after solemn deliberation, in an enlightened age, to elect their own Government."[33] Facing a large military force, the 8,000 insurgents began to disperse and return home.

Washington wondered where his secretary of war could be in the midst of domestic turmoil after an absence of nearly two months. He sent Henry a mild rebuke for exceeding his furlough. "Hearing nothing from you for a considerable time has given alarm," Washington wrote on Tuesday, September 30, "lest some untoward accident may have been the cause of it."[34] Washington wrote Knox that he was leaving for Carlisle, Pennsylvania with Hamilton to rendezvous with the militia.

Knox did not receive the letter at the time. Although he had emerged from his malaise, he was already on the road headed back to Philadelphia when the dispatch reached Maine. The impeccable timing that Knox had been blessed with all his life suddenly deserted him. As he traveled on the road to the nation's capital, Washington packed his bags and departed on his journey to confront the whiskey rebels without his secretary of war at his side. As both Knox and Washington traveled separate paths, communication between the two men faltered for the first time in Henry's long career. They seemed to be heading in opposite directions.

On October 6, Knox arrived in Philadelphia and sent word to Washington, offering to join him in Carlisle. Knox's dispatch demonstrated that he was hopelessly out of step with the rest of the administration during the crisis.

The rebellion was already subsiding. Washington wrote Henry that he had missed a great opportunity that might have been a historic highlight of his long military career. He likely would have been given command of the army had he returned in time. On October 9, Washington wrote to Knox: "It would have given me pleasure to have had you with me on my present tour, and advantages might have resulted from it, if your return, in time, would have allowed it. It is now too late."

The president politely conveyed his irritation: "I am very glad to hear of your safe return. We were apprehensive something more than common had happened from no one having received a line from you for a considerable time before I left the city."[35]

Washington returned to the capital by Tuesday, October 28. The usual warmth and affection that Washington and Knox had shared cooled after the Whiskey Rebellion. Observers once compared their relationship as being as close-knit as a marriage. Now their lives diverged. Although Knox had made great sacrifices for his country during his career, Washington could not afford to be sympathetic. The president perhaps felt that his own happiness had been subverted by duty. The difference, however, between Knox and Washington was that the president had Mount Vernon, an established estate, to return to after he left office. Henry's holdings consisted of uncultivated land that had little value until it could be developed and thousands of acres he had leveraged on credit. Unlike Washington, Knox could no longer be absent from his land without risking financial ruin. And most important of all, Knox had children while the president did not.

From the president's perspective, however, the needs of the country unquestionably came before those of any individual, and he had expected Knox to be attending his duties during the crisis in Pennsylvania.

On December 5, Knox confided in Winthrop Sargent, the secretary of the Ohio Territory, that he would resign from the government before the beginning of the year. He worked frantically to put his office in order before his departure and provided Congress with a flurry of reports on the wide scope of projects under his direction, including updates on the ongoing work to erect federal forts along the frontiers and the project to build a line of coastal defenses for the nation's harbors. He also provided reports on the ongoing efforts to organize, arm, and train the state militias.

He composed a detailed statement addressing the delays in the construction of the six frigates and the launch the U.S. Navy; his defensive tone reflected his frustrations in dealing with Congress. He pointed out that work had been postponed because funding for the project had not been made available until June 9, although the legislation was approved on March 25. The other obstacle had been the procurement of raw materials. Prior to the Revolution, the American colonies had relied on the British and its navy for protection and therefore the country lacked the infrastructure to build battleships. Knox was erecting the U.S. Navy from scratch. Few supplies were already stocked, and many of the raw materials had to be harvested, mined, or even planted in the earth and grown. He explained to Congress: "[The] wood of which the frames were to be made was standing in the forests; the iron for the cannon lying in its natural bed; and the flax and hemp, perhaps, in their seed. That the materials will be soon collected and the building vigorously pushed."[36]

During the Christmas holiday season, Knox told Washington of his plan to resign from the administration and to return to New England. Washington once again urged him to stay. But Henry had so often chosen duty and country over his family; he told Washington that he could no longer sacrifice the happiness of his wife and children. Two days after Christmas, Knox wrote a letter to Henry Jackson telling him to prepare for his arrival at the Maine estate: "I hope to be a free man on the first day of January, although both the measure and the time are strongly objected to."

After spending a few moments reflecting on his long public career, Knox sat down and wrote out his formal resignation on December 28. He reduced his reasons to paper for Washington, again citing "the indispensable claims of a wife and a growing and numerous family of children, whose sole hopes of comfortable competence rest upon my life and exertions, will no longer permit me to neglect duties so sacred. But in whatever situation I shall be, I shall recollect your confidence and kindness with all the fervor and purity of affection of which a grateful heart can be susceptible."[37]

Washington responded two days later, acknowledging Knox's long-standing desire to return to private life and accepting his resignation without argument. "I can only wish that it was otherwise," the president wrote. "I cannot suffer you however, to close your public service without uniting with the satisfaction which must arise in your own mind from a conscious rectitude, my most perfect persuasion, that you have deserved well of your country."[38]

Knox picked up his last paycheck of $750 on December 31 and signed a receipt for the last time as "HKnox, Secretary of War." In the opening days of January 1795, an anonymous letter appeared in publisher John Fenno's quasi-official Federalist, *Gazette of the United States*, which announced Knox's departure from the administration.

> Among the changes which are likely to take place in the offices of our general government, there is none which we have greater cause to lament than the resignation of the Secretary of War. When we recall the services, which he has rendered his country, whether in a military or political vein, his merits demand our warmest approbation and praise. The early Revolution, when many of the mushroom patriots of today stepped behind the scene; the important service which he afterwards rendered to the cause of liberty by his activity, zeal and perseverance, which were so conspicuous on every occasion, leave a deep impression on the mind of every friend of America. . . . In his private life, we find the integrity, zeal, candor and good sense. The late important victory of our Western Army proves beyond contradiction the wisdom of those measures devised by the Secretary of War preparatory to that end. Signed, a citizen.

ELEVEN

SOLDIER'S HOME

After Henry stepped down from the government, he and Lucy lingered in Philadelphia for six months while the finishing touches were applied to their home in the remote District of Maine. On June 1, 1795, the couple uprooted their six children, parted with friends, and bid farewell to the cosmopolitan capital before heading north for life in a secluded backwoods that was then an undeveloped territory of Massachusetts.

Although Lucy enjoyed life as a Philadelphia socialite, she welcomed the move to the sprawling estate because of a visceral tie to the land. The move to her ancestral estate allowed Lucy to plant roots in familial ground after two decades of estrangement from her heritage.

When Henry, Lucy, and the children reached New York City, they embarked aboard a packet sailing for Boston Harbor. After reaching their hometown, they were dined and toasted at a lavish banquet held in Henry's honor. The native son had left as a bookseller and had returned as a famous general and national political leader.

After a few days of relaxation, the Knoxes boarded a vessel that sailed 175 miles up the Atlantic coast, at which point they took a ferry along the winding St. George River, which the Indians called Segochet, or "a pleasant place." As they approached the remote hamlet of Thomaston on June 22, they could see their majestic mansion rising above the coniferous forest, elevated on a high bank overlooking the water. The white rectangular structure, which featured an oval center chamber and portico, was constructed of stone, brick, and timber. Montpelier's mammoth size was along the lines of a public building rather than a private home, and Knox could proudly beam that he had provided his family with the most impressive residence in all of New England. Although he had never toured Washington's Mount Vernon or Jefferson's

Monticello, his imagination seemed to have been fueled by descriptions of their homes. His abode would not suffer by comparison, regardless of the constraints on his pocketbook.

The Knoxes stepped off the riverboat ferry onto their own spacious front lawn, where a group of Thomaston residents had turned out with a welcome party even before they had the chance to cross the home's threshold. Over the previous year, the mansion's construction—in an area typified by rustic log cabins—naturally drew curiosity. One of the townspeople stepped forward with a prepared speech, welcoming the heralded general but regretting his absence from the national government: "We deplore the loss of our United Federal Government of an officer so distinguishedly deserving, so actively patriotic and so highly meritorious, as our late Secretary of War."[1]

Despite the air of civility, Knox's imprint on the community was already being felt, and some of the residents were uneasy about his arrival as he showed off his family. His daughter Lucy was a young woman of nineteen; Henry Jackson Knox was fifteen; followed by Julia, eleven; George, five; Caroline, four; Augusta Henrietta, twenty-one months; and Marcus Bingham, nine months.[2]

In planning Montpelier, Henry and Lucy had envisioned a grand yet delicately crafted cultural oasis. Henry demonstrated an eye for style, providing architect Ebenezer Dunton with detailed instructions that incorporated features meant to make the home visually memorable. As his family entered the house, they were ushered into an oval-shaped room as large as a public lobby that had been designed to accommodate entertainment for a large group of friends. Two white-marble fireplaces gave the area a feeling of warmth. The room's wooden doors had been carefully steamed and bent to fit the oval walls. Henry ordered special glass for the windows, which extended down to the floorboards so that guests could open any of the swinging windows and step out on the piazza to take in the panoramic view of the St. George River as it stretched for miles toward the Atlantic Ocean.

To the left of the home's first-floor oval, or "salon floor," Henry's library beckoned guests with the finest literature along with after-dinner diversions. Henry and Lucy took it upon themselves to set the community's tone for style and taste. His shelves were filled with 15,353 volumes, collected over years, including 364 books published in French. A billiard table was installed in the library from the firm of Benjamin Frothingham, Jr. In Lucy's "withdrawing room," she could host games of chess and whist. From the respected firm of

Longman & Broderip, the Knoxes ordered an expensive pianoforte, the first such instrument ever to appear in Maine.

In the evenings, the game room glistened from tiny bits of mica, which were metal chips, embedded in the wallpaper that sparkled in the candlelight. The house contained several guest rooms, including a "Gold Room" for visiting dignitaries, so called because of the gilded wallpaper, the gold-brocaded valances, and the gold-colored Aubusson rug.

Soon after, a cordial letter from Thomas Jefferson arrived. "Have you become a farmer?" Jefferson inquired politely. "Is it not pleasanter than to be shut up within four walls and delving eternally with the pen?" Jefferson portrayed himself as a simple planter on Monticello and gave little indication of his ambition to become U.S. president: "I am become the most ardent farmer in the state [of Virginia]," he told Knox. "I live on my horse from morning to night almost. Intervals are filled up with attentions to a nailery. . . . I rarely look into a book, and more rarely take up a pen. I have proscribed newspapers, not taking a single one, nor scarcely ever looking into one. My next reformation will be to allow neither pen, ink, nor paper to be kept on the farm. When I have accomplished this I shall be in a fair way of indemnifying myself for the drudgery in which I have passed my life."[3]

Farming was just one of a myriad of businesses that Knox was set to explore. His years spent planning large government projects had led him to believe that he could take on monumental tasks. As war secretary, he had planned the nation's fortifications, orchestrated military expeditions, planned coastal defenses, and established the U.S. Navy. No enterprise seemed to be beyond his abilities. He was accustomed to overseeing an army and giving commands. As he looked over the Waldo patent, he envisioned workers toiling in a variety of enterprises: lumberyards, fisheries, cattle breeding, brickmaking, farming, shipbuilding, lime burning, and other crafts. Three years earlier, he had sent a French mineralogist by the name of Monvel to inspect the land and determine the natural resources. He reported that limestone was plentiful along with thirty-one other minerals, thirty-two varieties of trees, and seventy-five different plants and herbs. Marble was also plentiful. Knox planned to carve a community out of wilderness, and he drew up plans for roads, churches, schools, libraries, shops, post offices, and homes, believing the land would yield a fortune if settlers planted roots and built up the area.

Yet unlike the government projects, he had to come up with the private funds to make his land and business ventures profitable before he was buried beneath mortgages, taxes, bills, and lawsuits. Already highly leveraged, Knox began to sell off even more land and to borrow from friends, such as Benjamin Lincoln. He placed advertisements in New England newspapers touting the region's healthy climate in an effort to attract settlers who might boost the value of property. In the meantime, Knox made few concessions to curtail his grand lifestyle.

The controversial diplomat Charles-Maurice de Talleyrand-Perigord, commonly known as Talleyrand, made a trip to Montpelier. After the French monarchy fell, Talleyrand fled to England where he lived with John B. Church, the brother-in-law of Alexander Hamilton. He was forced to leave England due to an expulsion order by William Pitt, and Church financed his trip to the United States and set up a meeting with Hamilton. Washington declined to receive him to avoid an awkward situation with France. Talleyrand made the trip to Knox's home in an effort to establish ties with influential American leaders.

That July, a Frenchman by the name of George Washington Motier Lafayette arrived in Boston as a political refugee. The son of the Marquis de Lafayette, he had been accompanied to America by his tutor, Felix Frestel. The young Lafayette traveled simply under the name George Washington Motier in order to conceal his identity.

Shortly after victory at Yorktown in 1781, the elder Lafayette had returned to Paris. When the stirrings of revolution began in France, Lafayette took a lead in the reform movement and was elected in 1789 to the legislature, the Estates-General. In June of that year, Louis XVI agreed to share power with the legislature, which was soon replaced by the National Assembly. Lafayette was elected to the assembly, where he presented a declaration of rights that he had cowritten with Thomas Jefferson. Lafayette was so enthralled with the spirit of liberty and equality that he denounced his noble title in 1790.

But the upheaval soon flamed out of control as idealism gave way to bloody carnage. Heads of murdered aristocrats were placed on pikes, and the bodies of nobles were dragged through the streets of Paris. Lafayette became dismayed at the revolution's violence. He rescued the queen, Marie Antoinette, from the hands of a mob in October 1789 and valiantly worked to save other aristocrats. The Jacobin party finally issued an order for Lafayette's arrest in 1792, which forced him to flee for safety. He was arrested in Rochefort, Belgium, and was imprisoned by the Austrian army. President Washington made repeated diplomatic appeals in vain to secure Lafayette's release.

In late August 1795, Knox made a business trip to Boston and was sought out by Lafayette's son, who instantly made a favorable impression. As the young student talked, Henry found him to be "a lovely young man, of excellent morals and conduct."[4] He was moved as he listened to the plight of Motier, who had come to America seeking help from his namesake, George Washington, but was uncertain whether he should contact the president. As a member of the Lafayette family, he had been deemed an enemy to the French government, and Washington could not acknowledge him without insulting France.

Knox wrote a confidential note to Washington on Motier's behalf. He had not written to the president since leaving the government and opened the correspondence by confessing to an uneasy "reluctance to break in upon your affairs." He then continued with encouraging words, telling Washington that the political storm over the controversial Jay's Treaty was finally subsiding in New England. In recent months, the president had been subjected to severe criticism for his approval of the treaty between the United States and Great Britain that had been negotiated by John Jay. Washington argued that the accord had averted another war with England. Nevertheless, riots erupted in Boston as angry demonstrators marched in the streets, crying that the treaty failed to stop the British practice of attacking American ships and impressing merchant seamen. In a port town such as Boston, many families had lost loved ones on the high seas. Feeling betrayed by the treaty, they demanded war with England.

Among the graffiti scrawled in protest was the cry: "Damn John Jay! Damn every one that won't damn John Jay! Damn every one that won't put lights in his windows and sit up all night damning John Jay!!!"[5]

Knox told Washington that protests had been fueled by Republican critics of the administration who enthusiastically supported the French Revolution. "The experience the good Citizens have had of their president, and their confidence in their government, has caused them to reflect—then to conclude and tacitly to acknowledge that the treaty although not so favorable as their wishes dictated; was not, so injurious to France and their own country as they had been led to believe."[6]

Knox told the president that he had found happiness in his wilderness retreat and that his prospects looked promising: "Mrs. Knox and my family and myself are entirely satisfied with our situation—we are surrounded with plenty."

In Philadelphia, Washington read Henry's words and denoted a tone of apprehension over their strained relationship. The president responded on

September 20 in an unequivocally warm tone: "My dear Sir: I received with great pleasure the letter you wrote me from Boston . . . as I always shall do any others you may favor me with. This pleasure was increased by hearing of the good health of Mrs. Knox and the rest of your family, and the agreeableness of your establishment at St. George's in the Province of Maine." Washington entreated Knox to spend his winter in Philadelphia, and thanked him for his heartening thoughts on the public reaction to Jay's Treaty. The president waxed philosophically over his ongoing conflict between "upright intentions" and the "approbation of my constituents." He confided that he could not publicly meet with Motier but would pay for him to attend college. "Assure [Motier] in the strongest terms, that I would be to him as a friend and father."[7]

The Knox family spent its summers in Montpelier and winters in Boston. In January 1796, Knox traveled from Boston to Philadelphia to bury his brother. He had placed William in the Pennsylvania Hospital in that city on January 14, 1795, two weeks after stepping down as war secretary. He had been William's father figure since he was three years of age in 1759, when Henry was just nine years old. They had grown up together and had faced an adult world at each other's side. But there was little Henry could do to help William as his mental condition worsened except to pay for his care. He died on December 30, 1795.

If Knox indeed did miss public life, he was too tied up in his financial ventures to return to government duty. He kept an interest in political news. On February 21, he sent Washington a list of candidates to help settle a border disagreement with Great Britain. The U.S. boundary was in dispute because of confusion over the true path of the St. Croix River. Instead of selecting one of Knox's choices for the appointment, Washington nominated Henry on March 31, 1796, as one of the commissioners, and the Senate confirmed the appointment on April 1.[8]

In writing to Knox on April 4, Washington acknowledged that "before this will have reached you, you must have seen in the gazettes, that I have taken the liberty (without a previous consultation) to nominate you the commissioner."[9]

With his business projects just getting off the ground, Knox felt he had no choice but to decline the appointment. In writing to Washington on April 14, he explained in an initial draft of the letter that "I shall have sixty workmen employed during the summer, in erecting mills and other buildings, opening slate and marble quarries, and in keeping lime and bricks. These and other things are experiments to raise a revenue while my lands are gradually selling at the least nimble prices."[10]

But Knox decided to omit this paragraph in the final draft of the letter and instead concisely wrote: "The appointment of commissioner would mar most effectually my plans for the summer and which are on an expensive train of execution."[11] Knox also told Washington that the duty of the commissioners created a conflict of interest due to his landholdings in Maine, and offered words of encouragement: "No chief magistrate ever possessed in a degree greater the affection and respect than you."[12]

Aside from his business interests, a personal dilemma forced Henry to bow out of any appointment. Two of his children came down with a disorder that was then called putrid sore throat and was later named diphtheria. The highly contagious disease caused children to vomit and suffer nausea, chills, and fever and to experience a sore throat and trouble swallowing. Henry and Lucy could do nothing to save three-year-old Augusta Henrietta and twenty-month-old Marcus Bingham. Both died on April 23, 1796. Six-year-old George also became ill. Four days later, the *Columbia Centinel* noted the deaths of the two children and the illness of a third against a tragic backdrop of repeated deaths in the Knox family: "Seven healthy, blooming children have been torn almost as suddenly from the same fond parents, who, with lacerated hearts, hang over the bed of another child, laboring under the same disease."[13]

Upon learning of the deaths of the Knox children, Washington wrote to the grieving parents on June 8 with "my sincere condolence on your late heavy loss. Great and trying, as it must be to your sensibility, I am persuaded after the first severe pangs are over you both possess fortitude enough to view the event, as the dispensation of providence, and will submit to its decrees, with philosophical resignation."[14]

Just as Knox had done so many times before, he threw himself into his work. He continued to plan projects as if he had a gnawing need to carry out large ideas and feel expansive. He soon employed more than 100 men in occupations such as quarrymen, brick-makers, carpenters, coopers, blacksmiths, farmers, gardeners, laborers, and millwrights. By the summer of 1796, his shipyards started building vessels to ship goods used in his businesses. He decided to use nearby Brigadier Island as an isolated breeding ground for improved strains of cattle and sheep. He imported sheep from England that were bred for their heavy wool and crossed them with domestically bred animals with success.

Henry continued to have faith in the inevitable profitability of the estate and had few reservations about spending future earnings on present expenses. He was generous to a fault, and too fond of entertaining for his limited income. During one hospitable mood, he opened his house to the entire Tarratine clan of the Penobscot Indians and set out a banquet of beef, pork, corn, and bread. The Indians stayed for several days until Knox's pantry became bare. He finally had to politely ask his guests to leave.

Knox kept himself constantly set in motion by pursuing one project after another and hosting nightly dinners as an escape. If the twin deaths in the spring of that year had not already been painful enough, in December George Washington Knox died shortly before turning seven years old, after years of poor health. Lucy was inconsolable, and Henry felt that she once again had suffered a permanent emotional wound that would never heal. After refraining from writing to Washington for several months, he felt obligated to notify the president that his namesake had died. Writing from his winter home in Boston, Henry wrote on January 15, 1797, saying that the boy had "always been sickly, having been born premature, but we flattered ourselves that his health would increase with his years. Unfortunate indeed have we been in the death of eight children, requiring the exercise of our whole stock of philosophy & religion [and every] other principle of support. However I hope we may say with propriety that God tempers his wounds to the shorn lamb. We find ourselves afflicted by an irresistible but invisible force to whom we must submit—But the conflict is almost too great for the inconsolable mother who will go mourning to her grave."[15] He told Washington that his financial prospects had been improving and that his land had doubled in value since his move to Thomaston.

Washington was preparing to leave the presidency when he responded to Henry on March 2 with words of solace: "From the friendship I have always borne you, and from the interest I have ever taken in whatever relates to your prosperity and happiness, I participated in the sorrows which I know you must have felt for your late heavy losses. But is not for man to scan the wisdom of Providence. The best he can do, is to submit to its decrees. Reason, religion and philosophy, teaches us to do this, but 'tis time alone that can ameliorate the pangs of humanity, and soften its woes."

As he moved toward retirement, Washington described himself as a "wearied traveler who sees a resting place, and is bending his body to lean thereon," stating that there were but a "few intimates whom I love, among these, be assured you are one."[16] Two days later, George Washington stepped down from office and walked away from power.

★ ★ ★ ★

In his inauguration speech on March 4, 1797, John Adams alluded to the controversy surrounding his election and the French government's open and very public support of Thomas Jefferson's candidacy. If France had been able to influence the American election, Adams said, then "[it] may be foreign nations who govern us, and not we, the people, who govern ourselves."[17]

Adams faced an undeclared naval war with France, whose seamen continued to attack and seize American ships on the high seas in response to Jay's Treaty with Britain. France refused to recognize the American ambassador, Charles Cotesworth Pinckney, and even threatened to have him arrested, which forced him to flee to the Netherlands.

The strained relations with France weighed on Knox's mind as he wrote to John Adams, his friend of nearly three decades. "I doubt whether I ought to congratulate you on being elevated to the chief magistracy of the United States," he cautioned, "for it is questionable, very questionable, whether there are not more thorns than roses in the situation." Henry suggested that Adams send Thomas Jefferson to France to restore harmony between the two countries. "I entertain so good an opinion of Mr. Jefferson's patriotism, as to believe he would not hesitate, and much less refuse the offer."[18]

In a confidential letter to Knox written on March 19, Adams claimed that he sought the presidency only to prevent unqualified candidates from leading the country. "To see such a character as Jefferson, and much more such an unknown being as Pinckney, brought over my head, and trampling on the bellies of hundreds of other men infinitely his superiors in talents, services, and reputation, filled me with apprehensions for the safety of us all." Adams shared Knox's apprehensions that full war could erupt with France. "I have it much at heart to settle all disputes with France, and nothing shall be wanting on my part to accomplish it."[19]

Knox maintained an interest in national affairs as the country continued to veer toward hostilities. He realized that if America and France went to war with each other, his life would take a drastic turn. If called into service, he would have to abandon his plans for the Maine property and once again leave his family and the comforts of home for the rigors of military life. As tensions in the country rose, however, he could take pride in the fact that during his tenure as war secretary, he had been able to maintain the army, build fortifications, and begin the construction of harbor and coastal defenses—all of which suddenly became vitally important as the threat of a French invasion loomed. And perhaps most important of all, Knox had been able to help establish a navy. On May 10, 1797, one of the original six frigates that he had helped plan was launched in Philadelphia under the command of Captain John Barry. Knox could read with pleasure the newspaper reports that chronicled one of the greatest spectacles that anyone in the capital could ever remember as an immense crowd of 30,000 showed up at Front and Water streets to witness the event. Critics claimed the vessel would split apart once afloat due to its excessive weight. At one o'clock the restraining blocks were knocked away from the keel and the 1,500-ton vessel slid into the Delaware River to great cheers. The hull remained firm, and Knox's gamble had paid off.

President Adams did not send Jefferson to France but instead recommended to Congress that a three-man delegation be dispatched. Adams delivered a belligerent speech to the House of Representatives on May 16, denouncing France for refusing to receive Charles Cotesworth Pinckney of South Carolina as the American ambassador and treating the United States as a colony rather than a sovereign country. The president recommended expanding the U.S. Navy and the militia as "effectual measures of defense."[20] In June, the secretary of state reported that France had captured 300 American commercial ships.

The quarrel continued to need remedy. The three-man American delegation of John Marshall, a U.S. Representative from Virginia, along with Elbridge Gerry and Pinckney arrived in Paris on October 4, 1797, where they received a cold reception. The French foreign minister turned out to be Talleyrand, who had previously toured America and been a guest in the homes of several prominent leaders, including Knox and Alexander Hamilton.

The resilient Talleyrand had returned to France after the Reign of Terror and found his way back into the good graces of the French Directory, which served as the executive branch of the government. He obtained the highly coveted appointment as foreign minister, and hoped to capitalize on his public position by extorting money from foreign ambassadors seeking an audience with the Directory. He told a friend: "I have to make an immense fortune out of it, a really immense fortune." During his first two years as foreign minister, he collected an estimated 13 to 14 million francs.[21]

Talleyrand condescendingly sent word to the American delegation that he would not meet with them in person but instead sent three emissaries, who were later referred in the commission's dispatches simply as "X," "Y," and "Z." The agents told Marshall, Gerry, and Pinckney that members of the French Directory were irritated by passages in Adams's speech and demanded that they be softened into a more respectful tone. Then the agents flatly told the Americans that as a condition to any treaty negotiations, the U.S. government would have to provide a "loan" to France. In addition, Talleyrand demanded a personal bribe of $240,000. The American delegation was stunned but realized that France had very little incentive to come to an agreement because of American neutrality in the war between France and Britain. One of Talleyrand's agents explained that "all nations should aid them, or be considered and treated as their enemies."[22] News of the affront was not immediately known in America because of the confidential nature of the talks, which were plagued by a series of postponements over the winter.

Knox was forced to wonder about his future as the prospect of war continued. The American effort to reach an accord with France that would protect U.S. commercial shipping interests, similar to the Jay's Treaty with Britain, was proving fruitless. On January 8, 1798, John Marshall formally rejected France's demand that the United States pay a bribe. When Talleyrand's agents warned that a refusal might trigger a war, Pinckney replied defiantly that the United States would pay "millions for defense, but not one cent for tribute . . . no; no; not a sixpence."[23]

Knox closely followed the newspaper reports chronicling President Adams's announcement to Congress of unsavory details of the XYZ correspondence on March 19. Around Boston, Knox heard growing anti-French sentiment, and many of his neighbors supported a war.

In response to the ongoing undeclared naval war with France, Congress created a separate U.S. Department of the Navy in May to increase the size of the fleet that Knox began in 1794. After Congress authorized President Adams to raise a 10,000-man volunteer army, Knox realized that he would likely be called for military service. To give the force legitimacy in the public's eyes, President Adams named George Washington as commander in chief.

Adams arranged to send Secretary of War James McHenry to Mount Vernon to notify Washington of his recall to service. When Secretary of State Timothy Pickering learned of this, he quickly drafted a letter to Washington suggesting that he use his influence with President Adams to appoint Hamilton as his top commander.

Hamilton meanwhile met with Pickering in Philadelphia to discuss army appointments. Pickering handed him a copy of his letter to Washington touting Hamilton, who did not voice any disapproval of the clandestine attempt to use Washington's prestige to force President Adams to appoint him virtual commander. Hamilton was troubled, however, that this move would have to come at Knox's expense.

When McHenry traveled to Mount Vernon, he unwittingly played a role in Pickering's conspiracy by delivering his letter among a pile of other dispatches. Pickering's note told Washington that New England leaders and several prominent members of Congress were demanding that Hamilton be appointed second in command.

Washington had already decided to accept command of the army under the conditions that he would not be required to leave Mount Vernon until actual fighting was imminent and only if he could pick his top commanders. His second in command would be the virtual leader of the army. Washington ranked his top choices in order: Hamilton, Charles C. Pinckney, who had served as one of his aide-de-camps during the revolution, and then Knox. Washington also considered the talents of Charles Pinckney, whose reputation was riding high due to his defiant stance with the French during the XYZ affair. Washington believed that if France invaded America, the southern states would be the most vulnerable and tempting target for the enemy. Recruiting officers from that area would be much easier if Pinckney, who hailed from South Carolina, played a major role in the army. Until reading Pickering's letter, Washington had not considered that Hamilton would walk away from his lucrative law practice and an annual salary of £4,000 to return to the army. He wrote Pickering that Hamilton's "services ought to be secured at *almost* any price."[24]

More than anybody, Washington was keenly aware of Alexander Hamilton's extraordinary abilities. He thought that Hamilton was one of the most gifted men of his age, even eclipsing Thomas Jefferson in Washington's estimation. Hamilton had been the dominant member of his cabinet and had married into the influential Schuyler family of New York. During the Revolution, Washington also had the opportunity to judge Hamilton's military judgment and ability. As an aide, Hamilton wrote many of the general's most important letters and often served as his proxy in dealing with officers. He became so adept at anticipating Washington's needs, so quick to grasp issues, plan strategy, and offer remarkably sound judgment and perceptive suggestions, that Washington must have believed that his aide could actually step in and fill his shoes. Washington thought that Hamilton's intuitive judgment was "great."

Regardless of the intrigues behind the appointments, of which an astute man like Washington must have been well aware, he chose Hamilton as the army's inspector general, giving him preeminence over Knox and Pinckney. In a July 14 letter informing Hamilton of his appointment, Washington confessed to some uneasy feelings over the likelihood that his choice would wound the pride of "General Knox, whom I love and esteem."[25] Hamilton was also fond of Knox and seemed to feel indebted to him. He confessed to Pickering in a letter of July 17 that he would be willing to serve under Knox, if necessary, but that he would prefer to be second in command. Hamilton would not serve under Pinckney, however. Pickering never disclosed Hamilton's generous offer to Washington, who was led to believe that Hamilton would absolutely refuse to serve under Knox. Instead, Pickering gave Washington the impression that Hamilton and Knox vied with each other for preeminence, which irritated Washington.

President Adams submitted Washington's list to the Senate, and the appointments to the rank of major general were confirmed on Wednesday, July 18, in the order of Hamilton, Pinckney, and Knox.[26]

From Mount Vernon, Washington had sent a delicately written letter to Knox announcing the arrangements of the new army on July 16. When the note arrived in Boston on July 29, Knox opened the dispatch feeling "delightful sensations of affection" for Washington. But as his eyes scanned the words, he was astonished to find himself ranked below Hamilton and Pinckney, both of whom had been his juniors during the Revolution. Washington disingenuously implied that he played little role in the arrangement and stated that "[Hamilton] in the public estimation, as declared to me, is designated to be second in command; with some fears, I confess, of the consequences; although I must acknowledge at the same time that I know not where a more competent choice could be made."[27]

The words stung Knox. He studied each phrase in an attempt to decipher what he believed were hidden political motives. He wondered if the arrangement was meant to insult him to a degree that he would be forced to resign and therefore be deprived a role in the army. Knox shot back at Washington in the most forceful letter he ever penned to his former leader. "For more than twenty years, I must have been acting under a perfect delusion," he complained. "Conscious myself of entertaining for you a sincere, active, and invariable friendship, I easily believed it was reciprocal. Nay more, I flattered myself with your esteem and respect in a military point of view. But I find that

others, greatly my juniors in rank, have been, upon a scale of comparison, preferred before me."[28]

To protect his seniority, Knox decided to seize upon an obscure rule
passed by the Continental Congress under the Articles of Confederation that
stipulated that an officer's former rank during the Revolution still determined
hierarchy in the army. In other words, Knox would outrank Hamilton and
Pinckney because he was the superior officer during the war. This appeared to
be a dubious claim since the Continental Army, the Continental Congress,
and the Articles of Confederation had all passed into history. When Knox's
letter protesting Hamilton's promotion over him reached Mount Vernon,
Washington "was not a little surprised." He took exception to the accusations, which he found "insinuating and unkind," that his friendship had been
less than genuine during their long association. Yet he wrote Knox on August
9 that the wounded tone of his letter had "filled my mind with disquietude,
and perplexity in the extreme; but I will say nothing in reply, intentionally,
that shall give you a moments pain." He again claimed that he had played
very little role in picking the ranking of the major generals and only learned
of his own appointment from newspapers, after the issue of rank had been
decided. Washington assured Henry that his affection for him was unabated:
"I earnestly wished on account of that friendship, as well as on the score of
military talents, to have had the assistance of you and Colonel Hamilton in
the arduous contest with which we are threatened."[29] Washington sent a private note to McHenry expressing his doubts over whether Knox would serve
in the army.

Knox was not without his supporters, however, and not the least of these
was the President of the United States. John Adams had gone home to
Quincy, Massachusetts, to attend to his ill wife, Abigail, who was rheumatic
and struggling for life. Adams more than likely met with Knox, who was then
in Boston, and Henry had the opportunity to tell him of his litany of complaints. Adams took a moment away from caring for Abigail on August 14 to
express the written opinion that "General Knox is legally entitled to rank next
to General Washington; and no other arrangement will give satisfaction."
Adams did not agree that New Englanders preferred Hamilton over Knox. In
a letter to Secretary of War McHenry, he ordered that Washington's ranking
be reversed, which would place Knox above Hamilton. "If it shall be consented that the rank shall be Knox, Pinckney, and Hamilton, you may call the
latter, too, into immediate service, when you please. Any other plan will occasion long delay and much confusion. You may depend upon it, the five New

England States will not patiently submit to the humiliation that has been meditated for them."[30]

John Quincy Adams, the son of the president and a future president himself, later traced the "first decisive symptom" of a schism in the Federalist Party to the rivalry created by the ranking of the major generals. Washington and the president were suddenly at odds. And during the ordeal, the Adams cabinet showed itself to be more loyal to Hamilton than to the president.[31]

Washington was irritated that he had been second-guessed by President Adams in a military matter, and he resented Knox's attempt to make a direct appeal to Adams. Washington decided to throw his political influence behind Hamilton as his choice as second in command. He sent a confidential note to Pickering on September 9 that warned: "How the matters stands between [Knox] and the President; and what may be the ultimate decision of the latter, I know not; but I know that the President ought to ponder well before he consents to a change of the arrangement."[32]

Washington then cleared the air in a forceful letter to Adams on September 25 in which he flatly stated that if he could not have Hamilton as his coadjutor, the president could fight the war without him. He explained that the task of choosing among Knox, Hamilton, and Pinckney had been acutely painful. "With respect to General Knox," Washington told Adams, "I can say with truth, there is no man in the United States with whom I have been in habits of greater intimacy; no one whom I have loved more sincerely, nor any for whom I have had a greater friendship. But, esteem, love, and friendship, can have no influence on my mind when I conceive that the subjugation of our government and independence, are the objects aimed at by the enemies of our peace; and, when, possibly, our all is at stake."

President Adams was besieged on all sides as his own cabinet pressed for Hamilton to take virtual control of the army. Oliver Wolcott, the secretary of the Treasury, wrote him on September 17, saying that Knox had a spurious claim and reminded him that Washington had agreed to serve only if allowed to pick his generals. Adams wrote a heated reply voicing his virulent antipathy for Hamilton but refrained from mailing it: "If I should consent to the appointment of Hamilton as second in rank, I should consider it as the most [ir]responsible action of my whole life, and the most difficult to justify. Hamilton is not a native of the United States, but a foreigner."[33]

Henry realized that he could not serve in the new army and decided to resign his commission. He felt that he had lost Washington's confidence, and the trust that fostered an intimate relationship for the past twenty-three years had been broken. Knox also felt that he could not serve under a cloud of suspicion. The accusation that he had caused the breach in their friendship wounded him. In his reply, Knox recalled that Washington was the only person among all his friends who advised him to accept "the appointment of the third major general." Knox felt that his offer to serve as Washington's aide had been more than generous and "arose from the sincere effusion of personal attachment, unmixed with regret or resentment. But the possibility being suggested by you of my harboring any secret 'gnawings' upon the subject of rank, precludes decisively my having the satisfaction proposed, of sharing your fate in the field. I will not detain you one moment longer, than to say in the presence of Almighty God, that there is not a creature upon the face of the globe who was, is and will remain more your friend than H. Knox."[34]

TWELVE

ATOMS UPON THIS ATOM

Knox could not afford to accept a position in the army. If friends counseled him not to accept "the appointment of the third general," they also warned that he could not step away from his Maine estate without incurring financial disaster. Many of his ventures were unfinished and had yet to turn a profit. Knox was having one of the most difficult financial years of his life. His household and businesses were costing $7,661.60 annually to operate while his enterprises were generating about $6,500. He employed more than 100 men. According to records for 1798, cattle slaughtered annually just to feed his household and work crew amounted to 15,000 pounds of beef, 900 pounds of tallow, and 2,500 hides. One beeve and twenty sheep were butchered each week, along with a bounty of fish, fowl, and game. Henry Jackson, Henry's wartime comrade who helped manage his estate, told Knox that he could not walk away from his business obligations to accept any role in the army without risking everything.

Plans for the new army became less important as John Adams lost all his enthusiasm for a war with France. Deciding instead to place his hopes in a diplomatic solution, he began to put together another peace mission to send to Paris. Although tensions remained high as French ships continued to capture American commercial vessels, America's new navy was proving itself. On February 9, 1799, U.S. captain Thomas Truxton, commanding the thirty-six-gun *Constellation*, captured a French thirty-six-gun frigate, *L'Insurgente*, off the island of Nevis, near the birthplace of Alexander Hamilton. *L'Insurgente* had plagued U.S. trade and had captured a merchant ship as recently as November. Knox could take pride in the victory and that his gamble on large frigates was proving farsighted in the undeclared naval war with France.

With the controversy over the army rankings now a moot issue, Hamilton decided that it was time to restore his relationship with Knox. In a March 14 letter, he confessed: "My judgment tells me I ought to be silent on a certain subject; but my heart advises otherwise, and my heart has always been the master of my judgment." Hamilton said he felt greatly pained by Knox's resignation and explained that he had not played a role in the rivalry that had been created between them. This claim was not without truth. Hamilton did offer to serve under Knox, but Pickering did not pass this information on to Washington.

Hamilton confided that "there has been a serious struggle between my respect and attachment for you and the impression of duty. This sounds, I know, like affection, but it is nevertheless the truth. In saying this much, my only motive is to preserve, if I may, a claim on your friendly disposition towards me, and to give you some evidence that my regard for you is unabated."[1]

The words provided Knox with great solace. Despite their differences, Knox had great respect and love for Hamilton. Their careers had become inextricably intertwined, and together they had shared some of the most significant moments in American history.

A similar friendly gesture came from Mount Vernon. In an effort to restore ties with Knox, Washington sent a letter on May 22 assuring him of the "sincere and affectionate esteem" that he retained for Henry. Knox immediately replied in kind.

★ ★ ★ ★

Knox focused his attention on the development of Thomaston in the hopes that the growing settlement would soon increase the value of his land. He became a familiar figure on the town's streets, invariably dressed in black and carrying his gold-handled cane, which he flourished while making points during conversation. His rich baritone voice gave listeners a feeling that he was accustomed to barking orders. He might have seemed imposing if not for his regard for the feelings of other people and his fondness for laughing. He wore a light silk hat, which he would often remove when in the shade. People took notice of the way he would unwind and rewrap the handkerchief over his mutilated hand carefully as if not to expose the injury from his teenage years.

The only drawback to his remote retreat was the absence of friends. He seemed to need constant companionship. Relationships in the eighteenth century often were maintained through cross-country correspondence, and years might pass without friends ever being able to meet in person. Knox kept in touch with many of his former comrades and remained active in the Society of Cincinnati. But he was social by nature and could not long stay away from society. The Knoxes continued to spend their winters in Boston. On December 22, he wrote to George Washington as one longtime friend to another. Making an introduction on behalf of a Boston friend, Knox wrote: "He like myriads of others, cannot die in peace, nor live with satisfaction, until they see you, who has done so much for them and for their Country!"

He reported that he was prospering and that his son, Henry Jackson Knox, was in the navy. "I am here and should be more happy in my pursuits than I have ever been were some embarrassments entirely dissipated. But this will require time. My estate with indulgence is competent, and greatly more, to the discharge of every cent I owe."

Knox had no way of knowing as he wrote these words that Washington had already died. Ironically he concluded the letter by saying: "I may not wish you the greatest blessing by wishing you a long life—because I believe firmly that while you continue here you are detained from a much better condition. But I pray fervently that your days on earth may be days of felicity without clouds of sickness or sorrow."[2]

On December 13, Washington had ridden about his estate and was caught in a light rain, after which he developed a fever and complained of difficulty in breathing. His condition worsened, and doctors bled him of twelve ounces of blood, causing him to deteriorate badly. He died on December 14, 1799, at 67 years of age, and was placed in the vault at Mount Vernon just days after Congress had begun sessions in the capital bearing his name.

In November 1800, a fire erupted at the War Department office in Washington, D.C. Nothing could be done to save the warehoused records detailing the careers of the former secretaries. Samuel Dexter, the current secretary of war, bemoaned: "All my papers have been destroyed by fire." Yet in letters, Knox did not express concern that his place in history might have been jeopardized.

Knox was not completely finished with politics, however. In the presidential election of 1800, Knox worked in support of the reelection of John Adams. The issues that divided the country continued to revolve around relations with France along with the unpopularity of the Alien and Sedition and Naturalization acts. In response to the number of French agents and spies known to be operating around the country and due the strong pro-French sentiment, Congress passed these drastic measures that curtailed free speech and civil rights. President Adams extended their use to silence critics of his administration by throwing a number of newspaper publishers in jail.

The military buildup in the face of the possible war had caused high taxes, and Adams was blamed by his opponents for being simultaneously too soft and too harsh in his dealings with France. When electoral ballots were counted on February 11, 1801, Thomas Jefferson and Aaron Burr both received seventy-three votes, followed by Adams with sixty-five and Pinckney with sixty-four. Six days later, the U.S. House ran through thirty-six ballots and remained deadlocked. The Federalist caucus backed Burr, but Alexander Hamilton used his influence to swing the election to Jefferson, who was chosen president. Burr became the vice president.

At the time, Knox would have had little reason to realize that election marked the end of prominence of the Federalists. From the mid-1780s until the defeat of John Adams, the Federalists had dominated American politics. Knox had been a vital cog in the party as its members had cemented the union, created and championed a national constitution, and had produced the first two U.S. Presidents while building up the nation's defenses and sparking its economy. But the party that centered itself on a belief in a vigorous federal government, strong national defense, and pro-British economic ties suddenly found itself too weak to ever again win a presidential election.

Part of the reason that the party could burn so brightly and yet would flare out so suddenly lay in its dependence on George Washington. The Federalist Party had been built by men who had been willing to subvert their careers to boost Washington's reputation in an attempt to unify the country. The Federalists were able to capitalize on the popularity of Washington—much to the dismay of Republicans like Jefferson—to gain national office. Jefferson viewed a personality-driven party as undemocratic in spirit.

Once Washington was no longer on the scene, much of the Federalists' strength dissipated. Fortunately for Jefferson, the leading Federalist, Alexander Hamilton, could not run for president because he was foreign-born.

Although disappointed at the defeat of John Adams, Knox was heartened by Jefferson's inaugural address, specifically by his reminder that "We have called by different names brethren of the same principle. We are all Republicans, we are all Federalists."[3]

In a March 16 letter to Jefferson, Knox admitted that he had backed Adams but praised the bipartisan stance of the new president's national address and expressed confidence in his colleague's character. Responding eleven days later, Jefferson voiced "the greatest satisfaction I learn from all quarters that my inaugural address is considered as holding out a ground for conciliation & union." Writing perhaps for the eyes of John Adams, he explained in detail that he would likely nullify many of the late-hour federal appointments the former president had made after discovering that he had been denied reelection. "I have opened myself frankly because I wish to be understood by those who mean well, and are disposed to be just towards me, as you are," Jefferson explained to Knox. "I know you will use it for good purposes only and for none unfriendly to me."[4]

In Massachusetts, Knox remained active in state politics, and ran in 1801 for a seat in the legislature, which was called the general court. During sessions, he appeared affably unpolished in debates and hesitant as a speaker. During his military career, he had been accustomed to carefully collecting his thoughts and reducing his opinions to paper. He was less comfortable in the impromptu arena of deliberations on the floor of the state house. Harrison Otis Gray, a former U.S. congressman who served alongside Knox in the state legislature, observed that Henry "did not possess the talent of debate, but was unaffectedly diffident of his oratorical powers. He was nevertheless a fluent and effective speaker. He had the gift of natural eloquence; his imagination was ardent, and his style sublimated perhaps to a fault." Knox tended to use flowery language. Yet Otis claimed that no one in the legislature commanded greater attention when speaking than did the booming General Knox. But even Otis believed that Knox was at his best in the company of the polished circles of high society.

To Knox's great satisfaction, President Jefferson reversed his earlier opposition to Henry's long-standing proposal for a national military academy. On March 16, 1802, Congress gave its approval for a military school for the corps of engineers and named Jonathan Williams, a grand-nephew of Benjamin Franklin, its superintendent. The United States Military Academy at West Point opened on Independence Day, 1802. Knox had continually advocated a military academy for the past twenty-five years. He had established the nation's first officer-training academy at his artillery headquarters at Pluckemin during the war, which was the forerunner to West Point. In 1783 and again during the Washington administration, he specifically proposed West Point as the site to build a military school, and he even went so far as to outline a course of study.

Knox's contribution to the U.S. military and his support for a military academy were recognized by his election to the United States Military Philosophical

Society, which was headquartered at West Point. The academy's superintendent, Williams, founded the society, using books he had inherited from his great-uncle. These volumes became its scientific library. The society's political and military goals were to build knowledge that would help develop nations around the world.

★ ★ ★ ★

On May 17, 1803, Henry Jackson Knox married Eliza Taylor Reed, the eldest daughter of the town clerk in Thomaston, Josiah Reed, who published their engagement as part of his official duties. The match was viewed as fortuitous by Henry and Lucy. Miss Reed was the granddaughter of a wealthy landowner, and their son's future prospects appeared bright. The bride was also intelligent and charming, known for her amiable personality.

Knox's daughter Lucy also became betrothed. On January 6, 1804, she married Ebenezer Thatcher of Newcastle, a brigadier general in the state militia. He was educated at Harvard as a lawyer and would later become a circuit court judge in the District of Maine. He was athletic and rugged, yet had a refined quality and was remarkably articulate. He also had impeccable Revolutionary War credentials as the son of Samuel Thatcher, a militia colonel who fought at the battles of Lexington and Concord.

In the spring of 1804, the sister-in-law of James Madison, Anna Cutts, made a visit to Boston and spent much of her time with the Knoxes. In the evenings, Lucy would lay out tables with games for guests to play. Henry refrained from participating in these amusements but would walk around the room, moving from one circle of guests to another playing host. Lucy was competitive by nature and kept her gaming skills sharp by constant practice. Cutts wrote to her sister, Dolley Madison: "We have very pleasant lodgings, and for my companion, the famous Madame Knox, who although very haughty, I find pleasant and sensible. Chess is now her mania, which she plays extremely well, only too often for my fancy, who am not of late so partial to it. Every morning after breakfast, there is a summons from her ladyship, which I attend, pins me to her apron-string until time to dress for dinner, after which she retires, again inviting me to battle. Out of twenty-one games, in only two, and a drawn game, has she shown me any mercy; she is certainly the most successful play I have ever encountered."[5]

Shortly before Knox turned fifty-four, he was appointed by Massachusetts governor Caleb Strong in June 1804 to the state's executive council, which served as the upper body of the legislature. Knox continued to play the role of a key advisor on state issues while he managed his property. Within weeks of his appointment, Knox received the shocking news that the sitting vice president of the United States had murdered Alexander Hamilton at a secluded spot along the Hudson River opposite New York City called Weehawken. During the Revolution, Knox had inspected that ground many times.

According to the *New York Evening Post*, Hamilton had crossed the river at seven in the morning on July 11, 1804, to meet Vice President Aaron Burr for a duel. Burr aimed deliberately, apparently to kill. His ball punctured Hamilton's body on the right side, causing him to lift involuntarily on his toes and turn to his left. Hamilton's pistol went off and sent a wild shot into the air. His wound was mortal and he died within minutes.

Upon learning of Hamilton's death, Knox broke down and cried inconsolably. Despite all the rivalry between the two men, a genuine affection endured. Their relationship had clearly been complex. They had shared the experience of war. Both had fought for a new constitution, both served in the nation's first administration and together strove to build the country. Both had been members of what Washington called "a band of brothers," and both had been in the intimate circle around Washington, who seemed to view both men as surrogate sons. Henry could remember the young Hamilton, whom he met during the heady days of 1776. At the time, Hamilton had been an ambitious captain in Knox's artillery corps, a soldier eager for glory and with a burning hunger to distinguish himself. Henry could remember Hamilton's bursting talent and infectious charm. He had cheered Hamilton's spectacular rise. Yet now the man who had shined so brilliantly was gone, and Knox mourned as if he had lost another brother.

The resiliency that Knox had shown throughout his life sustained him once again. Despite repeated blows to his optimism, he remained steadfastly sanguine over the future. He believed that his debts would soon be satisfied through his array of business ventures as well as from the sale of land, once the market for lots increased. Many settlers were moving into the area. Over the previous decade, the nation's population had exploded 35 percent to reach 5.3 million residents. Knox also began to consider another source of income. He believed that the supply of limestone on his property was endless and would someday reap a fortune. Although his early experiments with the stone had produced a lower-quality grade than he had hoped, he began to wonder if he should concentrate his efforts on excavating it and perfecting its processing. His belief was well founded. According to a geologist's report of the minerals in the community released three decades later, in 1838, more than $14 million of limestone lay less than twenty feet from the surface in the land around Thomaston. Marble was also found "in exhaustless abundance" along with granite of the highest quality in every color and shade needed for architecture. All these building materials could be easily transported by way of the river and its many inlets and bays. Demand for the valuable stone also appeared endless; markets stretched all along the Atlantic seacoast as far south as Havana. Even into the 1830s, the cost of transporting granite to New York did not exceed $2.50 a ton, while the stone sold for $7 a ton.[6]

As Knox accepted accolades and entered a tranquil period of his life, he contemplated his own mortality. To others, he expressed no doubts about the immortality of his soul. He considered his own significance, or insignificance, in a letter to his friend Samuel Breck, a Boston sail-maker, written early in 1806: "Years roll away, and soon we shall be numbered among those who have been atoms upon this atom of a globe and very soon after, it will be forgotten that we had here any existence. But this ought not in the least degree to cloud any of our present enjoyments, it being a condition of our nature."[7]

In July, Knox made great strides toward settling his debts. On July 24, he parted with thousands of acres of land in Hancock and Lincoln counties for $203,870, the proceeds of which went to pay off a mortgage. He also satisfied his debts to lenders. Knox turned his attention to his limestone operations, estimating that he could produce 30,000 to 40,000 casks a year.

Prosperity, he believed, was right around the corner.

In October, as he prepared for a business trip to Boston, he sat down for a meal. A chicken bone became lodged in his throat, and an infection and swelling quickly set in. It was immediately clear that his condition was life threatening. Doctors worked frantically. His son reported that everything that could be tried was tried. All was in vain. Henry Knox died on October 25, 1806, at the age of fifty-five, and a remarkable life came to an unexpected, sudden close.

His death was a crushing blow to Lucy. Throughout the war, she had been tormented with the constant thought of losing Henry in battle. She had endured the deaths of nine of her twelve children. Now, with the loss of her closest friend and confidant, she would be forced to carry on all the responsibilities of the estate alone.

The funeral of Henry Knox took place at Montpelier on October 28. His life was celebrated with full military honors. An artillery company led the procession, which included a company of cavalry and infantry. His coffin was transported to a tomb at a spot Knox had chosen. The shaded piece of ground was under a large oak tree on the couple's estate. As the mourners gathered about the gravesite, a musketry volley was fired into the air and standards were lowered.

In Boston, the *Columbian Centinel* marked his passing by recalling his military service, praising his virtues, and expressing Knox's conviction that his financial prospects were improving: "To his merits as a military chief and public man were joined those qualities which conciliate affection and engage esteem in private intercourse, which made him the delight of his family and the promoter of social happiness in the circles in which he moved. The affairs of his fortune which for some years had been perplexed and difficult, had taken a course offering him pleasant anticipations."

Memorials were offered in praise of Knox's virtues, which seemed to leave a deeper impression on those who knew him than even his remarkable achievements. One of the men who knew Knox well and had witnessed him in battle was Dr. James Thacher, a military surgeon. In his recollection of Knox, he focused on personality traits.

> Long will he be remembered as the ornament of every circle in which he moved, as the amiable and enlightened companion, the generous friend, the man of feeling and benevolence. His conversation was animated and cheerful, and he imparted an interest to every subject he touched. In his gayest moments, he never lost sight of dignity; he invited confidence, but repelled familiarity. His conceptions were lofty, and no man ever possessed the power of embodying his thoughts in more vigorous language: when ardently engaged, they were peculiarly bond and original, and you inevitably felt in his society that his intellect was not of the ordinary class; yet no man was more unassuming, none more delicately alive to the feelings of others.[8]

In Knox's will, which had been notarized on November 26, 1802, he expressed his religious convictions in the preamble, a common practice of the time. He proclaimed: "First, I think it proper to express my unshaken opinion in the immortality of my soul, or mind, and to dedicate and devote the same to the Supreme Head of the Universe; to that great and tremendous Jehovah who created the universal frame of nature, worlds, and systems of worlds in numbers infinite, and who has given intellectual existence to his rational beings of each globe, who are perpetually migrating and ascending in the scale of mind according to certain principles always founded on the great basis of morality and virtue; to this sublime and awful Being do I resign my spirit, unlimited confidence in his mercy and protection."[9]

At the time of his death, his home was valued at $100,000. This included the value of seven carriages and fifteen horses.

Knox had been driven since childhood to build a secure haven for his family. He wanted to be the stable rock that his father had never been for him. Yet his sudden death cut short his plans. His daughter Lucy would later point out that had her father "been permitted to attain the common age of man, the gradual rise in value of his property would have enabled him to realize all his anticipations."[10]

Knox's wife, Lucy Knox, became reclusive after his death, content to allow people to remember her from happier days. She stayed at Montpelier in Maine. Her independent streak sustained her, but without the social graces of Henry, her friendships were limited to a few close intimates. She gained a reputation of possessing a violent temper. To satisfy creditors, she was forced to sell off much of the remaining estate and many of her valuable possessions.

She was unable to lean on her son, Henry Jackson Knox, whose erratic habits and struggles with alcohol left him unable to sustain a living. His marriage dissolved after a few years, and his wife went to live with her mother in Uxbridge, Massachusetts. Eventually Henry Jackson Knox became destitute. In 1809, Timothy Pickering reported to Ebenezer Stevens, a colonel in the artillery corps during the revolution, that the son of Henry Knox had the ignoble misfortune of being tossed into "Debtor Prison No. 2" in Boston. In a gesture that Pickering described as "pathetic," Henry J. made a personal appeal to him, asking if any money was due from his stint in the navy. This amounted to a mere $43.50. Harassed by creditors, he moved to Windsor, Vermont, in an effort to turn his life around.

Henry J. Knox then entered medical school at Dartmouth College, and graduated in 1811. Trying to combine his naval experience with his elementary knowledge of surgery, he applied for a job as a surgeon's mate aboard the privateer ship *America* in hopes of one day reentering the U.S. Navy as a doctor. His earnings aboard the ship were seized by creditors, and he again plunged into depression and addiction. Henry J. Knox then took up employment as a clerk for his mother. His wife was able to obtain a divorce in 1818.

The family living at Montpelier could not help but hear the echoes of merrier days. Caroline commented to a friend in 1822 in offering an invitation to the mansion: "The glory of Israel has departed, the days of show and profusion are all gone and we are a plain, retired country family."[11]

Lucy Knox's health began to fail in the spring of 1824, and she became confined to bed in May. She suffered a great deal of pain and was rendered senseless for two weeks. Her agony became so unbearable that it took several people to hold her in bed. She reportedly imagined that she was once again young, dancing with Henry at a ball. She died at 3 A.M. on June 20, 1824, three days short of what would have been the fiftieth anniversary of her marriage. She was sixty-seven years of age, and had left her estate to be split between her three children, Henry Jackson Knox, Lucy Thatcher, and Caroline.

Henry J. Knox underwent a religious transformation in the last years of his life after hearing an evangelist speak in Thomaston. His sister Lucy was amazed at his metamorphosis, and wrote to her son that "you will be much surprised to hear that your Uncle Knox has lately become a pious man—his conversion is one of the most wonderful things I have ever met with . . . at length he felt irresistibly impelled to the study of the scripture—in which he had been hitherto almost an unbeliever—the more he read, the more he became confirmed in the truth."[12]

Henry Jackson died in Thomaston in 1832, so repentant of his life that he requested to be interred away from the family burial ground. In compliance with his wishes, he was laid to rest at a community cemetery in an unmarked grave.

Caroline married James Swan, who died within a few years from complications of alcoholism, and then married John Holmes, who became a United States Senator after Maine became a state in 1820. She lived at Montpelier until her death in 1851. Lucy Thatcher and her husband moved to Mercer, Maine, where he set up a law practice. Her family then moved to Bingham, Maine, where her husband died in 1842.

After Caroline's death, Lucy Knox Thatcher returned to Montpelier and lived there for three years before passing away. Her son, Henry Knox Thatcher, who later became a rear admiral in the U.S. Navy, did not have the time or interest in maintaining Montpelier and instead rented it out. The mansion eventually fell into disrepair and was finally demolished in 1871. The servants' quarters became the Thomaston railroad station. Because the home and property changed hands over the years, the grave of Henry Knox was relocated several times.

The name of Henry Knox, which during his lifetime was as widely known as any of the founding fathers', faded from the public consciousness but was never forgotten due to the many memorials to him. A fort bearing his name was built in 1844 at Prospect, Maine, not far from Thomaston. This first Fort

Knox was located at the narrows of the Penobscot River, opposite Bucksport. Joseph Totten, an army engineer who designed the fortification, took advantage of the abundance of quality granite in the area, and Fort Knox became the first fort in the state not built of wood and earth. During the Civil War, about ninety Union soldiers were stationed there. It remains a tourist attraction to this day.

As the country expanded to the west in the nineteenth century, Henry Knox was memorialized in the naming of counties in Illinois, Indiana, Kentucky, Maine, Missouri, Nebraska, Ohio, Tennessee, and Texas. The third largest city in Tennessee, Knoxville, bears his name.

Given his financial struggles, Henry Knox might have felt a tinge of satisfaction that the fort in Kentucky that bears his name has become synonymous with untold wealth. Since 1937, the U.S. Bullion Depository at Fort Knox has housed the bulk of the nation's gold reserves in its secure vault. Fort Knox is one of the largest installations in the U.S. Army, stretching more than 109,000 acres and housing 23,000 soldiers. A school to train officers for the Army Armor Corps is located there as well as the George Patton Museum of Armor and Cavalry.

In Thomaston, the memory of Henry Knox was vigilantly kept alive in the early twentieth century by the Henry Knox Chapter of the Daughters of the American Revolution, who looked for a time when the general could again be prominently memorialized in their town. In the 1920s, they launched an ambitious plan to completely rebuild the Montpelier mansion. Charitable donations poured in and ground for an exact replica was broken on July 26, 1929. Despite the economic depression that soon plagued the country, Montpelier was rebuilt. Painstaking efforts were made to match all the details of the original home, including the wallpaper, drapes, and furniture.

It was a fulfillment of the dream that Henry Knox had worked most of his life to achieve. In one of the last letters to his wife, he had written: "I hope our reunion will shortly be established, to separate no more."[13]

EPILOGUE

LEGACY

Henry Knox was a remarkably ubiquitous presence during America's founding generation. His life was replete with adventure, and an examination of his career provides a virtual tour of many of the most significant events of his time. Although Knox has been overlooked by historians for two centuries, even a cursory glance at his story reveals some of the most stunning achievements in American history.

In fact, it almost stretches credulity that one individual could play as many key roles in such a variety of historical events. As fate would have it, a nineteen-year-old Knox unwittingly walked directly into the unfolding Boston Massacre, a tragedy that he tried to prevent. Three years later, he was present among the patriotic men guarding the tea-laden ships in the days before the Boston Tea Party.

After the opening shots of the American Revolution were fired in 1775, Knox performed the heroic feat of dragging fifty-nine cannons from Ticonderoga more than 300 miles to the Cambridge shores opposite Boston. The guns gave the Continental Army and Knox's artillery the firepower needed to liberate Boston in 1776, thus enabling Washington to claim his first victory of the war. The achievement of supplying the guns and reopening Boston provided the colonies with the crucial military triumph needed to justify cries for independence in the heady spring days of 1776. It is doubtful that many of the colonies would have supported separation from Great Britain if the army had been unable to free Boston from occupation. The victory led patriots to believe that the British could be beaten in the field and that freedom was attainable.

If George Washington was the indispensable man of the Revolution, then Henry Knox was his indispensable man. As commander of the Continental

Army's artillery corps, Knox played a major role in every one of Washington's victories and received some of the war's most critical assignments. Knox directed the army's desperate evacuation of Brooklyn Heights over the East River for the safety of New York in the summer of 1776. He was charged with getting the patriot soldiers across the icy Delaware River on Christmas night, 1776, during the famous crossing, and his guns led the way at the successful charge at Trenton the next morning. He set up a military academy at his artillery headquarters in 1778 to train officers in strategy, tactics, logistics, and engineering. The school became a forerunner of the U.S. Military Academy at West Point. Every aspect of the nation's ordnance was placed under his authority. It was Knox's artillery corps that devastated the British at Yorktown in 1781, thus providing the victory that ended the war.

His achievements were no less conspicuous during peace. As secretary at war under the Articles of Confederation, he oversaw the federal response to Shays' Rebellion and was among the leading voices calling for a new constitution. Knox was among the small circle that swayed Washington into his decision to attend the Constitutional Convention, telling him that the country trusted his leadership. Knox even provided a plan for a bicameral national government and a draft of a constitution that was strikingly similar to the one adopted by the country in 1787 and ratified a year later.

Knox went on to serve in the nation's first administration as secretary of war alongside fellow cabinet members Thomas Jefferson and Alexander Hamilton. As head of the War Department, he helped launch the U.S. Navy, built frontier fortifications and coastal defenses, negotiated treaties and set policy with the American Indians. He advocated the building of a military academy at West Point, a proposal that would not be acted upon until 1802. The military historian and Knox biographer Callahan North wrote in the 1940s and 1950s that Knox more than anyone deserves the title of founder of West Point.

Yet despite all of his lasting achievements, the name of Fort Knox is more widely recognized than the exceptional man the installation memorializes. It seems like a comment on the fleeting nature of fame that one man could accomplish so much and yet fade from the public mind.

Knox's name is even less recognizable than that of many of his contemporaries, including Washington, John Adams, Benjamin Franklin, Thomas Jefferson, Alexander Hamilton, Samuel Adams, John Jay, Paul Revere, Patrick Henry, Molly Pitcher, Betsy Ross, John Marshall, and James Madison. The reasons appear to have less to do with the nature of his achievements than other complicated factors.

Knox is understandably overshadowed by George Washington, and he himself willingly relegated his career to a supporting role to the commander in chief during his lifetime. In his letters, Knox was quick to acknowledge his great debt to Washington. He believed that for the good of the country, Washington's reputation should be canonized in order to cement the union behind a single glorious leader and to raise American prestige in the eyes of the world.

Yet the success of the Continental Army was obviously due to the heroics of many brilliant patriots. Washington delegated a great deal of responsibility to subordinates, and he trusted no one with more critical assignments than Knox. In many instances, Washington depended on Knox to save the army, and in doing so, he placed the fate of the country in his hands. Imagine Washington's thoughts as he decided to chance everything on the ability of twenty-five-year-old Knox to find a way to drag nearly sixty tons of cannon from Ticonderoga over the Berkshire Mountains in order to keep alive the American cause. Consider that in Washington's most desperate moment, Christmas 1776, he turned to Knox and asked him to get the troops and tons of cannon across the freezing Delaware River in an attempt to surprise the Hessians at Trenton. If Knox had failed, what would have been the fate of the army or of American independence?

Washington's reputation as a military leader rests on the success of officers and soldiers such as Knox, who defied impossible odds and accomplished amazing feats. It may be tempting to believe that the men under Washington served in perfunctory roles as dutiful soldiers, merely following orders with little need of ingenuity, inspiration, and vision. This was certainly not true of Henry Knox.

He applied remarkable creativity and imagination to every endeavor. It is difficult today to envision the United States as the undeveloped country that it was in 1775, lacking heavy industry, foundries, gunpowder manufacturers, munitions, ordnance depots, arsenals, and government ships. At the time, the country even lacked the ability to cast cannons or excavate for iron, bronze, or copper. Under colonial rule, America was prohibited from developing the key tools to build an army or a navy.

Unlike any other artillery commander in American history, Henry Knox had no foundation to build on. He not only had to educate himself in the use of all the weapons at his disposal, but he also had to develop manufacturing and production processes to build them. No detail was too minute for him to grasp, and no strategy was too large for his imagination.

Knox, of course, did not have the benefit of a military school to guide his education. He taught himself strategy, tactics, and the calculus involved in firing cannons. He drove himself to learn every aspect of his craft, even setting up military laboratories and learning all the science behind making munitions.

As an artillery commander, Knox was innovative and skilled. He favored the use of highly mobile brass cannons rather than more powerful iron guns, and advocated using cannons to lead charges rather than in support of infantry. Napoleon would later use this same strategy to great effect in Europe.

As a military commander, Knox was well liked and respected by his men and by his colleagues in Washington's military family. He developed a wide circle of deep friendships, many of which lasted for years after the war. His corps was often cited as exemplary and as well trained as any in the Continental Army. To Knox's lasting credit, the American artillery corps performed on par with the formidable French at Yorktown and outdueled the British. According to the Marquis de Lafayette, Knox's gunners even exceeded their French counterparts.

Knox never led troops into battle. Throughout the war, he remained at Washington's side in a supporting role. As a strategist, he was well read and by all accounts possessed strong judgment. In planning for battle at councils of war, he leaned on the side of caution. Even when faced with tremendous political pressure, Knox insisted that the American army refrain from staking all in one decisive battle; instead it should remain on the defensive and invite the British to attack. Some critics, including Alexander Hamilton, thought that Knox was overly cautious and believed that Washington should take greater risks.

It is impossible to ascertain today the proper level of caution, but it can be noted that Washington did decide to wait patiently for the opportune moment and never gambled on a tempting offensive strike until blessed with favorable odds.

When that opportunity arose in 1781, Knox acted decisively and moved the American artillery from upstate New York to Yorktown, Virginia. At the Battle of Yorktown, he personally directed his artillery guns and was a hands-on commander who haunted the trenches and even aimed the cannons under fire. Knox was an exceptionally versatile commander, an expert in every branch of the service and a skilled engineer, artilleryman, strategist, and ordnance master.

As the war drew to a close and Washington stepped down from command, he turned the army over to Knox, who was given the assignment of reducing it to 700 men. He demonstrated a prophetic vision as a statesman. While serving as secretary at war under the confederation government, Knox realized that he needed to redefine perceptions about the army to suit the needs of a democratic republic. Many prominent American leaders wanted to disband the army completely and viewed any force as antithetical to representative government. Knox created a vision of a new kind of army in which soldiers were instilled with the nation's most cherished values. He believed that soldiers could be trained to fight to preserve political ideals rather than geographic boundary lines, to love liberty more than personal ambition, and to value honor above greed and the spoils of war.

That vision of the American soldier continues today. For the past two centuries, U.S. soldiers have exemplified patriotism and have professed an ardent love of liberty. Needless to say, American soldiers have marched into battle for the sake of defending the American principles of liberty, and many have given their lives for the sake of preserving freedom. Today, the very picture of patriotism is often that of a soldier. It is difficult to envision a time in America when politicians feared that soldiers would not feel a proper attachment to their country.

Knox was among the first who advocated drafting a new constitution to replace the Articles of Confederation. Even before the end of the Revolution, he wrote a letter to Gouverneur Morris recommending that a convention be held for that very purpose. Four years later, Morris would draft most of the language for the U.S. Constitution.

As war secretary in the Confederation government, Knox favored a regular army despite strong opposition from many in Congress. He argued the need for a force to deal with disputes between settlers and American Indians and suggested sending officers and soldiers to live in the frontier to help train militias.

Knox had mixed success as secretary of the United States Department of War during the Washington administration. He built up the army, laid out frontier fortifications in the West, and set up coastal and harbor defenses along the East Coast. But he had only uneven results in dealing with the Indian tribes. He established an enlightened policy for dealing with them, which later government leaders failed to follow or live up to. Knox held the rights of Indians to be equal with those of white settlers and demanded that crimes committed against the tribes be punished.

His warm, gregarious personality helped him negotiate several treaties with tribes in the southwestern region of the country and in the Ohio Territory. But

Knox oversaw two disastrous expeditions against the hostile Miami tribes near present-day Fort Wayne, Indiana. He was plagued by incompetent subordinates.

Perhaps his greatest achievement as war secretary was the launching of the U.S. Navy. Knox gambled on building super-size frigates, a move that many top shipwrights warned against. His intuition paid off as America soon became engaged in an undeclared naval war with France. American frigates that he requisitioned immediately established their presence on the high seas. Thomas Jefferson and James Madison, who each had opposed a navy, came to be thankful that Knox had won the political battle over the issue.

Knox found politics distasteful, and understandably did not enjoy the criticism leveled by the press. None of the major leaders in Washington's administration felt satisfied in their positions. The president regretted serving a second term, and Knox, Jefferson, and Hamilton turned in letters of resignation long before Washington left office. As a member of the Federalist Party, Knox was criticized in the Republican press controlled by Thomas Jefferson, who appears to have felt no personal animosity to Knox, only political antipathy. Knox's reputation through the years has undoubtedly suffered from the appraisals of Jefferson, who had little respect for military accomplishments. Washington's reputation also suffers from similar criticisms leveled by Jefferson. The validity of Jefferson's assessments of Knox must be weighed against his lifetime of remarkable achievements. As is the case with most praise or criticism, they each provide a prism too narrow in scope to render a full portrait of a life.

Henry Knox excelled at every task given him in service to his country. He placed the nation on solid footing in every venture he launched, from the artillery corps in the Continental Army to the navy in the 1790s. It is easy to take for granted his efforts simply because success is often quiet while failure is conspicuous, and it can be tempting to view the projects he guided as mystically destined for glory. Yet an examination of the historical record shows that his achievements were anything but foregone conclusions. He took great risks and remained a relatively obscure figure to historians because his endeavors were not plagued with problems. The fire at the U.S. War Office in November 1800 that destroyed all the department's records also served to obscure his record.

In the pantheon of Founding Fathers, exclusive membership often is reserved for the politicians who signed the Declaration of Independence or the U.S. Constitution. But on July 4, 1776, thousands of soldiers—Henry Knox among them—faced the most formidable army in the world. The contributions of soldiers standing in the field are no less significant than those of the delegates who penned their names to the Declaration. At the time the Constitution was adopted, Knox was serving as one of the few national officers in the country, and he had played a key role in spearheading the new framework of government. Knox's career crosses the traditional boundaries between soldier and statesman, and his contribution is difficult to categorize.

Perhaps it is best to imagine his booming voice piercing through the howling wind and falling snow, directing the shivering patriot soldiers as they embarked to cross the Delaware on Christmas night in 1776, and remember a man who risked everything he had for the sake of freedom and his country.

NOTES

CHAPTER 1—LOVE AND WAR

1. Henry Knox letter to David McClure, *Henry Knox Papers* [hereafter *HKP*], January 25, 1789.
2. Boston Latin School website, www.bls.org.
3. Samuel Adams, *The Writings of Samuel Adams*, ed. Alonzo Cushing [hereafter *Writings*], vol. 2, January 7, 1771.
4. George Bancroft, *History of America* [hereafter *History*] (New York: Harper & Brothers, 1882), vol. 3, p. 372.
5. Hiller B. Zobell, *The Boston Massacre* (New York: W. W. Norton & Company, 1996), p. 195.
6. Ibid.
7. Bancroft, *History*, vol. 3, pp. 374–375.
8. Ibid.
9. *Boston Gazette*, March 12, 1770.
10. Adams, *Writings*, vol. 2, January 7, 1771.
11. Francis S. Drake, *Life and Correspondence of Henry Knox* [hereafter *Life and Correspondence*] (Boston: Samuel G. Drake, 1873), p. 12.
12. Ibid.
13. Noah Brooks, *Henry Knox* (Cranbury, N.J.: Scholar's Bookshelf, 2000), p. 14.
14. Drake, *Life and Correspondence*, p. 16.
15. Ibid., p. 25.
16. Ibid., p. 16.
17. Ibid.
18. Brooks, *Henry Knox*, p. 24.
19. Wright & Gill to Henry Knox, *HKP*, July 14, 1774.
20. Brooks, *Henry Knox*, p. 14.
21. Thomas Jefferson, *The Writings of Thomas Jefferson* (Monticello ed.), vol. 1, pp. 12–13.
22. Brooks, *Henry Knox*, p. 25.
23. Ibid., p. 15.
24. Theodore Thayer, *Nathanael Greene, Strategist of the American Revolution* (New York: Twain Publishers, 1960), p. 67; Terry Golway, *Washington's General: Nathanael Greene and the Triumph of the American Revolution* (New York: Owl Book, Henry Holt and Company, 2006), p. 67.
25. Drake, *Life and Correspondence*, pp. 14–15.

26. Ibid., p. 127.
27. Alexander Hamilton, *The Works of Alexander Hamilton*, Federal ed. (New York: G. P. Putnam's Sons, 1904), vol. 1, p. 20.

CHAPTER 2—TICONDEROGA

1. Bancroft, *History of America*, vol. 4, p. 168.
2. Jane E. Triber, *A True Republican: The Life of Paul Revere* (Amherst: University of Massachusetts Press, 1998), p. 118.
3. Drake, *Life and Correspondence*, p. 18.
4. Ibid., p. 19.
5. George Washington, General Orders, July 29, 1775, *George Washington Papers* [hereafter *GWP*].
6. Ibid., July 10, 1775.
7. Drake, *Life and Correspondence*, p. 19.
8. *Journals of the Continental Congress*, vol. 2, p. 103.
9. John Adams to Joseph Warren, *Letters of Delegates to the Continental Congress*, in Paul Smith et al., *Letters of Delegates to Congress, 1774–1789*, CD-ROM ed. [hereafter *Letters of Delegates*] (Summerfield, FL: Historic Database, 1998), vol. 1, p. 652.
10. Samuel Adams to Elbridge Gerry, *Letters of Delegates*, vol. 2, p. 63.
11. John Adams to John Thomas, *Letters of Delegates*, vol. 25, p. 559.
12. Henry Knox to John Adams, *HKP*, October 26, 1775; Callahan, *Henry Knox*, pp. 34–35.
13. Ibid.
14. George Washington to John Trumbull, *GWP*, November 2, 1775.
15. *Journals of the Continental Congress*, September 20, 1775.
16. George Washington to Continental Congress, *GWP*, November 8, 1775.
17. John Adams to Henry Knox, *Letters of Delegates*, vol. 2, p. 329.
18. George Washington to Henry Knox, *GWP*, November 16, 1775.
19. Ibid.
20. George Washington to Philip J. Schuyler, *GWP*, November 16, 1775.
21. *Journals of the Continental Congress*, November 17, 1775, vol. 3, p. 358.
22. Henry Knox to George Washington, *GWP*, November 27, 1775.
23. Ibid., December 5, 1775.
24. John Hancock to George Washington, *Letters of Delegates*, vol. 2, p. 424.
25. Washington, General Orders, *GWP*, December 12, 1775.
26. Henry Knox to George Washington, *GWP*, December 17, 1775.
27. Callahan, *Henry Knox*, p. 46.
28. Henry Knox, *Henry Knox Diary*, Massachusetts Historical Society, entry for December 26, 1775.
29. Henry Knox to George Washington, *GWP*, January 5, 1776.
30. Philip J. Schuyler to George Washington, *GWP*, January 5, 1776.
31. Drake, *Life and Correspondence*, pp. 24–25.
32. Ibid.
33. Callahan, *Henry Knox*, pp. 51–52.
34. Ibid., p. 54.
35. John Adams, *Diary*, online at Masshist.org, entry for January 25, 1776.
36. General Officers Council, *GWP*, February 16, 1776.

37. Frank Moore, ed., *Diary of the American Revolution from Newspapers and Original Documents* [hereafter *Diary*] (New York: Charles Scribner, 1858), vol. 1, pp. 147–148.
38. George Washington to Continental Congress, *GWP*, March 7, 1776.
39. Ibid.
40. Moore, *Diary*, vol. 1, p. 154.
41. George Washington to the Continental Congress, *GWP*, March 19, 1776.
42. Thomas Jefferson to Thomas Nelson, *Letters of the Delegates to Congress*, vol. 4, p. 13.

CHAPTER 3—RAGAMUFFINS

1. *Journals of the Continental Congress*, vol. 4, p. 283.
2. George Washington to Henry Knox, *GWP*, April 3, 1776.
3. Henry Knox to George Washington, *HKP*, April 21, 1776.
4. Drake, *Life and Correspondence*, p. 27.
5. Alexander Hamilton, Artillery Company Report, *GWP*, April 20, 1776.
6. General Orders, *GWP*, May 7, 1776.
7. Ibid., May 15, 1776.
8. Ibid., May 20, 1776.
9. Robert Treat Paine to Henry Knox, *Letters of Delegates*, vol. 4, p. 109.
10. John Adams to Henry Knox, *Letters of Delegates*, vol. 4, p. 115.
11. Ibid.
12. Continental Army Court Martial, *GWP*, proceedings at New York City, June 26, 1776; General Orders, *GWP*, June 27, 1776; George Washington to the Continental Congress, *GWP*, June 28, 1776; *Pennsylvania Journal*, June 26, 1776; *Pennsylvania Evening Post*, July 2, 1776; Moore, *Diary*, vol. 1, pp. 177, 178.
13. Drake, *Life and Correspondence*, p. 28.
14. Ibid.
15. General Orders, *GWP*, July 9, 1776.
16. Ibid.
17. Ibid., July 10, 1776.
18. George Washington to the Continental Congress, *GWP*, July 22, 1776.
19. Robert Treat Paine to Henry Knox, *Letters of Delegates*, vol. 4, p. 473.
20. *Pennsylvania Journal*, July 20, 1776; Moore, *Diary*, vol. 1, pp. 187–188.
21. Ibid.
22. *Journals of the Continental Congress*, vol. 5, p. 607.
23. Robert Treat Paine to Henry Knox, *Letters of Delegates*, vol. 4, p. 555.
24. Henry Knox to Lucy Knox, *HKP*, August 11, 1776.
25. Brooks, *Henry Knox*, p. 60.
26. General Orders, *GWP*, August 13, 1776.
27. Adams to John Adams, August 16, 1776, in Samuel Adams, *Writings*, vol. 3; George Washington to the Continental Congress, *GWP*, September 24, 1776.
28. John Adams to Henry Knox, *Letters of Delegates*, vol. 4, p. 671.
29. *Journals of the Continental Congress*, vol. 5, p. 694.
30. Henry Knox to John Adams, *HKP*, August 21, 1776.
31. *Pennsylvania Journal*, August 28, 1776, Moore, *Diary*, vol. 1, p. 201.
32. Drake, *Life and Correspondence*, p. 29.

33. David Hacket Fischer, *Washington's Crossing* (New York: Oxford University Press, 2004), P. 21.
34. George Washington to the Continental Congress, *GWP*, September 2, 1776.
35. Henry Knox to Lucy Knox, *HKP*, September 5, 1776.
36. Drake, *Life and Correspondence*, pp. 30–31.
37. Ibid., pp. 31–32.
38. John Adams to Henry Knox, *Letters of Delegates*, vol. 5, p. 261; *Journals of the Continental Congress*, vol. 5, p. 838.
39. *Journals of the Continental Congress*, vol. 5, pp. 762–763; John Hancock to George Washington, *Letters of Delegates*, vol. 5, p. 230; John Hancock to Philip Schuyler, *Letters of Delegates*, vol. 5, p. 255.
40. *Journals of the Continental Congress*, vol. 5, p. 844.
41. Ibid.
42. George Washington to Henry Knox, *GWP*, November 10, 1776.
43. George Washington to the Continental Congress, *GWP*, November 14, 1776.
44. Drake, *Life and Correspondence*, pp. 33–34.
45. Ibid.
46. *Journals of the Continental Congress*, vol. 6, p. 1027.

CHAPTER 4—DELAWARE CROSSING

1. Henry Knox, "A Plan for the Establishment of a Corps of Continental Artillery, Magazines, Laboratories," *GWP*, December 18, 1776.
2. Ibid.
3. George Washington to the Continental Congress, *GWP*, December 20, 1776.
4. Ibid.
5. Henry B. Carrington, *Battles of the American Revolution: 1775–1781* (New York: Promontory Press, 1877), p. 267.
6. George Bancroft, *History of the United States*, vol. 5, p. 97.
7. Ibid.
8. David Hackett Fisher, *Washington's Crossing*, p. 206.
9. Callahan, *Henry Knox*, p. 83.
10. George Washington to the Continental Congress, *GWP*, December 27, 1776.
11. Drake, *Life and Correspondence*, p. 36.
12. George Washington to the Continental Congress, *GWP*, December 27, 1776.
13. Callahan, *Henry Knox*, p. 91.
14. Drake, *Life and Correspondence*, pp. 36–37.
15. Ibid.
16. Ibid.
17. George Washington to the Continental Congress, *GWP*, December 17, 1776.
18. Francis Lewis to Robert Morris, *Letters of Delegates*, vol. 5, p. 671.
19. *Journals of the Continental Congress*, vol. 6, p. 1043.
20. Drake, *Life and Correspondence*, p. 37.
21. Fischer, *Washington's Crossing*, p. 274.
22. Drake, *Life and Correspondence*, p. 37.
23. George Washington to the Continental Congress, *GWP*, January 1, 1777.
24. Drake, *Life and Correspondence*, p. 38.
25. Ibid.
26. Brooks, *Henry Knox*, p. 84.
27. Ibid.

28. Drake, *Life and Correspondence*, p. 40.
29. Ibid.
30. George Washington to Colonel Benjamin Flower, *GWP*, January 16, 1777.
31. George Washington to the Continental Congress, *GWP*, January 17, 1777.
32. Drake, *Life and Correspondence*, p. 41.
33. George Washington to Jonathan Trumbull, *GWP*, February 11, 1777; Drake, *Life and Correspondence*, p. 41.
34. George Washington to Henry Knox, *GWP*, February 11, 1777.
35. George Washington to John Hancock, *GWP*, February 14, 1777.
36. John Adams' Diary, *Letters of Delegates*, vol. 6, p. 334.
37. George Washington to Henry Knox, *GWP*, March 14, 1777.
38. Brooks, *Henry Knox*, p. 89.
39. George Washington to Samuel Holden Parsons, *GWP*, April 3, 1777; *Journals of the Continental Congress*, vol. 7, p. 262.
40. John Adams to Nathanael Greene, *Letters of Delegates*, vol. 6, p. 571; *Journals of the Continental Congress*, vol. 7, p. 266.
41. Drake, *Life and Correspondence*, p. 41.
42. Callahan, *Henry Knox*, p. 105.
43. Drake, *Life and Correspondence*, p. 42.
44. Ibid.
45. General Orders, *GWP*, May 8, 1777.
46. Drake, *Life and Correspondence*, p. 42.
47. George Washington to the Continental Congress, *GWP*, May 31, 1777; *Writings of George Washington*, Fitzpatrick ed., vol. 8, p. 145.
48. George Washington to Richard Henry Lee, *GWP*, June 1, 1777; *Writings of George Washington*, Fitzpatrick ed., vol. 8, p. 159.
49. John Adams to Nathanael Greene, *Letters of Delegates*, vol. 7, p. 163.
50. John Adams to Abigail Adams, *Letters of Delegates*, vol. 7, p. 207.
51. Charles Carroll to Charles Carroll Sr., *Letters of Delegates*, vol. 7, p. 189.
52. James Lovell to Joseph Trumbull, *Letters of Delegates*, vol. 7, p. 171.
53. John Adams to Abigail Adams and John Adams to James Warren, *Letters of Delegates*, vol. 7, pp. 207, 221.
54. Drake, *Life and Correspondence*, p. 42.
55. Ibid., p. 135.
56. *Journals of the Continental Congress*, vol. 8, p. 528.
57. James Lovell to Benjamin Franklin, *Letters of Delegates*, vol. 7, p. 292.
58. *Journals of the Continental Congress*, vol. 8, p. 537.
59. John Adams to Nathanael Greene, *Letters of Delegates*, vol. 7, pp. 305–307.
60. Drake, *Life and Correspondence*, p. 43.
61. George Washington to Phillipe Du Coudray, *Writings of George Washington*, Fitzpatrick ed., vol. 8, p. 396.
62. *Journals of the Continental Congress*, vol. 8, p. 553.
63. Ibid., p. 569.

CHAPTER 5—THE BATTLE FOR PHILADELPHIA

1. Henry Knox to Lucy Knox, *HKP*, July 26, 1777.
2. Marquis de Lafayette, "Lafayette Arrives in America," *America*, vol. 3, pp. 219–220.
3. Ibid.

4. *Journals of the Continental Congress*, vol. 8, pp. 592–593.
5. Marquis de Lafayette, *Memoirs of Lafayette*, online at gutenberg.org.
6. Henry Knox to George Washington, *Gilder Lehrman Collection*, online at GilderLehrman.org, letter of August 20, 1777.
7. Lucy Knox to Henry Knox, *Gilder Lehrman Collection*, August 23, 1777.
8. George Washington to the Continental Congress, *GWP*, September 9, 1777; George Washington, *Writings of George Washington*, Fitzpatrick ed., vol. 9, pp. 197–198.
9. George Washington to the Continental Congress, *GWP*, 5 o'clock, September 11, 1777; George Washington, *Writings of George Washington*, Fitzpatrick ed., vol. 9, pp. 206–207; Drake, *Life and Correspondence*, pp. 48–49.
10. Drake, *Life and Correspondence*, p. 47.
11. Ibid., pp. 48–49.
12. George Washington to the Continental Congress, *GWP*, at midnight, September 11, 1777; George Washington, *Writings of George Washington*, Fitzpatrick ed., vol. 9, p. 208.
13. Drake, *Life and Correspondence*, p. 47.
14. Ibid., p. 50.
15. Hamilton, *Works of Alexander Hamilton*, vol. 9, pp. 78–79.
16. Drake, *Life and Correspondence*, p. 50.
17. Ibid.
18. *Rivington's Gazette*, November 8, 1777, Moore, *Diary*, vol. 1, p. 331.
19. Drake, *Life and Correspondence*, p. 51.
20. Ibid.
21. Ibid., p. 53.
22. Ibid., p. 54.
23. Ibid.
24. Brooks, *Henry Knox*, p. 113.
25. George Washington to Richard Henry Lee, *GWP*, October 17, 1777; George Washington, *Writings of George Washington*, Fitzpatrick ed., vol. 9, p. 388.
26. Henry Laurens to Benjamin Huger, *Letters of Delegates*, vol. 8, p. 271.
27. *Letters of Delegates*, vol. 8, p. 314.
28. William Alexander, Lord Stirling to George Washington, *GWP*, November 25, 1777.
29. George Washington to Nathanael Greene, *GWP*, November 26, 1777; George Washington, *Writings of George Washington*, Fitzpatrick ed., vol. 10, pp. 106–107.
30. *Journals of the Continental Congress*, vol. 9, p. 958.
31. Henry Knox to George Washington, *Gilder Lehrman Collection*, November 26, 1777.
32. Ibid.
33. James Lovell to Horatio Gates, *Letters of Delegates*, vol. 8, p. 329.
34. *Journals of the Continental Congress*, vol. 9, pp. 971–972.
35. Ibid., pp. 972, 976.
36. Henry Knox to George Washington, *Gilder Lehrman Collection*, letters of December 1, 1777 and December 5, 1777.
37. Callahan, *Henry Knox*, p. 128.
38. *Journals of the Continental Congress*, vol. 9, pp. 1025–1026.
39. Harlow Giles Unger, *Lafayette*, (New York: Wiley, 2002), p. 60 .
40. Ibid.

41. John Sullivan to George Washington, *GWP,* letters of December 30, 1777, and January 2, 1778; Charles T. Whittemore, *A General of the Revolution: John Sullivan of New Hampshire* (New York: Columbia University Press, 1961), p. 79.
42. Callahan, *Henry Knox,* pp. 132–133.
43. George Washington to Henry Knox, *GWP,* January 8, 1778; George Washington, *Writings of George Washington,* Fitzpatrick ed., vol. 10, pp. 270–280.

CHAPTER 6—TURNING OF THE TIDE

1. Callahan, *Henry Knox,* p. 135.
2. Henry Knox to George Washington, *GWP,* February 4, 1778.
3. Elbridge Gerry to Henry Knox, *Letters of Delegates,* vol. 9, p. 45.
4. Ibid.
5. Henry Knox to George Washington, *GWP,* February 16, 1778.
6. George Washington to Henry Knox, *GWP,* February 21, 1778; Washington, *Writings of George Washington,* Fitzpatrick ed., vol. 10, pp. 489–490.
7. Drake, *Life and Correspondence,* pp. 55–56; Thayer, *Nathanael Greene,* p. 222; Terry Golway, *Washington's General: Nathanael Greene and the Triumph of the American Revolution* (New York: Owl Books, 2006), p. 164; Brooks, *Henry Knox,* pp. 114–115.
8. Ibid.
9. Thayer, *Nathanael Greene,* p. 226; Golway, *Washington's General,* p. 165.
10. George Washington to Henry Knox, *Writings of George Washington,* Fitzpatrick ed., vol. 11, pp. 26–27; George Washington to Henry Knox, *GWP,* March 5, 1778.
11. Henry Knox to George Washington, *GWP,* April 23, 1778.
12. Ibid.
13. Ibid.
14. George Washington to Gouverneur Morris, *Writings of George Washington,* Fitzpatrick ed., vol. 11, p. 306; George Washington to Gouverneur Morris, *GWP,* April 25, 1778.
15. *Journals of the Continental Congress,* vol. 10, p. 399; *Letters of Delegates,* vol. 9, pp. 516–517.
16. George Washington to Henry Knox, *Writings of George Washington,* Fitzpatrick ed., vol. 11, p. 407; George Washington to Henry Knox, *GWP,* May 17, 1778.
17. Henry Knox to George Washington, *GWP,* May 17, 1778.
18. Callahan, *Henry Knox,* p. 142.
19. General Orders, *Writings of George Washington,* Fitzpatrick ed., vol. 11, p. 361; General Orders, *GWP,* May 7, 1778.
20. *Journals of the Continental Congress,* vol. 11, p. 615.
21. Henry Knox to George Washington, *GWP,* June 18, 1778.
22. Drake, *Life and Correspondence,* p. 57.
23. George Washington to the President of Congress, *Writings of George Washington,* Fitzpatrick ed., vol. 12, p. 143; George Washington to the President of Congress, *GWP,* July 1, 1778.
24. Moore, *Diary,* vol. 2, p. 50.
25. Drake, *Life and Correspondence,* p. 59.

26. Hamilton, *Alexander Hamilton: Writings*, (New York: Library of America, 2001), p. 54.
27. Drake, *Life and Correspondence*, pp. 57–58.
28. Brooks, *Henry Knox*, p. 122.
29. General Orders, *GWP*, June 29, 1778; George Washington, *Writings of George Washington*, Fitzpatrick ed., vol. 12, p. 131.
30. George Washington to the Continental Congress, *GWP*, July 1, 1778; George Washington, *Writings of George Washington*, Fitzpatrick ed., vol. 12, p. 145.
31. Drake, *Life and Correspondence of Henry Knox*, p. 59.
32. George Washington to Gouverneur Morris, *GWP*, October 4, 1778; George Washington, *Writings of George Washington*, Fitzpatrick ed., vol. 13, pp. 21–22.
33. George Washington to Alexander McDougal, *GWP*, February 9, 1779; George Washington, *Writings of George Washington*, Fitzpatrick ed., vol. 14, p. 82.
34. James Duane to George Washington, *Letters of Delegates*, vol. 11, p. 524.
35. Drake, *Life and Correspondence*, p. 60.
36. Moore, *Diary*, vol. 2, p. 90.
37. *Journals of the Continental Congress*, vol. 13, pp. 201–206.

CHAPTER 7—FORTITUDE

1. Henry Knox to Lucy Knox, *HKP*, August 8, 1779.
2. George Washington to Henry Knox, *GWP*, July 12, 1779; George Washington, *Writings of George Washington*, Fitzpatrick ed., vol. 15, p. 411.
3. *GWP*, General Orders, April 6, 1780; George Washington, *Writings of George Washington*, Fitzpatrick ed., vol. 17, pp. 214, 286, 302, 468, and vol. 18, pp. 222–225; *Journals of the Continental Congress*, vol. 16, p. 161.
4. Alexander Hamilton to George Washington, *GWP*, January 14, 1780.
5. George Washington to Henry Knox, *GWP*, January 15, 1780; George Washington, *Writings of George Washington*, Fitzpatrick ed., vol. 17, p. 399.
6. Drake, *Life and Correspondence*, p. 62.
7. Ibid., p. 63.
8. Henry Knox to George Washington, *Gilder Lehrman Collection*, May 23, 1780; Henry Knox to George Washington, *GWP*, May 23, 1780.
9. *Journals of the Continental Congress*, vol. 17, p. 508.
10. Henry Knox, Ammunition Shortages, *GWP*, July 3, 1780.
11. George Washington to Continental Congress War Board, *GWP*, July 4, 1780.
12. Henry Knox to George Washington, *Gilder Lehrman Collection*, September 9, 1780.
13. Golway, *Washington's General: Nathanael Greene*, pp. 227–228.
14. Alexander Hamilton, *Works of Alexander Hamilton*, vol. 9, p. 151; Alexander Hamilton, *Hamilton: Writings*, p. 90.
15. Callahan, *Henry Knox*, p. 164.
16. Benedict Arnold to George Washington, *GWP*, September 25, 1780.
17. John L. Andre to George Washington, *GWP*, September 24, 1780.
18. George Washington, *GWP*, General Orders, October 1, 1780.
19. Moore, *Diary*, Moore ed., vol. 2, p. 213.
20. Ibid.
21. Callahan, *Henry Knox*, p. 165.
22. George Washington to John Mathews, *GWP*, October 23, 1780.

23. George Washington to John Sullivan, *GWP*, November 25, 1780; *Letters of Delegates*, vol. 16, p. 402.
24. George Washington to James Duane, *GWP*, December 26, 1780.
25. Drake, *Life and Correspondence*, p. 63; Callahan, *Henry Knox*, pp. 167–168.
26. Drake, *Life and Correspondence*, p. 64.
27. Circular to the New England States and George Washington to Henry Knox, *GWP*, January 5 and January 6, 1781; Washington, *Writings of George Washington*, Fitzpatrick ed., vol. 21, pp. 61, 76.
28. Henry Knox to John Lowell, *GWP*, January 16, 1781.
29. George Washington to Benjamin Lincoln, *GWP*, February 10, 1781.
30. George Washington to Henry Knox, *GWP*, February 7, 1781.
31. Henry Knox to George Washington, *Gilder Lehrman Collection*, February 13, 1781.

CHAPTER 8—YORKTOWN AND SURRENDER

1. Golway, *Washington's General*, p. 271; Bancroft, *History of the United States*, vol. 5, p. 504.
2. Golway, *Washington's General*, p. 286.
3. George Washington to Henry Knox, *GWP*, May 28, 1781; Washington, *Writings of George Washington*, Fitzpatrick ed., vol. 22, p. 126.
4. Henry Knox to William Knox, *HKP*, July 20, 1781.
5. Henry Knox to Lucy Knox, *HKP*, August 3, 1781.
6. Callahan, *Henry Knox*, p. 178.
7. William Knox to Henry Knox, *HKP*, August 22, 1781.
8. Henry Knox to William Knox, *HKP*, September 8, 1781.
9. George Washington to Board of War, *GWP*, September 29, 1781.
10. Nathanael Greene to Henry Knox, *HKP*, September 29, 1781.
11. Henry Knox to Lucy Knox, *HKP*, October 1, 1781.
12. Charles Cornwallis, "Report of the Battle of Yorktown," *America*, vol. 3, pp. 302–303.
13. Brooks, *Henry Knox*, p. 155.
14. Henry Knox to Lucy Knox, *HKP*, October 19, 1781.
15. Drake, *Life and Correspondence*, pp. 72–73.
16. George Washington, General Orders, *GWP*, October 20, 1781; Washington, *Writings of George Washington*, Fitzpatrick ed., vol. 23, p. 246.
17. Henry Knox to John Jay, *HKP*, October 21, 1781.
18. George Washington to the President of Congress, *GWP*, October 31, 1781; Washington, *Writings of George Washington*, Fitzpatrick ed., vol. 23, p. 308.
19. Nathanael Greene to Henry Knox, *HKP*, December 10, 1781.
20. *Journals of the Continental Congress*, vol. 18, pp. 1117–1120 and vol. 22, p. 143.
21. Henry Knox to George Washington, *Gilder Lehrman Collection*, April 21, 1782.
22. Ibid.
23. *Letters of Delegates*, vol. 18, p. 488.
24. Hamilton, *Works of Alexander Hamilton*, Federal ed., vol. 9, p. 185.
25. Brooks, *Henry Knox*, p. 167.
26. George Washington to Henry Knox, *GWP*, August 29, 1782; Washington, *Writings of George Washington*, Fitzpatrick ed., vol. 25, p. 91.
27. Washington, *Writings of George Washington*, Fitzpatrick ed., vol. 26, p. 475.

28. Henry Knox to George Washington, *Gilder Lehrman Collection*, September 10, 1782.

29. Washington, *Writings of George Washington*, Fitzpatrick ed., vol. 25, p. 150.

30. Henry Knox to Benjamin Lincoln, *HKP*, December 20, 1782; Brooks, *Henry Knox*, p. 169.

31. Samuel Osgood to Henry Knox, *Letters of Delegates*, vol. 19, p. 452.

32. James Madison to Edmund Randolph, *Letters of Delegates*, vol. 19, p. 5.

33. *Journals of the Continental Congress*, vol. 25, p. 850; James Madison's Notes of the Debates, *Letters of Delegates*, vol. 19, p. 571.

34. *Journals of the Continental Congress*, vol. 25, p. 852; James Madison's Notes on the Debates, *Letters of Delegates*, vol. 19, p. 580.

35. Alexander Hamilton to George Washington, *Letters of Delegates*, vol. 19, p. 690; Hamilton, *Works of Alexander Hamilton*, Federal ed., vol. 9, p. 222.

36. Henry Knox to Alexander McDougal, *HKP*, February 21, 1783.

37. Henry Knox to Gouverneur Morris, *HKP*, February 21, 1783; Brooks, *Henry Knox*, 170; Callahan, *Henry Knox*, p. 200; Drake, *Life and Correspondence*, p. 77.

38. Henry Knox to Alexander McDougal, *HKP*, March 3, 1783; Drake, *Life and Correspondence*, p. 79.

39. Joseph Jones to George Washington, *Letters of Delegates*, vol. 19, 746.

40. James Madison to Edmund Randolph, *Letters of Delegates*, vol. 19, p. 763.

41. Washington, *Writings of George Washington*, Fitzpatrick ed., vol. 26, p. 211.

42. Henry Knox to Alexander McDougal, *HKP*, March 12, 1783.

43. Henry Knox to Benjamin Lincoln, *HKP*, March 12, 1783.

44. Washington, *Works of George Washington*, Fitzpatrick ed., vol. 26, p. 225.

45. Ibid., p. 222.

46. Henry Knox to Benjamin Lincoln, *HKP*, March 16, 1783.

47. George Washington to Henry Knox, *GWP*, March 24, 1783.

CHAPTER 9—CONFEDERATION SECRETARY

1. Henry Knox to George Washington, *GWP*, April 17, 1783.

2. Henry Knox to George Washington, *Gilder Lehrman Collection*, September 17, 1783; Henry Knox to George Washington, *GWP*, September 17, 1783.

3. Henry Knox's Reply to Washington's Farewell Address to the Army, *HKP*, November 2, 1783.

4. George Washington to Henry Knox, *GWP*, December 4, 1783.

5. Benjamin Tallmadge, *Memoirs* (New York: Fraunces Tavern Museum Collection).

6. George Washington to Henry Knox, *GWP*, December 5, 1785.

7. Henry Knox to George Washington, *Gilder Lehrman Collection*, January 31, 1785; Henry Knox to George Washington, *GWP*, January 31, 1785.

8. George Partridge to Henry Knox, *Letters of Delegates*, vol. 22, p. 254.

9. Rufus King to Henry Knox, *Letters of Delegates*, vol. 22, p. 270.

10. Henry Knox to Charles Thomson, *HKP*, March 17, 1785; *Journals of the Continental Congress*, vol. 28, pp. 115, 129.

11. Henry Knox to Samuel Parsons, *HKP*, March 29, 1785.

12. Callahan, *Henry Knox*, p. 237.

13. David Ramsay to Henry Knox, *Letters of Delegates*, vol. 23, p. 187.

14. *Letters of Delegates*, vol. 23, p. 187.

15. Nathanael Greene to Henry Knox, *HKP*, March 12, 1786.

16. *Journals of the Continental Congress*, vol. 31, pp. 739–740.

17. Ibid., p. 752.
18. Henry Knox to George Washington, *HKP*, October 23, 1786.
19. George Washington to James Madison, *GWP*, November 5, 1786.
20. Henry Knox to George Washington, *HKP*, January 14, 1787.
21. Henry Knox to Stephen Higginson, *HKP*, January 28, 1787.
22. *Journals of the Continental Congress*, vol. 32, p. 39.
23. Henry Knox to Benjamin Lincoln, *HKP*, February 14, 1787.
24. George Washington to Henry Knox, *GWP*, March 8, 1787; Washington, *Writings of George Washington*, Fitzpatrick ed., vol. 29, pp. 171–172.
25. Henry Knox to George Washington, *GWP*, March 19, 1787.
26. Callahan, *Henry Knox*, p. 259.
27. Henry Knox to Winthrop Sargent, *HKP*, April 15, 1787.
28. Rufus King to Henry Knox, *Letters of Delegates*, vol. 24, p. 290.
29. *Letters of Delegates*, vol. 24, p. 352.
30. George Washington to Henry Knox, *GWP*, August 19, 1787.
31. Henry Knox to George Washington, *GWP*, December 11, 1787.
32. Henry Knox to George Washington, *Gilder Lehrman Collection*, February 14, 1788; Henry Knox to George Washington, *GWP*, February 14, 1788.
33. George Washington to Henry Knox, *GWP*, February 5, 1788.
34. Henry Knox to Marquis de Lafayette, *HKP*, April 26, 1788.
35. Doughty to Henry Knox, *HKP*, July 15, 1788.

CHAPTER 10—ILLUSIVE BUBBLES

1. Alexander Hamilton to Theodore Sedgwick, *Letters of Delegates*, vol. 25, p. 416.
2. *Letters of Delegates*, vol. 25, p. 417.
3. Alexander Hamilton to James Madison, *Works of Alexander Hamilton*, Federal ed., vol. 9, p. 321.
4. Henry Knox to George Washington, *Gilder Lehrman Collection*, December 21, 1788; Henry Knox to George Washington, *HKP*, December 21, 1788; Henry Knox to George Washington, *GWP*, December 21, 1788.
5. David McClure to Henry Knox, *HKP*, December 22, 1788.
6. Henry Knox to David McClure, *HKP*, January 25, 1789.
7. George Washington to Charles Thomson, *GWP*, April 14, 1789.
8. William Maclay, *Journal of William Maclay—United States Senator from Pennsylvania, 1789–1791*, pp. 129–130. Online at loc.gov.
9. Callahan, *Henry Knox*, p. 276.
10. Henry Knox to George Washington, *GWP*, January 12, 1790.
11. Maclay, *Journal*, p. 175.
12. Henry Knox to Josiah Harmar, *American State Papers, Indian Affairs*, June 7, 1790.
13. *American State Papers, Indian Affairs*, August 7, 1790.
14. George Washington to Henry Knox, *GWP*, November 2, 1790.
15. Ibid., November 19, 1790.
16. James D. Richardson, ed., *A Compilation of the Messages and Papers of the Presidents* (Washington, D.C.: U.S. Bureau of National Literature and Art, 1910), vol. 1, p. 78.
17. George Washington to Henry Knox, *GWP*, June 8, 1791.
18. Callahan, *Henry Knox*, p, 285.
19. Brooks, *Henry Knox*, p. 229.

20. Thomas Jefferson, *Writings of Thomas Jefferson*, Monticello ed. (Washington, D.C.: Thomas Jefferson Memorial Association, 1904–1905), vol. 1, pp. 350–351.
21. *U.S. House Journal*, 1st Ses., 3rd Congress, vol. 2, supplemental journal, NP, January 2, 1794.
22. Ian Toll, *Six Frigates: The Epic History of the Founding of the U.S. Navy* (New York: W.W. Norton, 2006), p. 45.
23. John Lehman, *On Seas of Glory: Heroic Men, Great Ships, and Epic Battles of the American Navy*, (New York: Touchstone, Simon & Schuster, 2002), pp. 73–74.
24. Ibid., p. 72.
25. *U.S. House Journal*, 1st Ses., 3rd Congress, p. 87.
26. Henry Knox to George Washington, *GWP*, April 15, 1794; *American State Papers, Naval Affairs*, vol. 1 p. 6.
27. Lehman, *Seas of Glory*, p. 78.
28. Thomas Jefferson to John Adams, *Thomas Jefferson Papers*, November 1, 1822.
29. Henry Knox to Henry Jackson, *HKP*, May 10, 1794.
30. *Messages and Papers of the Presidents*, George Washington (Washington D.C.: Federal Register Division, National Archives and Records Service, Government Printing Office, 1956), vol. 1, p. 151; Proclamation, *GWP*, August 7, 1794.
31. *Messages and Papers of the Presidents*, George Washington, vol. 1, p. 152; George Washington to Henry Knox, *GWP*, August 8, 1794.
32. Henry Knox to Lucy Knox, *Henry Knox Papers*, August 17, 1794.
33. *Messages and Papers of the Presidents*, George Washington, vol. 1, p. 154.
34. George Washington to Henry Knox, *GWP*, September 30, 1794.
35. Ibid., October 9, 1794.
36. *American State Papers, Naval Affairs*, vol. 1, p. 6.
37. Henry Knox to George Washington, *GWP*, December 28, 1794.
38. George Washington to Henry Knox, *Gilder Lehrman Collection*, December 30, 1794; George Washington to Henry Knox, *GWP*, December 30, 1794; Washington, *Writings of George Washington*, Fitzpatrick ed., vol. 34, p. 76.

CHAPTER 11—SOLDIER'S HOME

1. Callahan, *Henry Knox*, p.344.
2. Thomas Morgan Griffiths, *Major General Henry Knox and the Last Heirs to Montpelier* (Lewiston, ME: Monmouth Press, 1965), p. 48.
3. Thomas Jefferson to Henry Knox, *Thomas Jefferson Papers*, June 1, 1795.
4. Henry Knox to George Washington, *Gilder Lehrman Collection*, September 2, 1795.
5. Woodrow Wilson, *History of the American People* (New York: William H. Wise, 1931), vol. 3, p. 141.
6. Henry Knox to George Washington, *Gilder Lehrman Collection*, September 2, 1795.
7. George Washington to Henry Knox, *Writings of George Washington*, Fitzpatrick ed., vol. 34, pp. 310–311; George Washington to Henry Knox, *GWP*, September 20, 1795.
8. *Messages and Papers of the Presidents*, George Washington, vol. 1, p. 188.
9. George Washington to Henry Knox, *Writings of George Washington*, Fitzpatrick ed., vol. 35, pp. 12–13.
10. Henry Knox to George Washington, *Gilder Lehrman Collection*, April 14, 1796.

11. Henry Knox to George Washington, *GWP*, April 14, 1796.
12. Ibid.
13. Brooks, *Henry Knox*, p. 248.
14. George Washington to Henry Knox, *Writings of George Washington*, Fitzpatrick ed., vol 35, pp. 84–85.
15. Henry Knox to George Washington, *Gilder Lehrman Collection*, January 15, 1797.
16. George Washington to Henry Knox, *Writings of George Washington*, vol. 35, pp. 408–409; George Washington to Henry Knox, *GWP*, March 2, 1797.
17. *Messages and Papers of the Presidents*, John Adams, vol. 1, p. 220.
18. Henry Knox to John Adams, *Works of John Adams, Second President of the United States*, (Boston: Little, Brown and Company, 1853), vol. 8, p. 532.
19. John Adams to Henry Knox, *Works of John Adams*, vol. 8, p. 535.
20. *Messages and Papers of the Presidents*, John Adams, vol. 1, p. 226.
21. Ron Chernow, *Alexander Hamilton* (New York: Penguin Books, 2004), p. 549.
22. Charles C. Pinckney, "The XYZ Correspondence," *America*, vol. 4, p. 207.
23. Ibid., p. 208.
24. George Washington to Timothy Pickering, *GWP*, July 11, 1789.
25. George Washington to Alexander Hamilton, *GWP*, July 14, 1789.
26. U.S. Congress, *Senate Exec. Journal*, 5th Congress, 2nd Sess., July 18, 1798, p. 292.
27. George Washington to Henry Knox, *GWP*, July 16, 1798; Henry Knox to George Washington, *HKP*, July 29, 1789.
28. Henry Knox to George Washington, *HKP*, July 29, 1789.
29. George Washington to Henry Knox, *GWP*, August 9, 1798; George Washington to Timothy Pickering, *GWP*, September 9, 1798.
30. John Adams to James McHenry, *Works of John Adams*, vol. 8, 580.
31. Chernow, *Alexander Hamilton*, p. 557.
32. George Washington to Timothy Pickering, *GWP*, September 9, 1789.
33. John Adams, *Works of John Adams*, vol. 8, pp. 602–603.
34. Callahan, *Henry Knox*, p. 372.

CHAPTER 12—ATOMS UPON THIS ATOM

1. Hamilton, *Works of Alexander Hamilton*, Federal ed., vol. 10, p. 267.
2. Henry Knox to George Washington, *Gilder Lehrman Collection*, December 22, 1789.
3. *Messages and Papers of the Presidents*, Thomas Jefferson, vol. 1, p. 310.
4. Thomas Jefferson to Henry Knox, *Thomas Jefferson Papers*, March 27, 1801.
5. Morgan Griffiths, *Major General Henry Knox*, p. 46.
6. "Jackson's Geology of Maine," *North American Review* (Cedar Falls, University of Northern Iowa), 47, no. 100 (July 1838).
7. Callahan, *Henry Knox*, p. 379.
8. James Thacher, "Biographical Sketch of Henry Knox," *Military Journal*, available at www.american revolution.org.
9. Henry Knox Will, *HKP*, November 26, 1802.
10. Drake, *Life and Correspondence*, p. 118.
11. Callahan, *Henry Knox*, pp. 380–381.
12. Griffiths, *Major General Henry Knox*, p. 56.
13. Henry Knox to Lucy Knox, *HKP*, March 17, 1806.

BIBLIOGRAPHY

Adams, John. *Adams Family Papers including Autobiography of John Adams, Letters between John and Abigail Adams, the Diary of John Adams.* Boston: Massachusetts Historical Society. Electronic archive at (www.masshist.org).

———. Adams, John and Charles Francis. *The Works of John Adams, Second President of the United States: With a Life of the Author, Notes and Illustrations.* 10 Vols. Boston: Little, Brown, 1851.

Allan, Herbert S. *John Hancock: Patriot in Purple.* New York: Macmillan, 1948.

America—Great Crisis in Our History Told by Its Makers: A Library of Original Sources. 11 vols. Chicago: Americanization Department of Veterans of Foreign Wars of the United States, 1925.

American State Papers, Foreign, Indian Military and Naval Affairs. Washington, D.C.: Library of Congress.

Bancroft, George. *History of the United States from the Discovery of the American Continent. 6 vols.* New York: Harper & Bros, 1882.

Boston Latin School website, www.bls.org.

Brookhiser, Richard. *Alexander Hamilton: American.* New York: Free Press Touchstone, 2000.

———. *Gentleman Revolutionary: Gouverneur Morris, the Rake Who Wrote the Constitution.* New York: Free Press, 2004.

Brooks, Noah. *Henry Knox: A Soldier of the Revolution.* Reprint of 1900 Edition. Cranbury, New Jersey: The Scholar's Bookshelf, 2005.

Callahan, North. *Henry Knox, General Washington's General.* New York: A.S. Barnes and Company, 1958.

Carrington, Henry B. *Battles of the American Revolution: 1775–1781.* New York: Promontory Press, 1877.

Chernow, Ron. *Alexander Hamilton.* New York: Penguin Books, 2004.

Constitution of the United States of America

Copeland, David A. *Debating the Issues in Colonial Newspapers: Primary Documents on Events of the Period.* Westport, Connecticut: Greenwood Press, 2000.

Cushing, Harry Alonzo, ed. *The Writings of Samuel Adams.* New York: G.P. Putnam's Sons, 1904. Vol. 1, Electronic edition distributed by Fictionwise. 4 vols. 2–4, online at www.gutenberg.org.

Drake, Francis Samuel. *Life and Correspondence of Henry Knox.* Boston: Samuel G. Drake, 1873.

Eliot, Charles W. *American Historical Documents, 1000–1904. The Harvard Classics, vol. 43.* New York: P. F. Collier and Son Corporation, 1938.

Ellis, Joseph J. *Founding Brothers: The Revolutionary Generation.* New York: Albert A. Knopf, 2000.

———. *His Excellency: George Washington.* New York: Albert A. Knopf, 2006.

————. *American Sphinx: The Character of Thomas Jefferson.* New York: Albert A. Knopf, 1997.

————. *Passionate Sage: The Character and Legacy of John Adams.* W.W. Norton & Company, 2001.

Elliot, Jonathan, ed. *The Debates In the Several State Conventions On the Adoption of the Federal Constitution, as Recommended by the General Convention at Philadelphia, in 1787. 5 vols.* Philadelphia: J. B. Lippincott Company, 1901.

Federal Register Division, National Archives and Records Service. *Public Papers of the Presidents of the United States. 79 vols.* Washington, D.C.: Government Printing Office, 1956–.

Fischer, David Hackett. *Washington's Crossing.* New York: Oxford University Press, 2004.

Ford, Worthington, editor et all. *Journals of the Continental Congress, 1774–1789, 34 vols.* Washington, D.C.: Library of Congress, 1904.

Griffiths, Thomas Morgan. *Major General Henry Knox and The Last Heirs to Montpelier.* Monmouth, Maine: Monmouth Press, 1965.

Golway, Terry. *Washington's General, Nathanael Greene and the Triumph of the American Revolution.* New York: Owl Book, Henry Holt and Company, 2006.

Halsey, Francis W. *Great Epochs in American History, Described by Famous Writers From Columbus to Roosevelt.* 10 vols. New York: Funk & Wagnalls Co., 1912.

Hamilton, Alexander. *The Works of Alexander Hamilton,* Henry Cabot Lodge ed. 12 vols. New York: G.P. Putnam's Sons, The Knickerbocker Press, 1904.

Inaugural Addresses of the Presidents of the United States from George Washington 1789 to George Bush 1989: Bicentennial Edition. Washington, D.C.: Government Printing Office, 1989 (additional materials added 1997).

Jackman, William J. and Jacob H., Patton; and Rossitter, Johnson. *History of the American Nation. 9 vols.* Chicago: K. Gaynor, 1911.

Jefferson, Thomas. The Thomas Jefferson Papers Series, Manuscript Division, online at www.memory.loc.gov.

————. *The Writings of Jefferson.* (Monticello Edition) Deposited in the Department of State and Published in 1853 By Order of the Joint Committee of Congress. 6 Vols. Washington, D.C.: Thomas Jefferson Memorial Association, 1904–1905.

————. *Thomas Jefferson, Writings* edited by Merrill D. Peterson.(*Autobiography, Notes on the State of Virginia, Public and Private Papers, Addresses, Letters*). New York: Library of America, 1984.

————. *The Works of Thomas Jefferson.* 12 vols. (Federal Edition) Paul Leicester Ford editor. New York: G.P. Putnam's Sons, The Knickerbocker Press, 1904.

Journal of the executive proceedings of the Senate of the United States of America. Vol. 1, 1789–1805. Washington D.C.: Library of Congress.

Journal of the House of Representatives of the United State, 1789–1875. Washington D.C.: Library of Congress.

Lafayette, Marquis de. *Memoirs of Lafayette.* Online at gutenberg.org.

Ketcham, Ralph (Introduction). *The Anti-Federalist Papers.* New York: Signet Classics, 2003.

Knox, Henry. *Henry Knox Papers. 65 vols.* Boston: Massachusetts Historical Society.

————. *Henry Knox Papers.* New York: Gilder Lehrman Collection on deposit at the New York Historical Society.

————. "Plan for the General Arrangement of the Militia," *War Department Papers,* George Mason University, March 18, 1786

Larabee, Benjamin Woods. *The Boston Tea Party*. Boston: Northeastern University Press, 1979.

Lehman, John. *On Seas of Glory: Heroic Men, Great Ships, and Epic Battles of the American Navy*. New York: Touchstone, Simon and Schuster, 2001.

William Maclay. *Journal of William Maclay—United States Senator from Pennsylvania, 1789–1791*. Online at loc.gov

McCullough, David, *John Adams*. New York: Simon and Schuster, 2001

———. *1776*. New York, Simon and Schuster, 2005.

Madison, James; Hamilton, Alexander; and Jay, John. *The Federalist, or The New Constitution*. 2 vols. Chicago: Albert Scott & Company, 1894 cited in the American Reference Library (Orem, Utah: Western Standard Publishing Company, 1998)

———. *Journal of the Federal Convention*. 2 vols. Chicago: Albert, Scott & Co, 1893, originally published in 1840. Reprint. E.H. Scott.

———. *Letters and Other Writings of James Madison, Fourth President of the United States. In Four Vols*. Published by Order of Congress. 4 vols. Philadelphia: J.B. Lippincott & Co, 1865.

———. *James Madison Papers at the Library of Congress, 1741–1799* in Washington D.C., online at (www.memory.loc.gov).

Martyn, Charles. *The Life of Artemas Ward: The First Commander-In-Chief of the American Revolution*. Port Washington, NY: A. Ward, 1921.

Messages and Papers of the Presidents, George Washington. Washington D.C.: Federal Register Division, National Archives and Records Service, Government Printing Office, 1956.

Moore, Frank editor. *Diary of the American Revolution From Newspapers and Original Documents. Vols. 1 and 2*. New York: Charles Scribner, 1860.

Morison, Samuel Eliot. E., ed. *Sources and Documents Illustrating the American Revolution, 1764–1788, and the Formation of the Federal Constitution,*. Oxford: Clarendon Press, 1923.

Morris, Gouverneur. *The Diary and Letters of Gouverneur Morris*. Ann Cary Morris ed. Two vols. New York: Charles Scribner's Sons, 1888.

North American Review. "Jackson's Geology of Maine," Cedar Falls, University of Northern Iowa, 47, no. 100, July 1838.

Purcell, L. Edward. *Who Was Who In The American Revolution*. New York: Facts on File, 1993.

Purcell, L. Edward and David F. Burg editors. *The World Almanac of the American Revolution*. New York: World Almanac, 1992.

Purvis, Thomas L. *A Dictionary of American History*. Cambridge, Mass.: Blackwell Reference, 1995.

Richardson, James D., ed. *A Compilation of the Messages and Papers of the Presidents*. 10 vols. Washington, D.C.:U.S. Bureau of National Literature and Art, 1910.

Schlesinger Jr., Arthur M. (Editor). *The Almanac of American History*. New York: Barnes & Noble Books, 1993.

Smith, Paul, editor et all. *Letters of Delegates to the Continental Congress, 1774–1789*, 25 Vols. Summerfield, Florida: Historical Database, 1998.

Tallmadge, Benjamin. *Memoirs*. New York: Fraunces Tavern Museum Collection

Thacher, James. *Military Journal* at americanrevolution.org

Thayer, Theodore. *Nathanael Greene: Strategist of the American Revolution*. New York, Twayne Publishers, 1960.

Thayer, William Roscoe. *George Washington*. New York: Houghton Mifflin, 1922.

Toll, Ian W. *Six Frigates: The Epic History of the Founding of the U.S. Navy*. New York: W. W. Norton & Company, 2006.

Triber, Jane E. *A True Republican: The Life of Paul Revere*. Amherst: University of Massachusetts Press, 1998.

Tyler, Moses Coit. *The Literary History of the American Revolution, 1763–1783*. New York: G. P. Putnam's Sons, 1897.

Unger, Harlow Giles. *Lafayette*. New York: Wiley, 2002.

U.S. Congress. *Biographical Directory of the American Congress, 1774–1949: the Continental Congress, September 5, 1774, to October 21, 1788 and the Congress of the United States, from the First to the Seventy-third Congress, March 4, 1789, to January 3, 1949, Inclusive*. Washington, D.C.: U.S. Government Printing Office, 1950.

United States. National Archives and Records Service. *The Founding Fathers: Delegates to the Constitutional Convention*. Washington, D.C.: www.nara.gov/exhall/charters/constitution/confath.html, 1998.

Van Tyne, Claude Halstead. *The Loyalists in the American Revolution*. New York: Macmillan, 1902.

Wahlke, John C., ed. *The Causes of the American Revolution*. Revised ed. Boston: D. C. Heath and Company, 1967.

Washington, George. *George Washington Papers at the Library of Congress, 1741–1799*. Washington D.C., online at www.memory.loc.gov.

———*George Washington Papers*. New York: Gilder Lehrman Collection at the New York Historical Society.

———. *The Writings of George Washington from the Original Manuscript Sources, 1745–1799*. Jonathan Fitzpatrick ed. 39 vols. Washington, D.C.: U.S. Government Printing Office, 1931.

———. *Writings*. New York: Library of America, 1997.

Wells, William V. *The Life and Public Services of Samuel Adams: Being a Narrative of His Acts and Opinions, and of His Agency in Producing and Forwarding the American Revolution* 3 Vols. Boston: Little, Brown, 1888.

Charles T. Whittemore, *A General of the Revolution: John Sullivan of New Hampshire*. New York: Columbia University Press, 1961.

Woodrow Wilson. *History of the American People*. 5 Vols. New York: William H. Wise. 1931.

Woods, Gordon S. *Radicalism of the American Revolution*. New York: Vintage Books, 1991.

———. *Revolutionary Characters: What Made the Founders Different*. Reprint edition. New York: Penguin, 2007.

Zobel, Hiller B. *The Boston Massacre*. New York: W. W. Norton., 1970.

INDEX